TWAYNE'S WORLD AUTHORS SERIES

A Survey of the World's Literature

Sylvia E. Bowman, Indiana University

GENERAL EDITOR

FRANCE

Maxwell A. Smith, Guerry Professor of French, Emeritus
The University of Chattanooga
Visiting Professor in Modern Languages
The Florida State University

EDITOR

Nicolas Boileau

(*TWAS 91*)

TWAYNE'S WORLD AUTHORS SERIES (TWAS)

*The purpose of TWAS is to survey the major writers
—novelists, dramatists, historians, poets, philosophers,
and critics—of the nations of the world. Among the
national literatures covered are those of Australia,
Canada, China, Eastern Europe, France, Germany,
Greece, India, Italy, Japan, Latin America, New Zea-
land, Poland, Russia, Scandinavia, Spain, and the
African nations, as well as Hebrew, Yiddish, and
Latin Classical literatures. This survey is comple-
mented by Twayne's United States Authors Series
and English Authors Series.*

*The intent of each volume in these series is to present
a critical-analytical study of the works of the writer;
to include biographical and historical material that
may be necessary for understanding, appreciation,
and critical appraisal of the writer; and to present all
material in clear, concise English—but not to vitiate
the scholarly content of the work by doing so.*

Nicolas Boileau

By JULIAN EUGENE WHITE, JR.

University of New Mexico

Twayne Publishers, Inc.   ::   New York

Preface

MANY general studies on Boileau, critical in nature, are available to the specialist. Most of these are in French and assume that the reader has read Boileau's works. Few studies in English exist, and there are no translations available of most of his poems. This book, which makes neither claim nor pretense to any new discoveries, is designed primarily for an English-speaking audience of non-specialists, most of whom have not read much of Boileau beyond portions of the *Art Poétique*. The method used has been to study each poem or prose work by means of fairly close textual analysis and paraphrasing of Boileau's own words, with introductory and summary passages to situate the work in relation to contemporary events and the poet's entire production. Biographical information has been held to the minimum required for an adequate understanding of the man and his works.

In a study of limited length many items must, of course, be omitted. This book does not contain a long and involved history of the Quarrel of the Ancients and Moderns in all its phases but concentrates on the minimum amount of information concerning that period in which Boileau was a participant. The legend of the "quatre amis" has been sufficiently refuted, and continued mention serves only to prolong the existence of a false concept. No detailed analysis of his works, from an esthetic viewpoint, has been undertaken but rather an attempt to expose the general ideas they contain. Little attention has been given to the changes made by Boileau from one edition to another but concentration has been on the final version. Most of the names of figures relatively unknown today but mentioned by Boileau have been omitted, as inclusion and identification would be of dubious value to the general reader while the specialist can find them elsewhere.

I have naturally made use of studies by previous scholars and have borrowed freely from my predecessors. While all cannot be named here, I must acknowledge particular debt to the studies by Jules Brody, René Bray, Daniel Mornet, and Gustave Lanson. Each is a masterful piece of scholarship and, were it not for the fact that Brody's work is a more specialized study while the others are in French, this book would not be necessary. I have relied especially heavily on Brody in all matters concerning Boileau and Longinus and on Lanson for his critical insights. My debt to Bray and Mornet is less extensive but equally apparent.

If there has been a single thought or purpose informing the writing of this study, it has been to give a more balanced picture of Boileau than those extremes which see in him only a dogmatic apostle of reason or a poet and critic who does little more than reflect contemporary ideas and taste. I have tried to bring together in concise and clear form the results of recent Boileau scholarship in order to present a coherent and fair picture, in English, of Boileau as a person, as a man of ideas, and as a poet.

J. E. W.

Albuquerque, New Mexico
September 1967

Contents

Chronology

1636 Nicolas Boileau born in Paris, November 1.
1638 Death of Boileau's mother.
1643 Student at Collège d'Harcourt.
1648 Student at Collège de Beauvais (Paris).
1652 Boileau begins to study law.
1656 Admitted to the bar.
1657 Death of Boileau's father. He renounces the law.
1657– Composition of *Satire I* (including at this time *Satire VI*),
1664 which circulated in the salons.
1660 *Satire VI* detached from *Satire I.*
1660– *Satire VII.*
1661
1663– *Satire II.*
1664
1664– *Satire III, Satire V, Satire IV.*
1665
1665 *Dissertation sur Joconde, Dialogue des héros de romans.*
1666 First edition of *Satires.*
1667– *Satire VIII, Satire IX.*
1668
1668 Publication of a *Discours sur la satire;* together with *Satires VIII* and *IX.*
1669– Publication of *Epître I;* composition of *Epître II.*
1672 Work begun on *Art poétique* and *le Lutrin.*
1671 *l'Arrêt burlesque.*
1672 *Epître IV.*
1673 *Epître III.*
1674 New edition of his works, containing the *Satires*, first four *Epîtres, l'Art poétique*, first four cantos of *le Lutrin, Traité du sublime* (translated from Longinus). Composition of *Epître V.*

1675   *Epître IX.*

1676– *Epître VIII.*
1678

1677   *Epître VI* and *Epître VII.* After *cabale* over *Phèdre,* Boileau and Racine are named royal historiographers.

1681– Completion of Cantos V and VI of *le Lutrin.*
1683

1684   Boileau elected to Académie française, April 15.

1685   Purchase of a house at Auteuil.

1687   Beginning of Quarrel of the Ancients and Moderns, January 27.

       July–September, Boileau goes to Bourbon to take waters for his laryngitis. Corresponds with Racine.

1692– *Satire X.*
1693

1693   *Ode sur la prise de Namur; Discours sur l'ode; Réflexions critiques sur Longin.*

1694   Reconciliation with Perrault, brought about by Arnauld.

1695– *Epître X, Epître XI, Epître XII.*
1697

1698– *Satire XI.*
1700

1699   Death of Racine, Boileau's closest friend.

1701   New edition of his works, his favorite and the last he personally corrected; contains important *Préface.*

1705– *Satire XII.* Refused *privilège* for publication.
1708

1711   Death of Boileau in Paris, March 13.

CHAPTER 1

Boileau the Man

A long literary tradition, already begun in his own lifetime and continued until the present, especially in the classroom, has made of Boileau a formidably cold, correct, and stiff figure. Much of this misconception of his real personality has been the result of a too dogmatic interpretation of his critical writings, in particular the *Art poétique* (*Art of Poetry*). Further support has been added to this attitude by an excessive preoccupation with his later years, when he was burdened with ill health, deaths of his friends, anxiety over the misfortunes of France, attacks by the Jesuits, and the ordinary tendency in old age toward serious and even melancholy reflection. A more balanced approach to Boileau's entire life, as revealed in his works, his friendships, his personality and character shows another facet of the man. In addition to the traditional figure of marmoreal austerity, handing down literary judgments from the heights of Parnassus, we see a loyal friend, a lively wit, a fierce but forgiving enemy, an honest, upright, and sincere gentleman.

I *Early Years (1636–1657)*

There is little in the circumstances of his birth, his family, and his youth to indicate a dogmatic Boileau, the apostle of reason and common sense. However, his inclination toward satire and his lack of tenderness for women might be suspected from an examination of his early childhood and his family. Born on November 1, 1636, at Paris in a house in the court of the Palace of Justice, opposite the Sainte Chapelle, Nicolas Boileau displayed those qualities which characterize the French bourgeoisie—uprightness of life and habits, common sense, self-control, a sense of the concrete, and a mocking spirit. The place of his death, like that of his birth, is located on the Ile de la Cité in the Seine River, the heart of the city. Boileau had the satirical humor of a Parisian and a Parisian's prejudice against the provinces. The frame of his poems is Paris—its streets, its mud, its odors, its noise, the taverns, the Palace of Justice, the Sainte Chapelle.

The Boileau family was composed mostly of law clerks attached to the Palace of Justice, on both the paternal and maternal sides. Far from hiding his origins once he had become an eminent man of letters, Boileau proclaimed his descent from several generations of law clerks in *Epîtres* V and X. The family claimed minor nobility going back to Jean Boileau, secretary to the king and notary, who had been given patents of nobility in 1371. This claim was upheld in a court case in 1699 and Boileau, in his correspondence with Brossette, his Lyonese Boswell, evidenced some pride in this vindication of his family's claim.[1] With this exception, he makes no mention of his nobility, nor did he ever seek to make his way in society by virtue of it. On the contrary, as evidenced particularly in *Satire* V as well as in scattered references in other poems, he recognized that true nobility is a matter of behavior rather than ancestry. His family connections gave him a familiarity with the chicanery which often entered into the practice of law, as well as the verbosity and specious reasoning of contemporary lawyers. This furnished background or subject matter for several of his works, notably the *Arrêt burlesque* (*Burlesque Injunction*), and *Epître II*.

Boileau's early years were spent as a semi-orphan, because of the death of his mother when he was only eighteen months old. His father Gilles, widowed for the second time, did not remarry and the infant Nicolas grew up without the love and tender care of a mother, in a home ruled by an ill-tempered and scolding nurse. Fifteenth and next-to-last of his father's brood, he scarcely knew real family life or true affection. Perhaps this lack of maternal care and warmth, coupled with the harsh treatment he received from an ignorant and imperious domestic, may be reasons for his failure to appreciate the tender and maternal side of women.

Beginning his studies at the age of seven at the Collège d' Harcourt, young Nicolas was forced to leave school at the age of fourteen because of kidney stones. He underwent an operation, poorly performed, for removal of these stones but was left with considerable discomfort for the rest of his life. Unlike Molière, Boileau was not permanently soured on the medical profession. He has uncomplimentary things to say about some doctors, especially in 1687, when an attack of laryngitis left him unable to speak for some months. He also had some good friends in the medical profession, notably M. Félix who was the king's personal surgeon. The kidney stones and recurrent attacks of kidney colic, as well as later respiratory ailments (possibly asthmatic bronchitis), probably resulted in a more sober and reserved mode of life and attitude than might be expected in a youth. His health was a constant source of concern to Boileau, and some traces of hypochondria may be deduced from his later letters to Racine and Brossette.[2]

After convalescing from his operation, Nicolas continued his studies, this time at the Collège de Beauvais. His studies were the usual ones for the schools of the day, based primarily on reading the authors of antiquity and writing commentaries on them. Boileau became an excellent Latinist and better than average in Greek. Had his teachers done no more than teach him Greek and Latin, he owed them a considerable debt of gratitude, for love and admiration of the ancients was the key to his future taste and literary doctrine. Boileau also confessed later, somewhat shamefacedly, that he enjoyed reading the lengthy novels of love and adventure which were in vogue at the time. His initial liking for these novels did not last, and seems to have inspired in him a more exact critical sense which enabled him to see how ridiculous most of them were. His imitations of Horace, Juvenal, and Persius show his familiarity with the Latin satirists. Like many another schoolboy he also tried his hand at original verse—love poems, drinking songs, epigrams, enigmas, and even a romantic melodrama with giants. These early endeavors may indicate some poetic talent, but certainly not the talent for which Boileau was to become famous.

The young Nicolas was originally destined for a career in the church. Indeed, he had been tonsured from the age of eleven and began to study theology on leaving the *collège* in 1652. It seems that he lacked the necessary zeal and vocation for a career in the church. There can be little doubt of his religious faith, which increased with age, but it was a simple and austere faith which brooked no theological splitting of hairs or ecclesiastical pettiness. He had in his character much of the severe morality of the Jansenists and was on terms of warmest friendship with some of them, notably the leaders Arnauld and Nicole. Although he attacked the casuistry of the Jesuits, he also had many close friends in the Society, ranking Bourdaloue the Jesuit second only in his esteem and admiration to Arnauld the Jansenist.[3] He also associated with known free-thinkers, especially early in his career. Because of the Jesuit-Jansenist controversy, the frequent spiritual revivals on a nearly national scale, and the eminence of such great churchmen as Bossuet, Bourdaloue, Fénelon, Arnauld, etc., Boileau was, like nearly everyone else in the latter half of the seventeenth century, deeply interested in matters of religion, theology, and morality. This pre-occupation may be seen in many of his works, notably *Epître III*, to Arnauld, *Epître XII, Sur l'Amour de Dieu (On Love for God)*, and *Satire XII, Sur l'Equivoque (On Ambiguity)*. *Epître XII* and *Satire XII* were written in the midst of controversy with the casuists among the Jesuits, a battle which was to darken and embitter Boileau's later years. *Le Lutrin (The Lectern)* shows a more humorous and ridiculous side of churchmen in their petty jealousies and squabbles for pre-eminence. Boileau was not, then, inclined to the partisan spirit and hair-splitting niceties of theological dispute.

From theology he passed to the study of the law, which was hardly more to his taste. His antipathy for the maze of common law, the lawyers' and clerks' abuse of rhetorical and formal language, and the prevalent chicanery are apparent in many of his poems, especially *Satire I* and *Epître II, Contre les Procès (Against Lawsuits)*. The law was more repugnant to his mind than to his conscience, as had been the case with theology. The fault was probably in the method of teaching the law as a trade rather than a science. To a mind like Boileau's, which sought universality and underlying principles, the philosophy of the law was absolutely necessary for any appreciation of its practical application. In spite of his distaste, he entered the office of his brother-in-law, the law clerk Dongois, and was admitted to the bar in 1656. It is doubtful if he ever had a case in court. His stay at the Palace of Justice was certainly not wasted. In addition to the familiarity with the milieu already gained from his family connections, he was able to see the workings of court and *Parlement* at first hand and to conceive some idea of the role of the law courts under a monarchy.[4]

The death of his father in 1657 put an end to Nicolas' quandary over his future career as well as his boredom in Dongois' office.

His inheritance gave him the liberty and material independence to permit him to follow his natural inclination for poetry. Boileau was prudent with the twelve thousand crowns he inherited. At this time the city of Lyons was borrowing money for the Hôtel de Ville (City Hall) at rates which were very favorable to lenders. Boileau placed about one-third of his money *en fonds perdu* (principal not recoverable) at twelve and one-half per cent, receiving for life an annual income of fifteen hundred francs. Frugal with himself, he was generous to others. A bachelor, his furnishings were modest and his habits were orderly and simple. He did not need to write or accept patronage in order to earn a living; to do so would have been in conflict with his lofty concept of literature and the dignity of the poet. Boileau received no money from the publishers who were enriched by the sale of his works. His only other source of income was the royal pension he was to receive about twenty years later (1677). Financial independence bore early fruit, for it is from the year of his father's death that the composition of his first *Satire* may be dated.

II *Boileau the Satirist and Polemicist* (1657–1668)

An inclination toward satire seems almost a characteristic of the Boileau family. Nicolas, at the time he began his literary career, already had three brothers known in Paris society for caustic wit —Boileau-Puymorin, Jacques, and especially Gilles. The latter was so well-known that Nicolas adopted the name Despréaux (of the meadows) to avoid confusion; to his contemporaries he was known as either Boileau-Despréaux or, more usually, simply Despréaux. The name derived from a small property owned by his father near the village of Crosne. Contemporaries who used the name Boileau generally referred to Gilles, who already had a considerable reputation as a writer, primarily of satires, and who was elected to the Academy in 1659—twenty-five years before Despréaux. It was rumored that Chapelain, literary arbiter of the day and charged by Colbert with drawing up the royal pension list, helped Gilles enter the Academy and included him on the pension list in order to protect himself from Gilles' caustic pen.[5] A brother who was in the Academy and a friend of Chapelain could have been of inestimable aid to a novice in literature, but Boileau and Gilles did not get along at all well. In addition to writing satires which made fun of Chapelain's poetry, Nicolas also alienated Gilles, mentioning him in one of his satires as an unaffectionate brother and rhyming epigrams against him. Boileau was simply unable to be a friend of anyone protected by Chapelain. One may suspect that Boileau decided that the best method of calling attention to himself and beginning his own reputation was in attacking this acknowledged chief of the reigning literary party. In any case, one cannot accuse him of having used his brother to further his own interests. In later life, Nicolas and Gilles were reconciled.

Jacques Boileau, doctor of theology of the Sorbonne, later dean of the cathedral of Sens, and still later canon at the Sainte Chapelle through Nicolas' influence, was also a writer. He published Latin treatises which shocked by the boldness of their thought and expression, besides his reputation as a caustic wit. Nicolas and Jacques got along well and, indeed, became quite close in later years.

It has been difficult for students and specialists alike to understand why Boileau attacked Chapelain and his coterie so vehemently. As René Bray has pointed out, Boileau and Chapelain had much in common regarding literary doctrine and critical theory.[6] Daniel Mornet also emphasizes the role of Chapelain as the leading architect of classicism before Boileau.[7] It was Chapelain who preached with the greatest authority obedience to reason and the rules and distrusted most obstinately the caprices of the imagination. Mornet's conclusion is that Boileau's primary motive was to call attention to himself and thereby insure his success. There is surely some truth to this interpretation, but it fails to take into sufficient account the basic character and personality of Boileau, who had a life-long reputation for probity, honesty, and uprightness. It should also be noted that Boileau did not attack Chapelain on the basis of his literary doctrine but on the basis of taste— at best Chapelain's poems are worthless and at worst, e.g., *La Pucelle* (*The Maiden*), they are soporific. With few exceptions the same criticisms may be made against the other authors attacked by Boileau. That these attacks aided in establishing a reputation for Boileau, although a not very desirable one, is undeniable. However, we need not conclude that both his desire for attention and a natural malice were Boileau's only motives. It was his good fortune that those who were considered the arbiters of contemporary taste were also abominable poets and deserved to be casti-

gated. Nor should we lose sight of the fact that, with two or three
exceptions, the judgments of Boileau also have been those of
posterity. There have been few critics whose literary evaluations,
whether based on a systematic doctrine and theory or simply on an
instinctive taste, have been so consistently right.

Having alienated Chapelain and his protectors, most of the
members of the Academy, and most of the writers whom Chapelain had included on the pension list, Boileau stood in need of
friendship. He was not long in acquiring allies and devoted
friends, among them two of France's greatest authors, Molière
and Racine. An early friend also was Antoine Furetière who led a
joyous life as *habitué* of the leading cabarets but who was also a
well-known poet and satirist, writer of *Le Roman bourgeois* (*The
Bourgeois Novel*), and author of a *Dictionary* which not only
competed with that of the Academy but was better in many ways.
Boileau's relations with Molière, Racine, and La Fontaine have
long presented thorny problems to scholars.[8] The successful attempt to demolish the legend of the "four friends" (Racine, Molière, La Fontaine, with Boileau as their mentor) has introduced
other problems, such as the extent of Boileau's friendship with
each of them individually, the dates of beginning and ending of
these friendships and, in view of the definitive split between Racine and Molière in 1665,[9] the question of a three-way relationship between them and Boileau. It is not the purpose of this book
to attempt to resolve these questions. Most of the doubt centers
on La Fontaine, who seems to have belonged to an entirely different literary milieu. Boileau was at least acquainted with La Fontaine's work as early as 1663–64 when he wrote the *Dissertation
sur Joconde* defending La Fontaine's version of that story. Since
both were on the same side in the Quarrel of the Ancients and
Moderns, it is possible that they drew closer to each other then,
but even this is problematical. Boileau was definitely a friend of
Molière until the latter's death in 1673, and the beginning of their
friendship probably dates from 1662–63, since Boileau's *Satire II*
(1664) was addressed to Molière. Boileau and Racine met as
early as 1663 and were friends in 1671. This friendship became
deep and intimate in 1675–77 and remained so until Racine's
death in 1699. Racine was Boileau's dearest friend and the feeling
was reciprocated by the younger man. Among this group of
friends there were also others, such as the brilliant Chapelle who

drank too much. All of them were of quite different temperaments but all had at least one thing in common—their dissatisfaction with the fashionable literature of the period, whether emphatic or precious, *romanesque* or burlesque.[10]

These friends met irregularly, sometimes in homes, but more frequently in one of the popular cabarets—the Mouton Blanc, the Croix de Lorraine, the Croix-Blanche, or the Pomme de Pin, which had been a favorite of Villon two hundred years before and of the satirist Mathurin Régnier earlier in the seventeenth century. These cabarets were what the cafés and English coffeehouses later became—clubs for *beaux esprits* and men of letters. It was at these friendly gatherings that such items as *Chapelain décoiffé* (*Chapelain "De-wigged"*) and *La Métamorphose de la perruque de Chapelain en astre* (*The Metamorphosis of Chapelain's Wig into a Star*) were composed in the midst of conviviality and drink, each contributing amusing lines under the inspiration of the moment. Boileau was surely not seduced by these companions but chose them from a natural inclination and for the kind of life they led. Loving good cheer, he spent several happy years leading what his enemies referred to as a debauched and scandalous life. Boileau was also a gourmet and knew how to set a fine table. Plainly, he had a less serious side, which he showed in the conviviality of good company.

Cabaret society was not the extent of Boileau's social life. He became a welcome guest at the leading salons of the nobility and also frequented those of the actress La Champmeslé and the famous Ninon de Lenclos. He was on friendly terms with some of the leading free-thinkers of the day, notably the aged La Mothe Le Vayer. At the opposite pole of religious and philosophical thought was the "academy" of the pious Lamoignon, attended by such eminent Jesuits as Rapin, Bouhours, and Bourdaloue. Here also, though somewhat later, Boileau was welcomed and considered a regular. There is doubtless much exaggeration in contemporary descriptions of the "Bacchic academies" which met in the cabarets, but there also remains some truth.

These, then, were Boileau's friends—people from all walks of life and every philosophical persuasion, Jesuits and Jansenists, writers and barristers, nobles and bourgeois. It was to this society that he first began to read his *Satires* and it was the encourage-

ment and appreciation he received from these friends that led him
to continue.

It is during this period of his life that Boileau composed his first
nine *Satires,* and it is interesting to note that, though satirical
traits may be found in all his works, he composed no formal satires between *Satire IX* (1667) and *Satire X* (1693). Never in a
hurry to get into print, Boileau did not publish the *Satires* until
1666, although several appeared in various anthologies. After the
appearance of a pirated edition in Rouen, Boileau decided to publish an authentic collection in 1666 of the first seven *Satires* and a
Discours au roi (*Address to the King*). The *Satires* had already
circulated in manuscript form, and Boileau read them in salon
and cabaret society. Many contemporaries attest to Boileau's gift
for reading aloud and for mimicry, which doubled the pleasure of
hearing his poems read aloud by their author. This talent also
helped to gain him entry and popularity in some of the literary
salons. Because of the habit, common in the century, of circulating literary works in manuscript form, not to mention Boileau's
constant revisions and changes from one printed edition to another, it is difficult to assign an exact date of composition to many
of his poems.

During the period from 1657 to 1668, in addition to the first
nine *Satires,* Boileau also composed the *Dissertation sur Joconde*
(*Dissertation on Joconde*) in 1663–65, and the *Dialogue des héros
de romans* (*Dialogue of the Heroes of Novels*) in 1664–65. In the
former he defends a version by La Fontaine of a story from Ariosto against those who preferred a version by a certain M. Bouïl-
lon. In the latter, he attacks the popular adventure novels, especially those of Mlle de Scudéry.[11] Out of respect for her, it was not
published until after her death, but it was known in manuscript
form. With the exception of these two pieces of excellent literary
criticism, Boileau became known to the public primarily as a satirist. His *Discours au roi* of 1663–64 was probably called to Louis
XIV's attention, but Boileau's access to court did not come until
later. Because of his acid pen, Boileau had made many enemies,
besides succeeding in calling attention to himself. But there were
also a large number of people in the new generation who were
ready to support his cause of taste and naturalness in literature.
Apart from the friends already mentioned, he had some powerful

partisans at court, e.g., La Rochefoucauld, the Duc de Vivonne, Mme de Thianges, Mme de Montespan. It was at about this time that Boileau resolved to curb the vitriol of his satire and seek to set forth some more positive ideas, especially in the field of literary theory.

III   Literary Maturity; Boileau the Critic and Theorist (1669–1677)

Contemporaries had been violently denouncing Boileau for the negative nature of the criticism in his *Satires*. It was not enough, they felt, simply to approve or disapprove. One must say why. In short, Boileau was accused of capriciousness in his judgments and taste. In the period from 1669 to 1677 we notice an attenuation of the satiric vein and a corresponding increase in critical doctrine and theory, in which Boileau attempts to demonstrate the foundations of his taste and judgment. Although literary satire is to be observed in nearly all Boileau's writings throughout his life, there is a noticeable decrease in this type and in the satire of bourgeois life, and an increasing number of poems dealing with moral questions. Most important of the events of this period are his regular attendance at the Lamoignon "academy," his introduction to the court, and the publication of his *Art poétique* in 1674.

The transformation which led Boileau to become serious and even a bit severe may be partially explained by the natural evolution of his temperament and thought. If a mocking wit is characteristic of the Paris bourgeois, there is an equally important quality of seriousness and morality. Having become known, Boileau now wanted to substitute for his reputation as a sharp satirist that of a learned poet and profound moralist. He also came under the influence of new milieux and new friends, especially that of the Lamoignon "academy." Lamoignon, universally respected for his piety and uprightness of life as well as for his intellect and culture, was president of the Paris *parlement*. Dating primarily from 1667, Lamoignon held regular meetings in his home, where erudite men met to discuss literature, morality, philosophy, physics, astronomy, and so on. In spite of the gravity and piety of the host, the conversations had little of the pedantic or austere about them. During this period of Boileau's literary evolution, when he had already begun the *Art poétique* (begun in 1669; completed in 1674), it is almost certain that he exchanged ideas and insights with Rapin, who was engaged in writing *Reflections on Aristotle's Poetics.* Boileau was a regular guest and was treated by Lamoignon not only as a poet of merit but as an intimate friend. It was Lamoignon who provided some of the inspiration which led Boileau to strive toward more serious and methodical works. Father Bouhours, author in 1671 of *Conversations between Ariste and Eugene,* was also an influence on Boileau. His lack of dogmatism in judging literary works and the importance he attached to the *je ne sais quoi* (*nescio quid,* "I know not what") is reflected in Boileau's translation of Longinus' *Treatise on the Sublime* (1674).[12]

Le Lutrin (*The Lectern,* 1674) grew directly out of a conversation which took place at a meeting of the Lamoignon group. In a discussion of epic poetry, always a lively topic in view of the many contemporary and unsuccessful attempts to provide France with a great national epic (*La Chanson de Roland* was lost), Boileau maintained that a good epic should not be burdened with a lot of material. As an example he cited the wrath of Achilles, which had sufficed for the *Iliad* of Homer. One of those present then related a recent squabble among the clerics of the Sainte Chapelle, and Boileau was asked, jokingly, if he thought he could compose an epic with such scanty material. Boileau's reply, almost without thinking, was "Why not?" On his return home he thought more about it, began to write, a few lines at a time, and in 1674 published the first four cantos of *Le Lutrin,* a sort of heroic-comic, mock epic.

It was also during this period that Boileau composed the *Arrêt burlesque* (*Burlesque Injunction,* 1671). Hearing that the Faculty of Theology of the Sorbonne was about to request the Paris *parlement,* presided over by Lamoignon, to hand down an injunction forbidding the teaching of any philosophy save that derived from Aristotle, Boileau drew up a mock injunction, in formal legal terminology, which is one of the most amusing things he ever wrote. His brother-in-law, Dongois, managed to slip it in a pile of papers on Lamoignon's desk, much to the president's amusement. Somehow the Sorbonne got wind of it and, because the satire and irony were so absolutely devastating, the request for the injunction was withdrawn. Thus, in spite of his resolve to be more serious, we see from the composition of *Le Lutrin* and the *Arrêt burlesque* that Boileau had by no means lost either his satirical bent or his sense of humor. It would be well for those who tend to see Boileau only as the cold, staid, and humorless author of the *Art poétique* to remember that these two comic pieces were composed at the same time as the more serious and doctrinaire work. It is perhaps unfortunate that Boileau was eventually to succeed in establishing a reputation for learned wisdom and serious meditation if his more amusing side has to suffer neglect.

Boileau's transformation of 1669 is thus by no means total. If he temporarily abandons the satiric form, he does not abandon the satiric inspiration, nor was he ever to do so completely. As the first period of his literary production was characterized by the publication of nine *Satires,* this period saw the publication of nine *Epîtres.* Boileau changed his form but could not alter his genius, which was basically satirical. Many of his *Epîtres,* especially *Epître I, Au roi* (*To the King*), are rather like satires, both moral and literary. Basically, however, the epistle has a different goal from the satire—the latter offends while the former flatters. Horace had conceived of the epistle as a letter in verse on a moral or philosophical subject. The seventeenth century generally preserved this idea, and Boileau certainly had Horace in mind when he began to write in this form. Three of his first nine *Epîtres* are addressed to the king, Boileau's way of praising a monarch whom he sincerely admired. If *Epîtres I, IV,* and *VIII* seem flattering today, they did not seem so to Boileau's contemporaries, who accused him of niggardliness in his praise of the Sun King.

Boileau had already written a *Discours au roi* in 1663–64 and would have had access to the court, either through Molière and Racine or by means of his protectors in the ranks of the nobility. He seems not to have wanted to take advantage of his openings at court, perhaps until he had succeeded in attenuating his reputation as a polemicist. Louis XIV was already acquainted with Boileau's poetry and enjoyed it, but it was probably not until after the composition of *Epître IV, Le Passage du Rhin* (*Crossing of the Rhine*) in 1672 that Boileau was formally presented at court by the Duc de Vivonne. The king was pleased, both with Boileau's poetry and his personality, and granted him a pension of two thousand francs a year, together with official permission to print all his works. With this permission, or *privilège,* the publisher Thierry printed an edition of Boileau's works in 1674. Boileau thanked the king officially in 1675 by means of *Epître VIII,* and he began to draw his pension only in 1677. The poet did not

forfeit his frankness or independence when he received royal protection and favor. His praises of the king were sincere and, as
much as possible under an absolute monarchy, Boileau kept his
freedom of judgment. Boileau's honesty and frankness did not
alienate the king, whose own upright spirit and firm common
sense appreciated these same qualities in the poet. In 1677 Louis
commanded Boileau and Racine to stop other tasks in order to
concentrate on writing the history of his reign. This appointment
as royal historiographer ushers in the period of Boileau's career as
an official, as well as the time of his most intimate friendship with
Racine.

IV *Official Career* (*1677–1686*)

Boileau's literary production during his active period as royal
historiographer was very slight, limited to the two final cantos of
Le Lutrin (1681–83). Not all of his time was spent in collecting
and writing the royal history, however. As a famous author it was
his responsibility to oversee the publication of new and augmented editions of his works. In Boileau's case this was not an
inconsiderable task, since it was his habit to rewrite his poems
from one edition to another. Nevertheless, the collection of the
royal history was very time consuming. Boileau and Racine, emi-
nently unqualified for the task the king had set them, did their
best. They had treaties and campaigns explained to them. They
interrogated the great siege engineer Vauban, the Marshal of
Luxembourg, the war minister Louvois, and others who participated in the events of the time. They collected memoirs and tried
to arrange the facts in some semblance of order. They attempted
not only to record the facts but also to understand the reasons
behind events, often the hardest part of the job. The most difficult
thing of all was having to accompany the king on his campaigns.
The poets' nearly complete ignorance of things military, their in-
eptness on horseback, their understandable lack of any inclination
to place themselves in positions of danger—all these caused a
great deal of teasing, both in the field and at court. Epigrams and
anecdotes about them circulated, to the delight of their enemies.
It is unfortunate for the historians of the reign of Louis XIV, but
possibly fortunate for our good opinion of Boileau and Racine,
that nothing survived of their history. Their manuscripts allegedly
perished in a fire in 1726. At his death Boileau sent an apology to

the king that he and Racine had not done a better job in an undertaking for which both were little qualified by nature or temperament.

There was a marked decrease in Boileau's literary efforts during
his later years. Besides the time spent in his duties as historiographer, illness and controversy, not to mention the infirmities of age,
may account for much of his seeming indifference toward his writing. As an official personage he seems to have thought that a gentleman had better things to do. It is well to remember that, despite Louis' generous pensions and his reception of some writers
at court, the profession of author was still slightly regarded. Louis
XIV made nobles of his six former fencing masters but he never
ennobled any writers. As a matter of fact, it was the fashion of the
time, even among poets, to decry the writing of poetry as a serious
occupation and to pretend a disdain and nonchalant attitude toward the "trifles" they dashed off. Writing was considered a pastime, indulged in moments of leisure, but unworthy of the full-
time attention of a gentleman. Elevated to the responsible and
official position of royal historiographers, Racine and Boileau also
had to maintain a certain façade of gentility.

Never really robust in health, Boileau eventually ceased to accompany the king on his military campaigns, leaving it to Racine
to suffer both the fatigues and the "glories" of camp life. Tor-
mented most of his adult life by respiratory ailments, Boileau
suffered an acute attack of laryngitis in 1687 which lasted some
months and rendered him almost completely speechless. He tried
every remedy known to the medical science of his day, including
apricot cough syrup and she-asses' milk, all to no avail. He even
spent some time at the spa at Bourbon. Louis XIV, exhibiting a
touching concern for Boileau's health, told Racine to inform Boileau of his interest and to tell him that his voice would return on
its own, when he least expected it.[13] Such was to be the case, although the illness incapacitated him for a time. Indeed, it appeared a convenient opportunity for Boileau, weary of the pomp
and circumstance of court life, to frequent Versailles less. Never a
natural courtier like Racine, he preferred now to allow himself to
be almost forgotten by the king.

In 1684 Boileau had been elected to the French Academy, an
honor which had been long overdue. He was already forty-seven
years old and had published his best work. His closest friend, Ra-

cine, had been a member since 1673 and, although Boileau consistently refused to seek a seat for himself, he deserved membership. In 1683, on the death of Colbert, a place became vacant and
La Fontaine presented himself as a candidate, promising the
members that he would reform and write no more salacious stories. He feared the concurrence of Boileau and asked him not to
solicit the chair. Boileau's reply was that if the Academy chose
him for the honor he would not refuse, but that he would do nothing actively to obtain it. The Academy was thus divided between
the two, with Boileau's enemies doing everything possible to dis-
credit him. On the first ballot La Fontaine received sixteen votes
to seven for Boileau. The choice could not be definitive until after
a second ballot, which had to be preceded by the king's acceptance of the chosen candidate. Louis XIV was not happy with the
choice of La Fontaine. Not wishing to influence the Academy directly, he simply put off making his wishes known. About the
same time the death of a M. de Bezons left another chair vacant,
to which Boileau was duly elected. This pleased Louis XIV, who
now permitted the seating of La Fontaine as well. During this
conflict the two poets remained outside the debate, showing no
resentment toward each other.

Even though a member, Boileau never felt completely at home
in the Academy meetings and was never satisfied with what the
Academy was doing. Nor did Boileau's enemies among the membership, many of the same men he had attacked in his *Satires*,
enjoy the presence of one whom they considered forced on them.
Boileau knew this, of course, and was often quite rough in his
remarks about the Academy. In truth, the group was not at this
time what one would call an illustrious assemblage. Boileau felt
that the Academy was not fulfilling the functions it had been as-
signed at its founding, i.e., the composition of a Dictionary, a
Grammar, a Rhetoric, and a Poetic. Of all these the Academy exe-
cuted only the writing of the Dictionary. To combat their inertia,
Boileau proposed translations from the ancients, corrected and
approved by the Academy, to be read by the public as examples
of good style. He also proposed that the presses of the Louvre be
used to publish good editions of the French classics. Neither of
these proposals was accepted.

Boileau had just been admitted to the Academy when Louvois
put him and Racine in the Academy of Inscriptions and Medal-

lions, nicknamed the "Little Academy." Its functions were limited
to selecting inscriptions for public monuments, designs for the
royal tapestries, coin designs, the embellishment of Versailles, and
the like. Boileau was zealous in these duties and was much more
enthusiastic and regular in attendance than at the meetings of the
Academy. He and Racine brought to the new position a taste for
simplicity and naturalness which had been hitherto unknown.
Even here Boileau found controversy, this time with one of the
older members, Charpentier, who was fond of long, emphatic, and
bombastic inscriptions. It was he who had written the inscriptions
for the paintings of Louis XIV's victories in the grand gallery at
Versailles. Boileau's taste was shocked, and the king was so impressed with his written opinions that he ordered Charpentier's
inscriptions effaced and new ones composed by Boileau and Racine put in their place. In this matter of inscriptions, as in his
poetry, Boileau consistently exhibited his taste for the simple and
natural over the bombastic and rhetorical.

In 1685 Boileau purchased a small house with a large garden in
Auteuil, not far from the Bois de Boulogne, and at that time located in the country. He enjoyed this property and it was the
garden there which is the subject of one of the two poems he
composed in honor of Nature. After 1687 he was able to live there
only during the warm months when there was no danger to his
respiratory system. He received his friends there and the place
seems to have had a calming effect on him. He kept it until old
age and illness finally forced him to sell it in 1709. His years of
relative peace were not to last, however, for his latter years were
also those of greatest conflict.

V Latter Years; Adversary of the Moderns and the Casuists (1687–1711)

Literary historians have often been inclined to picture the latter
years of Boileau with overemphasis on the seriousness, the bitter
controversies, and the tinge of sadness natural to old age. It
should be pointed out that, in spite of infirmity, conflicts, dissatisfaction with the turn of literary events, and the death of his
friends, Boileau's last years were not all morose. He continued to
exercise his function as royal historiographer, although he accompanied the king on no more campaigns. In 1692 his pension as
historiographer was reduced to one-half that of Racine, which

Boileau considered fair. He continued to frequent court for some time, but at irregular intervals, and he finally came to depend almost entirely on Racine as intermediary in his dealings with the court. After 1690 he went rarely to Versailles, and after the death of Racine in 1699, he went only one more time—to receive the king's instructions concerning the history.

In spite of his poor health, Boileau was able to remain calm and philosophical as well as mentally alert. His respiratory ailments developed into a chronic asthma, he became deaf, his sight grew worse, he suffered attacks of vertigo, and he was subject to dropsy and general weakness. By 1709 he was no longer able to walk unaided. Yet his letters, especially to Brossette, remain remarkably placid and resigned. His illness and age did not prevent him from working hard on another edition of his works nor from composing his last three *Satires*, the last three *Epîtres*, an *Ode sur la prise de Namur* (*Ode on the Capture of Namur*) and nine *Réflexions critiques sur Longin*. Although his poetry lost much of its original verve, the intellectual content and the morality were as solid as ever. He never completely lost the habit of satire, and even in his old age his wit could be cutting when his indignation was aroused.

Boileau had always set great store by friendship and was the type of person who never lost a friend. Thus it seems fitting that a great sadness as well as a great joy of his latter years should be connected with his friends. The death of Racine in 1699 was a heavy blow to Boileau. The two had been acquainted for nearly forty years and had been on terms of intimacy for about twenty-five years. The tone of their correspondence, especially during Boileau's stay at Bourbon, tells us much about their relationship. Like most letters of the time, which the writers knew would often be passed on or read aloud to mutual acquaintances, there is in them a ceremonious politeness and avoidance of confidences. But their friendship was solid and their mutual devotion unceasing. Right up to his death Racine went frequently to Auteuil, often with his wife and children. Boileau seems to have been genuinely fond of Racine's children, which was a considerable accomplishment for a confirmed old bachelor. He sermonized them, corrected their Latin compositions, talked with the boys about their future careers and moral life, and played ninepins with them—a game at which Boileau always excelled. After Racine's death, Boi-

leau maintained close relations with the children, continuing to
advise them. A certain sad and wistful loneliness now crept into
Boileau's life, not uncommon in elderly people who see their
friends dying off one by one. Another contributing factor to this
attitude was the fact that Boileau was unhappy with the direction
literature was taking, and tended to regard himself as the last of
the generation that had produced Molière, La Fontaine, and Racine.

Boileau always had a special feeling for the city of Lyons because of the annual income he received from his investment in her
municipal bonds, which had been paid unfailingly in good times
and bad. He welcomed any distinguished visitors to Paris from
Lyons as a mark of gratitude to the city he regarded as his foster
mother. In 1698 he received a visit from a young lawyer, Claude
Brossette, of Lyons. Brossette was an impassioned admirer of Boileau's works, asked for his friendship, and revealed his project of
writing a commentary on Boileau's work for the benefit of posterity. The old man was flattered by Brossette's adulation and enthusiasm. Although Brossette had to return to Lyons and returned to
Paris only once more, in 1702, their relationship developed into a
fast friendship by means of an extensive correspondence which
lasted until Boileau's death. These letters, along with the correspondence with Racine, are indispensable to a complete understanding of Boileau both as a writer and as a person. Boileau
rarely tired of answering Brossette's questions and asked only that
the commentary be an *imperceptible* apology. It is in these re-
sponses to Brossette's inquiries that Boileau's poetic vanity is most
visible. Perhaps this concern may be excused as an old man's long-
ing for immortality and his feeling that Brossette's apology would
be an important legacy to posterity. Boileau's memory was at
times surely faulty, but we may be certain that he never deliberately falsified anything to Brossette—this would be too contrary to
his lifelong character. Brossette's commentaries, although inval-
uable, are thus not always completely trustworthy.[14] Sometimes
Boileau is jesting and does not reveal his thought completely.
Brossette was not always scrupulous in his reporting and sometimes added ideas of his own. In any event, this friendship and
admiration helped brighten Boileau's later years, as did other
friendships, notably with Le Verrier, whose commentary on his
works Boileau took the trouble to correct in his own hand. These

indications of appreciation and loyalty were welcome interludes in the two great quarrels in which Boileau participated—the Quarrel of the Ancients and Moderns and the controversy with the casuists among the Jesuits.

The Quarrel of the Ancients and Moderns, in all its phases and ramifications, is much too complicated a story to detail, either here or in the chapter devoted to it in this book (Chapter 5). An ardent admirer and staunch supporter of the ancients, Boileau was placed in a position which made it difficult for him to defend them adequately because of his admiration and genuine devotion to such moderns as Corneille, Molière, Racine, and La Fontaine. Indeed, he himself was a modern writer, and his work was used by some of the more subtle of the partisans of the moderns to prove their point. The nine *Réflexions sur Longin, Satire X,* and the *Ode sur la prise de Namur* were all written in the heat of the quarrel, and all have some connection with it. Boileau's main opponents were, first Desmarets de Saint-Sorlin, and later Charles Perrault. His best-known allies were also the greatest writers of the time—Racine, La Fontaine, La Bruyère, and others. It is an interesting and perhaps unparalleled phenomenon in the history of literature to see the greatest modern writers united in defense of their rivals, the ancients. It will suffice here to state that the end of this phase of the Quarrel of the Ancients and Moderns resulted in a standoff. Boileau did not defend the ancients adequately because he was really a modern himself. Perrault's arguments were more rational but were based on a fundamentally false analogy between the sciences and the arts. Against his arguments Boileau was able to gain at least a stalemate because of his superior reputation and authority. Fortunately, perhaps, he did not live to see the reopening of the Quarrel and its final phases.

The quarrel with the Jesuit casuists reached a climax during the final period of Boileau's life, but it was one which had been building for a long time. In the eyes of the Jesuits, Boileau had long been guilty of one unforgivable sin—admiration for the Jansenists and especially for their acknowledged head, Antoine Arnauld. If it is somewhat difficult for us to understand Boileau's ardent interest in religious quarrels, we should remember that in the seventeenth century nearly everyone was an amateur theologian of sorts, and people were passionately interested in religious questions. In the continuing battle between Jesuits and Jansenists public opinion was divided, with much bitterness and vehemence on both sides.

Doctrinally Boileau had no fixed position. In the area of morality, his life and ideas resembled more the austerity and strictness of the Jansenists. Thus his quarrel was with the lax morality of the casuists rather than on any question of dogma or doctrine. He was a sincere admirer of the Jansenist Arnauld but also had some very close relationships with the Jesuits. Jesuit friends came to visit him often at Auteuil and members of the Society of Jesus had been his friends at Lamoignon's "academy." Nevertheless, he managed to irritate the Jesuits on several occasions when he consistently maintained that the *Provincial Letters* of Pascal, the Jansenist apologist, were the greatest masterpieces of modern prose style, surpassing even his beloved ancients. It should also be noted that the attacks made on Boileau did not come from any of his Jesuit friends or any others of the more famous and respected Jesuits of the time.

Epître XII, Sur l'amour de Dieu (*On Love for God,* 1695–97) and *Satire XII, Sur l'équivoque* (*On Ambiguity,* 1705–8) were the two poems which provoked open warfare with the casuist faction. While he attacked casuistry in several other poems, Boileau had always taken precautions to state that he was not attacking the Jesuit order itself but only the lax morality which resulted from the practice of casuistry by some of the members. In spite of these precautions, the Jesuits took *Epître XII* as an act of hostility. The doctrine (preached by certain Jesuits) that fear of punishment, without love for God, is sufficient for true penitence, offended not only Boileau's sense of morality but also his common sense. He could not resist writing a scathing satire against this idea. A fuller discussion of the moral and theological issue will be found in Chapter 3. Here it suffices to note that Boileau was attacked in an article in the *Journal de Trévoux,* a semi-official Jesuit organ, in 1703. He replied with a few strongly worded epigrams. Some of his Jesuit friends intervened and peace was made for the time being. The Jesuits saw, however, that even though Boileau made a distinction between respectable Jesuits and the casuists, the public did not. Another article appeared in the *Journal de Trévoux,* ostensibly in praise of Boileau but actually loaded with irony and innuendo. A furious war of pamphlets and epigrams began; *Satire XII* caused a scandal when it began to be read

aloud and circulated in manuscript form. Despite the approval of
the Archbishop of Paris and the Chancellor of France, Boileau
was made to realize that publication of the satire was not desired
at the time.

In 1709 Father de la Chaise, a friend and defender of Boileau,
died and was replaced as confessor to the king by Father Le Tellier, a violent adversary of the Jansenists. Because of Le Tellier's
influence with the aged and now pious monarch, Boileau was refused a *privilège* for publication of an edition of his works which
was to contain *Satire XII*. Boileau refused to deny authorship of it
or to publish the edition without it, so it was not published until
after his death. Defeated, saddened, and increasingly infirm, Boileau lived for two more years at the home of his confessor, Father
Lenoir, in the cloister of Notre Dame. Here he died on March 13,
1711 at the age of seventy-four, leaving his possessions to his family and friends and setting up an endowment for the poor in six of
the city's parishes. He was buried in the Sainte Chapelle. During
the Revolution his remains were removed to the Muséum des
Monuments Français, and during the Restoration he was reburied
in the abbey of Saint-Germain-des-Prés.

VI *Character and Personality*

Boileau the man may be best characterized as upright and sincere. He was serious but pleasant, with a fine sense of humor.
There is nothing really unusual or outstanding about Boileau's
personality or character. He might even be considered typical of a
young man reared in an upper middle-class family whose members exhibited the qualities usual to the Parisian bourgeoisie.
These were seriousness, strict morality, old-fashioned common
sense, and a slightly mocking spirit which can see the humor and
the sham behind façades of respectability or pomp. When no
longer subject to parental control, Boileau did as many young
men do for a while, enjoying a happy life of tavern society with
friends of a devil-may-care nature. Growing older, his innate
sense of seriousness and decorum reasserted itself. As we have
seen, the desire to distinguish himself in his chosen field led him
first of all to attract attention to himself and gain a hearing, then
to try to establish a solid reputation. As this reputation increased,
he became more serious, less radical in his thought and satire,
more conservative in his habits and theories, more restrained in

his pronouncements. Boileau's reputation and personality have been unintentionally distorted by an almost inevitable tendency to emphasize his works of morality and critical theory, especially the *Art poétique*, to the detriment of his lighter vein. Reading of the *Art poétique* should be tempered by a study of the delightful *Arrêt burlesque*, the *Dialogues des héros de romans*, and *Le Lutrin.*

Perhaps the best indication of Boileau's real personality may be gained by an examination of his friendships. He had the reputation of never having lost a friend and of counting former enemies among his friends. His friendship with the passionate Racine for over a quarter of a century would seem to give the lie to any impression of Boileau as cold. Such warmth and devotion may be inspired only by one who is warm and devoted in turn.

Although his frugality in his personal habits was well-known, Boileau's generosity was equally proverbial. It is reported that, on hearing that Corneille's pension was about to be cut off, Boileau immediately rushed to Madame de Maintenon to request her to intervene with the king on the dramatist's behalf, stating that he would rather sacrifice his own pension than permit such an act of ingratitude.

It was common practice among younger sons, especially of the nobility, to hold ecclesiastical benefices without ordination to the priesthood, but Boileau's sense of honesty and integrity would not permit him to retain a benefice he had held from the time he was destined for a career in the church. He not only gave up the benefice but also returned all the money he had been paid for the period of eight years that he had held this ecclesiastical "living."

Sincerity and independence of mind were fundamental to Boileau's character, and nowhere were these traits put to a more severe test than in his dealings with Louis XIV, a monarch who delighted in flattery and with whom it was unwise to disagree. On one occasion, the story goes, the king showed Boileau a poem of his own composition and asked his opinion of it. Constitutionally unable to say anything he did not believe, Boileau demonstrated a wit and presence of mind which show that he was not such a poor courtier after all. "Sire," he said, "nothing is impossible for Your Majesty. You wanted to write a bad poem and you have succeeded." [15] On another occasion the courtiers were discussing the current affectation in speech of using the word *gros* (fat; large in bulk) as a substitute for *grand* (great; large in height). Even the king judged that the substitution was acceptable, but not Boileau. "Sire," he retorted, "posterity will surely be able to make the distinction between Louis the Fat [Louis VI] and Louis the Great [Louis XIV]."

Boileau's sense of humor is most easily demonstrated in such works as *Le Lutrin,* the *Arrêt burlesque,* the *Dialogue des héros de romans,* and many of the *Satires.* His part in the composition of the *Chapelain décoiffé* also indicates a fun-loving disposition.

On the debit side of the ledger it must be mentioned that Boileau was not always completely fair to those he named in his satires. His greatest weakness as a critic is the fact that he had sometimes not read the works of those he condemned. Too often he criticized on the hearsay evidence of his friends. Too often, needing a name for a rhyme or a name of a certain number of syllables for his meter, he accepted without question a name furnished by friends, or simply picked one at random with the required number of syllables or sound from one of the many anthologies of poetry popular at the time. Boileau's great passion in life was the love of good books and the hatred of poor ones, and sometimes he became overly zealous and consequently unfair. Most often, however, he would change a name in a poem if he were informed that he had not been just in his original inclusion of it. And it is truly amazing how seldom his judgment was wrong. He was correct in denouncing the unnatural, precious, emphatic, burlesque, and ridiculous style wherever he observed it.

All in all, Boileau's fundamental generosity, honesty, integrity, and sincerity far outweigh his vanity and hasty judgments. He was a warm and devoted friend and was able to inspire reciprocal sentiments. His sense of humor, wit, and talent for reading aloud and mimicry made him a welcome guest in the salons. His seriousness, knowledge, intelligence, and reasonableness were attractive to his fellow guests in the more intellectual and serious gatherings, such as the Lamoignon circle. When at court, Boileau was able to retain the esteem of the king, without having to sacrifice his sincerity or independence of spirit. As a host in his house at Auteuil, his guests were numerous, his table was faultless, and his conversation was the delight of all who attended. As a social figure, Boileau had the knack of being able to adapt himself easily to the company he was in and to move effortlessly among all classes and types of persons. He was, then, a person whose company anyone would enjoy, providing he was not a vain and pompous author.

CHAPTER 2

Boileau the Satirist

SATIRE was Boileau's natural talent and, in spite of changes in form, some satire is always present in his work. This is true even in such a serious and theoretical work as the *Art poétique*, where he cannot resist occasions to poke fun. A study of all the *Satires* together followed by all the *Epîtres*, while preserving unity of literary genre would lead to disunity of thought and ideas. Since many of the *Epîtres* are also satires and since many of the *Satires* contain moral and religious ideas, a division on the basis of thought and subject is more logical than one based on form. This approach also has the advantage of a parallel to the life and thought of Boileau, whose earlier period of literary production (1657–68) contains a preponderance of satire, while the period of maturity (1669–77) saw the composition of most of his moral epistles. There is, obviously, a certain amount of duplication. In such cases, works will be discussed in the category which seems most applicable and, in some instances, a work may be examined in more than one category. For further convenience, the satirical works will be discussed as literary satires or as satires of manners.

I *Satires of Manners*

Boileau's works which may be considered as primarily satires of manners are *Satires I, III, VI, X, Epître II, l'Arrêt burlesque*, and *Le Lutrin*. Some of these are satirical of bourgeois manners in general, while others are more specifically directed toward ridiculing certain groups of society.

Satire I

Satire I, of which *Satire VI* was once a part and later detached, is primarily a satire of the manners of the city. A single literary reference appeared in an unauthorized version and was subsequently removed. The division of the satire into *Satire I* and *Satire VI* is a natural one, for in the former it is primarily people with which Boileau deals, while in the latter it is the physical conditions of the city. In *Satire I* Boileau follows the model of Juvenal, who had treated the same subject in his *Satire III*, describing the departure of the poet Umbricius from Rome to Cumae. Boileau's poem is thus aptly subtitled *le Départ du poète* (*The Departure of the Poet*). Damon, the gentleman-poet, is constrained to leave Paris in indignation, for the manners of the city shock him, and true merit is not properly appreciated. Boileau attacks particularly the *nouveaux riches,* opportunists, and shady financiers.

After an introductory description of Damon's miserable condition, the rest of the poem comprises his angry farewell to the city. Since merit and intelligence are no longer fashionable, he has decided to leave. The city is now fit only for those who, by means of their ill-gotten riches, have purchased for themselves titles of nobility. The poet, unable to deceive, pretend, lie, and flatter, is too proud to sell his verse to the highest bidder. Damon then imagines that someone may reprove him for being so intractably virtuous and point out the need for adaptability, especially when one is poor. In a "century of iron" this is the only way an author might hope to accomplish any reforms of manners. The king has begun to help poets by means of the royal pensions, but one cannot even approach the source of the royal bounty because of the crowd of starving rhymsters. Formerly it was stylish to have a court poet, but today the finest wit and most polished author will never attain the status enjoyed by the court jester.

In such circumstances Damon wonders if he should try a different career, perhaps the law. The very thought of wandering through the confused labyrinth of chicanery, where innocence is oppressed by legal formality, makes the poet doubt his own sanity. His only choice is to leave a city where Fortune makes war on Honor and Vice claims sovereignty, walking about with mitre on its head and crosier in hand. Any decent man would be angry at the manners of Paris and, in spite of Apollo and the Muses, would learn to rhyme for the sole purpose of condemning such odious abuses. Anger alone would provide the necessary inspiration. This attitude is typical of one who has a satirical spirit, and Damon is fearful lest the spirit of satire have an embittering effect on him. He has decided that it is best for him to leave.

Boileau the Satirist

Satire I shows considerable boldness in attacking the financ[ ]
parvenus, lawyers, and the bad taste of the court, and in personi-
fying vice with the ecclesiastical mitre and crosier. The satire is
even more barbed when one considers that, whether accurately or
not, his contemporaries saw in some of the figures well-known
personages of the day. While Satire I often seems weak in comparison with later productions, one may already observe the mordant hyperbole of a master. The same theme, treated differently,
is also found in Satire III of Mathurin Régnier, but Boileau is
much closer to Juvenal, to whose satire he added little except the
substitution of Parisian for Roman actuality.[1]

Satire VI

Satire VI alone would suffice to qualify Boileau as one of the
great poets of the city of Paris along with François Villon and
Baudelaire. Boileau here adds his own originality, while borrowing from Juvenal's Satire I and from Régnier. The poem contains
much actuality, and the noise, mud, and inconvenience of Paris
give a picture of the city which is marvelously alive—the slums,
traffic jams, incessant noise of a large city. The satire is subtitled
l'Embarrass de Paris (The Confusion of Paris). It contains many
excellent lines, much verve and picturesqueness, and is easy to
remember. Compared to most similar works of his contemporaries, it is a masterpiece of purity and naturalness.

The poem opens with the poet's lament over his inability to
sleep in the city. (Boileau, who inhabited an attic room in his
brother's house, surely must have passed many a sleepless night
because of the noise.) It seems as if some demon has gathered all
the cats of the city on his roof, and the bats and rats have joined
in a compact with them to keep him awake. Hardly have the
roosters crowed at dawn when a neighboring iron-worker gives
him a headache with the resounding blows of his hammer. Carts
begin to move through the streets, masons commence their work,
shops open, and the church bells ring.

If this were all, the poet would be grateful, but it is even worse
when he leaves the house. Wherever he goes he must push and
shove his way through crowds. He is elbowed, his hat is knocked
off, and his progress is slowed by a funeral procession. Lackeys,
scolding one another, cause the dogs to bark and the passers-by to
curse. Street pavers block the passage and workmen repairing

roofs permit slate and tile to fall on unwary pedestrians. A large cart threatens to crush the crowd, knocks a wheel off a passing carriage and overturns it in the mud. Twenty more carriages immediately arrive on the scene and the traffic jam is made worse by a herd of cattle on the way to market. All are determined to get through, cattle lowing and men cursing. Not knowing what else to do, the poet takes a chance of being run over, jumps over water flowing in the streets, tries to push his way through, and ends by being knocked over by a horse. He escapes as best he can, now unable to keep his appointment in his muddy garments. While drying off in a corner, a rain begins to fall which would shame the original Flood. The street becomes a river which must be crossed on a narrow board.

As soon as night falls and the marketplaces are quiet, the thieves come out of their lairs and take over the city. In comparison to Paris at night, the loneliest forest is a place of security. Woe to him who has business on the streets at night, for he must either sacrifice his purse or his life. As for the poet, he goes to bed at sundown. But hardly has he extinguished his candle when a pistol shot breaks his window and someone screams, "Help! Murder!" Or a house in the neighboring section catches fire, making of the area a second Troy, complete with pillaging, until houses are knocked down to stop the fire's progress. By the time he returns home it is already dawn and sleep is impossible. Only with sufficient money for a new apartment far from the street can one sleep in Paris. The poet, who has neither heath nor hearth to call his own, must dwell wherever he can.

Satire VI thus exhibits a realism and actuality which are quite different from the abstractness of many of his other works. It also demonstrates Boileau's ability to evoke a living picture of the "downtown" of a large and busy metropolis, however satirical.

Satire III

Satire III, le Repas ridicule (The Ridiculous Meal) stands in a long and honorable tradition of satires on a similar subject. It contains both ridicule of bourgeois manners and some literary satire. Horace (*Book II, Satire VIII*) and Mathurin Régnier (*Satire X*) had both treated the theme of the ridiculous meal, but in different fashions. Boileau follows both models to some extent, probably imitating Horace for the meal and Régnier for the dispute. In addition to the mockery of the would-be gourmet, the poem contains a lesson in good taste. The adventure novels with their silly compliments, the insipid tragedies of Quinault, the worthless writings of Cotin, are among the literary productions attacked and ridiculed.[2] The neatness of Boileau's style, the correctness of his verse, the measure and precision of his execution surpass Régnier. Although this satire is not Boileau's best, it contains many well-turned phrases, new and picturesque expressions, wit, and pleasantry.

Satire III takes the form of a dialogue or interrogation, in which the poet is represented by the letter *A* and the gourmet guest at the ridiculous meal by the letter *P*. Each interlocutor has only one speech. The poet, catching sight of his friend on the street and perceiving him to be in a state of agitation, wants to know the cause of his chagrin. The gourmet, catching his breath, informs his friend that he has just left the home of a fool who has tried to poison him. For more than a year this person had been trying to invite *P* to a meal. The previous day he finally caught up with him and succeeded in gaining his acceptance by the promise of an excellent wine, Molière to read *Tartuffe*, and the appearance of Lambert, the renowned composer and musician.[3] Seduced by the promise of seeing Lambert, the gourmet went at high noon (the hour of the main meal during the seventeenth century). He was immediately greeted by his host with the news that neither Molière nor Lambert would be present. Disappointed and disgusted, but captured, the gourmet followed the host to an upper chamber which the heat of the summer sun had turned into an oven. Other guests present were two gentlemen from the provinces, assiduous readers of the popular adventure novels. They greeted him with all the high-flown and lengthy compliments they had learned from Mlle de Scudéry's novel *Artamène, ou le grand Cyrus*.

The first course of the dinner is served, to the horror of the gourmet. Boileau's description of the food and wine is delightful in its realism, and the meal is composed of dishes which even a normal appetite would find unpalatable. Moreover, the table where they are seated is so small that they cannot help but elbow one another. The host, meanwhile, praises each dish and extols the ability of the cook, while the two country bumpkins agree that it is a superb meal.

One of the guests proposes to drink to the host's health, and a red wine is poured into glasses still showing fingerprints from earlier use. The guests then join in a drinking song, even though none has a voice. ¶The conversation finally turns to poetry, and the provincials judge as if they were seated on Mount Parnassus: the host praises Théophile de Viau and Ronsard, while one of the provincials, with a learned air, extols La Serre[4] and *la Pucelle* of Chapelain, even though he cannot help yawning as he reads it. He sees no merit in Voiture[5] but concedes that Corneille is sometimes "pretty." He is unable to understand why Racine's *Alexandre* is praised, and prefers the heroes of Quinault, who even say "I hate you!" tenderly. All are incapable of understanding why a certain young satirist (Boileau himself in *Satire II*) has criticized Quinault, and they agree that the satire is rather dull.

Another of the guests, himself a poet, agrees that Quinault is a profound wit, but claims that there are others equally good. An argument ensues between this poet and one of the men from the provinces, heated by wine and anger. Angry speech progresses to a brawl, with dishes thrown and hair pulled. While the others are attempting to separate them, the gourmet slips quietly out the door.

Satire III, then, is a fine example of a satire of manners combined with literary satire. Using the ridiculous meal for its own comic and mocking effect, Boileau also makes of it the framework for a literary satire in which he gives opinions opposite from his own to obvious fools who are incapable of intelligent literary judgment.

Satire X

Satire X, Contre les femmes (*Against Women*), 1692–93, was published twenty-five years after *Satire IX* (1667–68), the last of Boileau's first group of poems in this genre. There is some indication, however, that he had the initial idea as early as 1665–67. There is a connection also between the publication of *Satire X* and the Quarrel of the Ancients and Moderns, but this relationship will be discussed in Chapter 5. Here it will be considered as a satire of manners with both moral and literary overtones. Containing 738 lines, *Satire X* is by far the longest poem of Boileau in this form, more than twice as long as *Satire XII*, the next longest.

Boileau received much criticism on account of this satire, from women and their partisans as well as from Bishop Bossuet, who claimed that it was inimical to the state of matrimony. The satire was defended by Antoine Arnauld, and Boileau considered this defense, by a man whom he admired so much, as the glory of his career. The vices of women are represented with an extraordinary verve and wit. Boileau's animosity is partially inspired by the fact that the majority of the women of the day, unable to read the ancients except in translation, favored the side of the moderns in the Quarrel. Part of the poem was sent to Racine for his opinion and corrections and, contrary to Boileau's instructions, Racine showed the verses to the prince de Condé and the prince de Conti, both of whom were utterly charmed. Their praise was relayed to Boileau, who was encouraged to continue his composition and to read it in society.

In an *Au lecteur* (*To the Reader*) which precedes the satire, Boileau excuses himself to the ladies for taking the liberty of painting their vices. Since his tableaux are so general, he does not fear offending women, but rather hopes for their curiosity and approval. He is at least certain that he will be praised for having treated his subject without employing a single word which might shock modesty. (This decency is a characteristic of Boileau's poetry.) His apology ends with the hope that the ladies will find his satire no more shocking than they do the sermons which are preached on the same subject every day.

Satire X takes the form of an address by the poet to his friend Alcippe, who is about to get married. The initial satirical device is to give praise and then take it away. Thus the poet congratulates his friend on having decided to settle down. Marriage has its pleasures—wifely caresses, seeing children growing up around the house, a wife's tender and solicitous care of her husband's slightest illness. The friend will not be, the poet hopes, one of those jealous fellows who think some secret lover is always ready to console his wife. The poet readily admits that there have been many faithful wives like Penelope, and one can still find some today. He can even cite three in Paris! The new bride will soon make another. At least this is to be hoped, but the poet warns his friend to be sure and warn his wife when he intends to return from a trip. It has often happened that a husband who did not take such precautions found on his return. . . . The poet realizes that his friend will not be satisfied with gossip, so he resolves to explain. He is wise enough in the ways of the world to know what a ridiculous figure the cuckolded husband makes. He is the butt of jokes in epigrams, songs, rondeaux, fables, satire and comedy, written by such famous men as La Fontaine, Molière, Villon, Saint-Gelais,[6] Ariosto, Marot, Boccaccio, and Rabelais. None of these has ever prevented anyone from getting married. To be happy in marriage, everything depends on the choice one makes of a wife.

Boileau then proceeds to chronicle some of the faults of bachelorhood. Nephews are so anxious to get an uncle's money that they seem to be dividing it already under his very eyes. When they receive the news that their dear uncle has passed away, they will shed a forced tear for the sake of appearances and then quickly seek consolation. Moreover, the bachelor must remain at home alone at night with valets who are often treacherous thieves. When he goes to bed he cannot help but think of the stories of tragic murders committed to get money. Left alone, man soon becomes miserable, so one should not censure matrimony, life's sweetest bond. And bond it is, make no mistake about that. Marriage is a yoke—which is needed by man, who otherwise might freely indulge his passions. To be truly free, man must be chained.

There are many pitfalls waiting for the innocent new bride, and Boileau proceeds to catalogue most of them here. The operas of Quinault and Lully,[7] with their libidinous morality (*morale lubrique*) make love appear so attractive that its importance is exaggerated beyond reason. Society itself holds many temptations, and neither Venus nor Satan will permit relationships to remain as chaste as in the novels like *Clélie,* which are the continual diet of the salons. Then there are those wives who like the glamor and scandal of vice, though not attracted to vice itself. These women will flirt just for the thrill of it and to irritate their husbands. They are also spendthrifts, who lavish money on fancy clothes, cosmetics, and elaborate coiffures. Still worse is the wife who becomes a compulsive gambler and may eventually bankrupt the family. (Gambling was the vice of the seventeenth century.) Perhaps even worse than a gambling wife is the parsimonious one, who can reduce her husband to poverty in the midst of wealth simply by her unwillingness to part with a cent. Her reputation for avarice may cause them both to be murdered by robbers.

Boileau, recapitulating, notes that he has painted three basic portraits—the woman without honor, the flirt, and the stingy

woman. He will now proceed to describe more specific types. Cat-
alogued here are many types—the nag, the jealous wife, the hypo-
chondriac, the learned type (cf. Molière's *Femmes savantes*), the
affected or *précieuse* (cf. Molière's *Précieuses ridicules*), the
snob, the religious bigot and falsely pious woman. In connection
with the latter type, Boileau furnishes a delightful description of
the directors of consciences (*directeurs de consciences*), who
were lavishly cared for in the homes of the religious bigots in
exchange for smoothing the way to paradise by a permissive attitude which justified all the lady's faults and sins.[8] Even worse
than the religious bigot is what Boileau calls the bilious bigot,
who is so severe she thinks hating mankind is synonymous with
loving God.

Alcippe protests that the poet can see no good in women and
has surely by now exhausted his satiric vein. The poet replies that,
far from having painted a complete tableau, he has enough left to
write several volumes. For example he has not even mentioned
several types—the atheist, the whimsical, the malign, the imperti-
nent, the old woman who expects her husband to behave like a
young lover, the beauty who smells of garlic and tobacco. There is
also the lady who turns her husband's home into a gambling den,
and the woman who perpetually quarrels with her children and
takes out on them the venom she feels towards her husband.
Other types are the superstitious, the pedant, and the boring
bourgeoise, whose cat is her sole topic of conversation and who
talks all the time and says nothing. There are thousands of them,
but he is tired and will spare Alcippe at least three-fourths of
them.

Alcippe is now sure that the poet is joking and indulging in a
tour de force of wit. To put an end to it he states that his bride-to-
be has none of the faults the poet has enumerated. If she should
ever change, however, he will immediately separate from her. A
separation is not so easy to bring about, says the poet, because the
wife must consent to it. And she will not want to give up the
pleasure of persecuting him. Since Parisian custom and law are so
favorable to women, the husband will soon be visited by her lawyer with a whole volume of her claims, and she will want to take
him to court. Arbitration will be out of the question because she
really doesn't want her rights but the pleasure of a lawsuit. She
would prefer to dispute in court over a little piece of land than get

a whole estate uncontested. If the husband cannot find some way to keep her out of the courts, he will be reduced to poverty and, what is worse, be forced to take her back.

Satire X thus treats manners, morality, and even some literary satire. In his criticism Boileau paints more than a dozen portraits of feminine vice, some of which may be considered universal and others particular to the society of the day. In such types as the flirt, the nag, the jealous wife, the stingy wife, we are able to recognize familiar portraits. Boileau does not, of course, intend to intimate that his tableau represents a majority of women. These are, however, eternal forms of vice which may also exist in men, and it is well to avoid them. Women whose virtue may be ruined by too much opera or too many novels, the excessive gambler, the affected (précieuse) wife, and the compulsive litigant, although they may also exist in any time, are more particularly types found in the France of the latter half of the seventeenth century. To Boileau and his readers, they were just as real and just as universal as the others, particularly among the upper classes, where money and leisure were available for indulging these vices. Contemporaries who condemned Boileau for having made fun of marriage and modern critics who reject his attitude toward women incline to read into the poem too much personal bitterness. They give the poet too little credit for observation and detachment. The writing of a satire against certain easily recognizable vicious traits and types of women does not necessarily indicate a misogynist, nor is every old bachelor automatically unhappy and deprived of desired affection. Boileau could and did criticize men in just as acid a fashion, but this criticism is scattered throughout his work rather than concentrated in one poem. There is no reason to consider Satire X as anything more than an unusually acute observation of the manners of certain women of his milieu.

Epître II

Epître II is a curious and almost accidental work, containing both moral and literary material. Originally found at the end of Epître I as the fable of the litigants and the oyster, it was deemed unworthy of an epistle addressed to the king. Having detached it from its original position, Boileau wanted to retain it and was obliged to write an introduction to lead into the fable proper. Actually there are two introductions, one to the abbé des Roches, advising him to steer clear of lawsuits, and another which precedes it and is an attack against the poet Linière.[9] The poem opens with the author talking to himself. What is the use of awakening his Muse, since no one wants to listen to his rules of correct writing nor follow Reason which speaks through him. The poets say his writing is no better than theirs, and Linière challenges him to a contest to see who can most quickly fill with verse a sheet of paper. (Linière had been a former friend who had made fun of the dryness and faulty taste of *Epître IV* and Boileau is here taking his revenge. He was not easily appeased since in Canto II of the *Art poétique,* in the original text of *Epître VII,* and in *Epître X,* he continues to reproach Linière with lack of talent, love of drink, and even impiety.)

Boileau then begins his introduction to the fable, advising des Roches to stay away from lawsuits. In a suit it is not the litigants who gain but only the lawyers, clerks, and judges. If des Roches should ever be tempted, then he should remember the lesson in the fable of the litigants and the oyster. Two hungry travelers meet an oyster and begin to quarrel over who shall have it. Justice, scales in hand, happens to be passing by, and the travelers ask her to decide the case. Justice takes the oyster, opens it, swallows it, and hands each of the travelers half a shell. She informs them that, at the Palace of Justice in Paris, they live off others' foolishness. *Epître II* is certainly one of Boileau's poorest poems. The same topic was also treated by the great fabulist La Fontaine with, as might be expected, much better results. In *Epître II,* as in *Satire X, Against Women,* Boileau directs the barb of his satire against a vice which had become almost endemic to seventeenth-century society. The writers of the period are nearly unanimous in their condemnation of this love of litigation which had reached the point, among the upper classes, of a favorite indoor sport and a status symbol.

L'Arrêt burlesque

The *Arrêt burlesque* (*Burlesque Injunction*) is one of the most amusing and least-known pieces Boileau ever wrote. In subject matter it is a satire of the philosophers, doctors of the Faculty of Medicine, and theologians of the Faculty of Theology of the Sorbonne. These had sought from the Parlement of Paris an official ban on the teaching of any philosophy save that of Aristotle as interpreted by St. Thomas Aquinas. In form it mimics the style current in law circles and used in drawing up briefs, edicts, and official documents. This legalistic style with its *whereas, aforementioned, party of the first part,* and the like was, as indeed it still is, virtually unintelligible except to the initiated. The poem contains, then, a double-edged satire against the attitude of the Sorbonne toward the newer philosophies of Descartes, Gassendi, Malebranche, and against the legalistic language of official documents. This language was one of the aspects of the legal profession with which Boileau was well acquainted and which contributed to his abandonment of the study of law.

The Faculties of Theology and Medicine intended to present an official request to Lamoignon, president of the Parlement of Paris, that an injunction be handed down prohibiting the teaching of any philosophy except Aristotle/Aquinas. As mentioned earlier, the *Arrêt burlesque* was composed by Boileau and the poet's brother-in-law Dongois slipped it into a pile of papers on Lamoignon's desk. The president was, of course, highly amused and, when word of the injunction spread in society, the Sorbonne shame-facedly declined to submit the request, at least for the time being.

The *Arrêt burlesque* is written as if issued by the supreme court of Parnassus, on behalf of the masters of arts, doctors, and professors of the University of Stagyra[10] in favor of the maintenance of the doctrine of Aristotle, sometime professor of Greek at the College of Lyceum and preceptor to his late majesty of quarrelsome memory, Alexander the Great. Laced liberally with participial phrases, *whereas, aforementioned,* and so on, the entire first paragraph contains only one sentence. A certain unknown person called Reason, with the aid of partisans of Gassendi, Descartes, Malebranche, and Pourchot,[11] has dared to enter the university and attempt to oust Aristotle by forcing him to submit his doctrine to reasonable examination. This procedure is in direct opposition to the laws of the university, where Aristotle has always been recognized as a judge from whose decisions there is no right of appeal. Moreover the same Reason, without the consent of Aristotle, has wanted to introduce changes and innovations manifestly contrary to Nature, such as transferring the center of the nervous system from the heart, where Philosophy had located it, to the brain. Furthermore Reason, by means of a completely null procedure, has permitted the blood to travel with impunity throughout the whole body through the veins and arteries.[12] This has been done with no more right or qualification than the proof of experiment, whose testimony has never been received as valid in the university. With enormous insult and damage to the Faculty of Medicine, Reason has successfully undertaken to cure numerous cases of fever by means of pure wine, powders, quinine, and other drugs unknown either to Aristotle or Hippocrates, his predecessor. Even worse, these cures have been brought about without bleeding or purging, and Reason has never been officially admitted to the *corpus* of the Faculty of Medicine. These cures obviously are the result of diabolical intervention.

In the matter of philosophy, Reason has sought the banishment of formalities, materialities, entities, and virtualities stemming from the teachings of Duns Scotus.[13] Such action, if successful, would totally subvert Scholasticism, which draws from these teachings all its mystery and all its substance.

Having heard and considered the request of the university, the court decrees that the aforementioned Aristotle shall remain in full possession and enjoyment of the schools, and it is ordered that he shall henceforth be followed and taught by the regents, doctors, masters of arts, and professors of the university. This decree does not mean that they are required to read Aristotle or understand his language or ideas. Furthermore, the heart is hereby directed to continue to be the seat of the nervous system and all persons, of whatever profession or condition, are directed so to believe, all experimentation to the contrary notwithstanding. It is expressly forbidden to the blood to wander through the body and circulate in vagabond fashion, under penalty of being abandoned to the whims of the Faculty of Medicine. Reason is enjoined to cease and desist immediately from effecting cures by means of drugs unknown to the ancients. If an irregular cure has been made by means of said drugs, it is permitted the Faculty of Medicine, following their ordinary methods, to restore to the patient his original illness and then treat it according to accepted rules. As for philosophy, the court restores to Scholasticism all its former renown and prestige.

In order to prevent any future occurrences of this sort, the court banishes, in perpetuity, Reason from the aforementioned university. Reason is henceforth forbidden to disturb Aristotle under penalty of being declared a Jansenist or a partisan of novelty. The decree of the court shall be read on the occasion of the next assembly for an academic procession.

The *Arrêt burlesque* alone, with its sustained irony and humor, should suffice to dispel the traditional picture of a dour and ascetic Boileau. It should also provide food for thought to those who, on the basis of the Quarrel of the Ancients and Moderns, see Boileau as a stern and narrow partisan of the ancients. Boileau is the partisan of *reasonableness* wherever it appears. In the *Arrêt burlesque* he attacks the superstitious veneration of the Sorbonne for the Scholastic interpretation of Aristotle in spite of reason and experiment. Even so great an ancient as Aristotle, "master of those who know," must not be blindly accepted solely on the basis of the authority of his name and tradition.

Le Lutrin

Le Lutrin (*The Lectern*) contains elements of satire of several varieties. Basically it is a satire of manners against the clergy, with an opportunity for literary satire in the episode of the Battle of the Books. The circumstances of the composition of *Le Lutrin* have been related in Chapter 1. It was a work in which Boileau became progressively more interested as he composed it, and he took considerable pride in it as a new form of the burlesque genre. The usual device of the genre was to have noble figures speak the common language of peasants. Boileau's method, exactly the reverse, was to have common people use the language of the heroes of epics. The device is not, of course, original with Boileau, but it was at least uncommon. Boileau often directed vehement attacks against the writers of traditional burlesque, mainly on the grounds that the genre was contrary to nature and that Dido and Aeneas speaking like peasants or bourgeois was an insult to the ancients. *Le Lutrin* actually has the same effect of comic burlesque, but Boileau evidently did not feel that his method offered any offense to the great epic writers.

The Sainte Chapelle of Paris, located on the Ile de la Cité, was a part of Boileau's daily scenery. There were three main dignitaries of the Sainte Chapelle, the *Trésorier*, the *Chantre*, and the *Vicaire*. The Trésorier, a bishop or archbishop appointed by the king, was the Superior of the college of canons, and the leading dignitary. The Chantre was a canon, elected to his position by the chapter assembly of the other canons, whose main duty was to attend all services both day and night and to oversee the performance and functions of the choir, chaplains, and other clerics. The Vicaire was a canon who was curate of the lower chapel and substituted for the Trésorier when services were held there. In August 1667 the Trésorier, Claude Auvry, Bishop of Coutances, had a dispute with Jacques Barrin, the Chantre. To show his authority, the Trésorier had a lectern placed in front of the choir stall of the Chantre, preventing him from seeing or being seen, as well as interfering with his direction of the choir. The Chantre, aided by other canons, removed the lectern by force. The conflict was finally taken to a court of law and was arranged by Lamoignon to the mutual satisfaction of both parties: the lectern was replaced for twenty-four hours to satisfy the Trésorier, and then removed permanently, at the orders of the Trésorier, to satisfy the Chantre. Lamoignon, pious but with an excellent sense of humor, told the affair to his circle of friends. Boileau's malicious spirit, aided and abetted by the dare, could not resist the temptation for satire. Moreover, it gave him the opportunity to try his hand at a long poem.

Boileau was a realistic poet and was tempted by a subject familiar to any inhabitant of the Ile de la Cité. He had known for a long time of the quarrels which had been going on in the Sainte Chapelle, for they had agitated the entire neighborhood. As a matter of fact, he brings into the 1667 affair reminiscences of prior events and other quarrels dating back as early as 1658. The characters of *Le Lutrin* are not exact copies of actual persons and, except for Claude Auvry, the Trésorier, Barrin, the Chantre, and Didier Delamour, the wigmaker, cannot be identified with certainty. Boileau probably began work on *Le Lutrin* in 1669. The next year he was reading passages from it to his friends and was still doing so in 1672. The unfinished poem, consisting of the first four cantos, was included in an edition of Boileau's *Oeuvres diverses* in 1674. Boileau claimed that he had secret reasons for not including Cantos V and VI. We do not know what these reasons were, but the entire poem was published in 1683. In the *Avis au lecteur* (*Notice to the Reader*), Boileau takes precautions to avoid scandal or excessive criticism. He claims that the poem was composed on the occasion of a slight difference of opinion between the Trésorier and the Chantre but that the remainder of the poem

is pure fiction; not only are the characters made up but he has
created them just the opposite from the way they exist in real life.
Although there is certainly much fiction, there is not as much as
Boileau says, and he deceived no one.

The *Lutrin* opens in almost exact imitation and parody of the
Aeneid of Virgil—"I sing of the combats, and that terrible prelate," recalls the "Arma virumque cano" of Virgil's opening line. In
spite of all Boileau's invective against those who parodied the ancient epics, the first line of *Le Lutrin* follows the same method.
Boileau then briefly sets forth his basic subject of the lectern
placed in the choir and the ensuing quarrel. In true epic manner
he invokes his Muse and asks her to relate to him the reason for
the quarrel. He also calls upon Lamoignon, hero who had rid the
Church of a nascent schism, to animate his project—and try to
keep from laughing.

The Sainte Chapelle of Paris is calm and her canons, ruddy and
plump with health, enjoy their laziness. The canons are more interested in soft beds and good food than in the Holy Offices, and
have the services sung by hired substitutes. But the goddess Discord, looking over her empire of strife and contention, sees the
peaceful church which seems to defy her power. Determined to
sow the seeds of discord, the goddess takes the form of an old
cantor and goes to find the Trésorier. This prelate is ensconced in
his down bed, enclosed by curtains to keep out the light and, fortified by lunch, sleeps lightly while waiting for his dinner. His
complexion is the picture of self-indulgence—he has a double
chin, and his weight makes the mattress groan. Discord awakens
him and instills jealousy by describing the Chantre, who has already begun to take over some of his functions and prerogatives
and will soon gain the Trésorier's crosier and mitre. The Trésorier
roars like a bull stung by a wasp and, rising from his warm bed,
begins to quarrel with his servants. Discord has done her work
well. His almoner reminds the bishop that his dinner will get cold
and that he did not become a prelate in order to work. While the
Trésorier eats his dinner, the almoner goes to round up all his
partisans, who assemble to receive his commands.

Like a general speaking to his loyal troops, the Trésorier exhorts
his followers. Will they permit the Chantre to usurp all his rights?
This very morning—a goddess has revealed it to him—the Chantre had the temerity to pronounce the *Benedicat vos*. Sidrac, eld-

est of the canons, has a plan. In front of the Chantre's customary place in the choir there used to be a huge lectern which hid the Chantre while leaving the Trésorier in full and resplendent view of all the chapter. The lectern was removed, but is still in the sacristy, where it has languished for thirty years. Sidrac suggests that, under cover of night, three of the Trésorier's partisans replace the lectern in the choir. If the Chantre should dare remove it, the Trésorier can take disciplinary action. It would be preferable to destroy the harmony of the chapel than to permit the bishop's prerogatives to be abused—this is the spirit of the Church. Since they are in Paris, the fashionable thing to do would be to institute a lawsuit. The prelate is pleased with this solution, and lots are drawn to see who will be the three to replace the lectern. Brontin, Delamour the wigmaker, and Boirude, the sacristan, are chosen. The assembly disperses and the prelate, now calmed, goes back to bed until suppertime. So ends Canto I.

Canto II opens with Rumor, in the form of a bird, visiting the wigmaker's wife to frighten her at the thought of the danger her husband will incur by aiding in the transfer of the lectern. Reminding her husband of all the sweet nights they spent together, both before and since their marriage, she tries to prevent him from exposing himself to danger. The wigmaker is well aware of her love, but marriage does not make him a slave to her wishes. He will not give up the great honor of moving a lectern, and she should help to strengthen his courage for the task ahead. He then leaves to join his companions. Armed with various carpenters' tools, and fortified with a bottle, the three proceed to their task.

Discord, with shouts of joy at seeing her plans about to be carried out, awakens Indolence, or Sloth, whose habitual dwelling is the Abbey of Cîteaux. Here she is served by Pleasure, Voluptuousness, and of course Sleep. Night tells Sloth about the undertaking, sponsored by Discord, and Sloth laments the fact that Discord has succeeded in inspiring so much action. Exiled from Paris because of Louis XIV's activity, Sloth had hoped to find refuge in the Church and especially in the monasteries. However, monastic reforms have become popular, and only Cîteaux and the Sainte Chapelle offer her a refuge. Now a lectern is going to introduce activity into the latter! She is about to ask Night not to permit it, but the effort has been too much for her, and Sloth, tired of talking, sighs and stretches, closes her eyes, and falls asleep.

In Canto III, Night hastens to Paris. Hoping to cause the failure of Discord's plan, she places an owl in the lectern just as the three chosen ones are preparing to move it from the sacristy to the choir. The three champions, full of wine and audacity, arrive in the chapel and light a candle. They enter the sacristy and are about to remove the lectern when the owl flies out, hooting, blowing dust, and extinguishing the candle with the blast from his wings. Frightened, they flee, but Discord has seen everything and, assuming the form of Sidrac, succeeds in rallying them. Anger succeeding fear, the three light their candle again and return to the sacristy, where they see that they have only been frightened by an owl. The lectern is taken to the choir.

Canto IV, which begins the next morning, opens with the narration by the Chantre of a horrible nightmare. He dreamt that a dragon in the shape of a giant pulpit followed the Trésorier from the sacristy and placed itself in front of his stall in the choir. The dream caused him to wake up frightened. Dressing in haste, the Chantre rushes to the choir. Boileau here calls again on his Muse to inspire him with words to describe the rage of the Chantre. His first reaction is to quit his position, but this would permit his enemy to enjoy his defeat. He decides rather that the lectern must be knocked down and, raging, he attempts to do so. At this time the canons appear and advise him that the destruction should be accomplished by all the canons. The chapter is called into session by the Chantre in spite of great difficulty in rousing these lazy clerics from their profound sleep. The canons are finally awakened by the rumor that a sumptuous feast has been prepared for them, and they hasten to the chapel.

Alain, one of the canons who is so learned that he understands Latin, announces that such a foul deed can only have been committed by a Jansenist. He advises them to search through all their books to see if some theologian has not mentioned the subject of lecterns. Evrard, a gourmand, is furious at the idea of reading at his advanced age. He reads the Bible itself no more than he reads the Koran, and all he needs to know is what annual rents are due to the chapel from the tenants on its lands. His arm alone, without benefit of Latin, is strong enough to overturn the lectern, after which they may eat and drink. The canons proceed to demolish the lectern and hide its remains in the Chantre's quarters.

Canto V, added along with Canto VI in 1683, contains the famous Battle of the Books. Sidrac receives the news of what has been done to the lectern and immediately informs the Trésorier, who dresses and finds his partisans waiting for him outside his room, ready to abandon the choir for good. The Trésorier decides that this would be useless and resolves instead to consult the Sibyl in her nearby cave. This cave refers to the Palace of Justice, and the Sibyl is Chicanery who dwells there. Chicanery, in order to ruin litigants, spends her time consulting the books of law, common law, and precedent. She devours houses, palaces, castles, and in exchange for piles of money returns a worthless mass of papers. The scales of justice are unable to maintain their balance in the presence of this monster, Chicanery.

The old Trésorier addresses her as "Queen of lengthy lawsuits" who renders the law powerless, and begs her, in honor of his lifetime spent engaged in litigation, to hear his prayers. Chicanery prophesies that the lectern will be replaced after great battles, but they must beware of permitting any accord to be established. She breathes into their souls the spirit of litigation and dissension, and they prepare to return to the chapel.

Meanwhile the partisans of the Chantre are enjoying the promised meal when the goddess Rumor announces to the Chantre the result of the Sibylline oracle. They leave the chapel and rush to the Palace of Justice. The opposing forces meet on the street in front of the bookstore of Barbin, and here the battle is joined, with bad books as missiles. The battle seems to be a standoff until the Trésorier thinks of a stratagem which gives him the victory. He bestows on his enemies his episcopal benediction, which forces them to kneel. The Trésorier returns to the church to enjoy the fruits of his victory, while the Chantre and his partisans retire in confusion. Here ends Canto V.

Canto VI is in a different, and no longer comic vein. Piety, who had retired to the monastery of the Grande Chartreuse in the Alps, hears the cries of her desolate subjects and, followed by Faith, Hope, and Charity, leaves her retreat. She goes to Paris to petition Themis, goddess of Justice, to bring an end to the quarrel, which is an offense to piety. Hypocrisy, she laments, has taken on her name and voice, and monsters of impiety are usurping her authority. In the early days of Christianity the faithful sought martyrdom and fled from the honors of this world. As soon as the Church had triumphed over paganism, sealing the cement of her altars with the blood of the faithful, a dangerous calm settled. The burning zeal of faith has now become lukewarm and faith is becoming heavy under the burden of sin. Monks have abandoned the hair shirt, canons have become indolent, prelates have been too much attracted by worldly honors. Ambition has chased out Humility and lodged Vanity in her place. Discord has been introduced into the sacred cloisters and has induced Piety's subjects to frequent the law courts. Discord has marched under the banner of Piety, and false doctors (casuists) have flattered sin and tried to prove that God approved of it. Fear now occupies the place of Charity, and the need for love of God, for true penitence, passes as something new and unheard-of. Now Discord has taken over the chapel erected in honor of piety by the most saintly of kings (Louis IX), and Piety calls upon Themis to put an end to it and justify heaven to mortals.

Themis promises aid, reassuring her that even if the piety of people seems to have disappeared, the Church itself is built of eternal mortar. Even Hell cannot shake her firm foundations. In the Palace of Justice there is a man who watches over the reputation of Justice. This honorable man is Ariste (Lamoignon), president of the Paris Parlement. Chicanery is powerless against him, Truth fears no imposter, and the inheritance of the orphan is not devoured by the guardian. Piety should know him, for he has been formed by piety from his early years. Themis advises Piety to go to Ariste in person, for she will be recognized and honored by him and his whole family. Piety does so, and informs Ariste of the situation in the Sainte Chapelle. Ariste sends for the Chantre and the Trésorier. Here again Boileau calls on his Muse for aid in recounting how Ariste was able to bring accord to the two rivals. Rather it is now up to Ariste himself to tell how he rendered the Chantre obedient so that the lectern was replaced and how the Trésorier, satisfied with this mark of respect, removed it immediately. Boileau is satisfied at having been able to write six cantos on the subject, making a second Ilion of a lectern. Now that he must describe and praise the hero of the action, he is confused and speechless before the enormity of the task. Thus Le Lutrin ends in praise of Lamoignon, not only in the case of the Sainte Chapelle, but in all instances in which a lawsuit comes before him as president of the Parlement of Paris.

In Le Lutrin, Boileau multiplies his attacks of moral, political, and literary order, against clerical manners, against the law courts, and against literary figures. The episode of the Battle of the Books serves as an excellent opportunity to make fun of detested authors, and the entire poem is rife with satire of every sort. However, *Le Lutrin* is, properly speaking, a burlesque poem still in the tradition of a genre which had been very popular, especially in the decade from 1650 to 1660, and which had included many parodies of Virgil, Homer, Lucan, Ovid, and others. In his *Satires* and in the *Art poétique* Boileau condemned the genre, but his use of it shows an apparent contradiction between theory and practice which Boileau attempted to excuse on the grounds of his method. As stated earlier, the invention is really quite slight and had existed earlier. The very nature of the burlesque is that it is based on contrasts: the subject contradicts the tone; the action's importance is not in proportion to the narration of it; and the characters are not in accord with the language they speak.

There is also, apparently, some contradiction in Boileau's use of the *marvelous* and his critical opinions. According to the *Art poétique* and other critical documents, Boileau believed that the *marvelous* of heroic poetry should be drawn from ancient mythology and fable. He opposed the use of the *Christian marvelous* in heroic, epic poems on Christian subject matter, and especially did he condemn the mixture of the two. Yet in *Le Lutrin* he uses allegories like Sloth and Night and even pagan divinities like Discord and Themis. For these reasons he has been accused of following the example of Ariosto, whom he condemns elsewhere.

Upon closer examination, however, these apparent contradictions may be explained, or at least attenuated. Boileau's primary objection to the burlesque genre is that it is contrary to nature, i.e., that Dido and Aeneas, for example, would not act and speak like mule skinners. It does not seem so contrary to nature that a group of pompous clergymen, vain, envious of each other, and jealous of every small prerogative, should attempt to use, with ridiculous results, the lofty and pompous speech of the highest class. On this score Boileau's defense of his form because of his method has some validity. Another reason for his denunciation of the burlesque was due to his deep affection and admiration for the ancients. This reverence did not permit him to approve of a form or method which seemed to him to be disrespectful to his beloved Homer and Virgil. To have Dido and Aeneas, characters created by Virgil and associated with his name, speak like peasants was almost an insult to the *Aeneid*. Use of the same characters as used in the ancient epics made comparison unavoidable. By utilizing the reverse method—having clerics and wigmakers use a lofty tone—the language of the ancients is not diminished. By not using the characters of the ancient epics, the comparison is not so much invited. The method also afforded Boileau an opportunity to make fun of some of the heroes of the popular adventure novels of the day, who spoke of nothing more important than love, yet in a language usually associated with the noblest sentiments.

Further study of his use of the *marvelous* also reveals that Boileau is much less at variance with his doctrine than has generally been suspected. The use of the allegorical characters Sloth and Night needs no excuse or explanation, since the practice has a long and honorable tradition in poetry on Christian subjects. The pagan goddesses Discord and Themis are simply a continuation of the allegory. Each represents a quality common to pagan antiquity and to Christianity, commonly known by their Greek appellations and probably also allegorical in ancient Greece. Boileau does not, it will be noted, utilize any of the traditional, anthropomorphic gods of the Greek pantheon. Thus, neither in his use of the burlesque form as he adapted it nor in his use of the *marvelous* is Boileau as much in contradiction with his own literary doctrines as has been commonly supposed. Nor was he criticized in his day for having made fun of the ancients.

Le Lutrin is probably the best revelation of Boileau's true temperament. He had already begun to try to present an image of himself to the public as a more serious person than the author of the first nine *Satires*, but love of satire was stronger in him than the desire to appear learned and wise. Criticism of the law and of those engaged in the practice of it was by now traditional enough, and there was little risk involved. The ridicule of churchmen was more audacious, although this aspect should not be exaggerated, since the century was well able to avoid confusing the Church with some of her unworthy ministers. Nevertheless *Le Lutrin* is far from being a poem of religious zeal, and Boileau often fails to make a clear and adequate distinction between the abuses and the institution. To have done so would, of course, have been contrary to his artistic purposes and would have had the effect of weakening the satire.

Boileau does not have the epic genius, but he does exhibit in *Le Lutrin* some of the talent of a good story-teller. He has a certain flair for the comic without possessing the comic genius of a Molière. The poem is also very worthwhile as a satire or a series of satires. It contains a great deal of realism, in which the poet shows himself to be an excellent and observant painter of the manners of certain clergy, bourgeoisie, and people connected with the law courts. His descriptions seem living and true to the reader. Here, as is often the case with Boileau, his innate artistic sense and talent make up for his weakness as a poet, in the lyric definition of the term.

II *Literary Satire*

Most of Boileau's writing, whether primarily moral, critical, or satires of manners, contain some literary satire. Some of this type have already been mentioned in the previous section of this chapter. This section will examine those works which are primarily literary satire, reserving works of literary criticism, theory, and doctrine for a later chapter. No purpose will be served in including a complete list of all the authors who were condemned by Boileau. Instead, attention will be directed to the important figures who incurred Boileau's ire, and to some of the fundamental reasons why they were satirized, often so vehemently. This portion of the chapter may then serve as background to the chapter on his literary criticism and theories, by presenting a series of negative examples of items drawing the disapproval of Boileau.

Satire VII

Satire VII, le Genre satirique, is the first of these satires of a literary nature (1660–61), but already assumes the existence of several poems written in the satiric genre. This may, of course, be attributed to Boileau's practice of reading his satires aloud and even circulating them in manuscript before finally placing them in their definitive form. In the opening line Boileau calls upon his Muse to join him in changing style and in abandoning satire. The habit of abuse is a wicked trade and often is ultimately most dangerous to the one who indulges in it. A boring eulogy or a cold encomium may decay in the bookseller's stall, dust and book-worms its only enemy, with no fear of public judgment. An author, on the other hand, who causes laughter at the expense of others, is blamed by the very persons who want to read him, making enemies of those who laugh at what he has to say. Too much sincerity outrages a reader easily, for the mirror held up by the satirist too often shows a reader his true visage. Such a reader may admire each satiric shaft, but in the depth of his soul will fear and hate the satirist.

For these reasons, Boileau calls on his Muse to rhyme in praise of some great and worthy hero. The effort, however, is in vain, for the poet is unable to find a rhyme for use in praising. The only rhymes he can find for this purpose are colder than those of Chapelain's *la Pucelle*. It might be noted here that Jean Chapelain was the author most frequently criticized by Boileau. A leading critic and figure in the literary society of the day, Chapelain was also in charge of compiling the list of recommendations of writers for royal pensions. His verse was most often harsh and lacking in animation, but he enjoyed a considerable reputation in the literary salons and as a critic—the latter largely deserved. *La Pucelle* was for a long time, during the process of composition, touted as France's greatest epic, and its appearance was awaited with eager anticipation by those who respected the author and had heard him read portions of it in society over many years. When the first portion was finally printed, it turned out to be almost unreadable in its stiffness and soporific in its tedium. Chapelain, both because of his eminent position and because he was a poor writer, thus came in for the lion's share of Boileau's ire. From the critical point of view, however, their ideas on literary theory were basically the same.

An attempt to praise, then, is torture to the poet, and the paper remains blank before him. But when it comes to mocking, he recognizes his true poetic talent. Apollo is ready to hear his prayer and the proper words run to take their places on the page. To illustrate this, Boileau proceeds to utilize the names of several second-rate authors to make his rhymes and fill out the syllable count of the verses. He feels that his mind is working under the inspiration of genius, and for every word he needs a thousand are ready and waiting. In the midst of such poetic furor, he is unable to spare anyone and his verve runs away with him. Merit is precious to him, but a fool displeases and the very sight of one hurts his eyes. Boileau compares himself to a hunting dog who bays at the first scent of his prey and can never stop until it is caught. Making a critical judgment of his own talent, at least at this particular stage in its development, Boileau states that he is able to attach a rhyme to the end of some lines and often dresses up in verse his mischievous and clever prose. Although this is by no means a complete critical judgment, it is often true as far as it goes. The poet goes on to state that if he is worth anything, it is due to this talent.

Whether his life be short or long, or whatever his condition, Boileau must write verse of a satirical nature. Someone may warn that he may be in danger from those he criticizes, but Boileau replies that neither Horace nor Juvenal met a tragic end. Besides, he is relatively unknown since his verse has not been printed and is heard only because he forces himself to read his poems from time to time to some importunate friend. Finally, it is his pleasure and he must satisfy himself; he cannot speak well of some people and he is unable to remain silent. As soon as a pleasant or amusing idea comes to him, he cannot resist setting it down on paper. This compulsion is like an irresistible torrent which sweeps him away.

Satire II

Satire II, A Molière, is a eulogy of the great comic author, as the title indicates. Boileau was a friend and admirer of Molière, and *Satire II* is the first public statement by Boileau of this admiration. The appearance of the satire was at an apropos time, for Molière was in the thick of the controversy over the *Ecole des femmes* (*School for Wives*), and had written and presented the *Critique de l'Ecole des femmes* in June of 1663. Boileau's *Satire II* was composed in the summer of 1663, and showed that the young satirist had the courage of his convictions and was able to support his friends when they needed him most. It should be remembered that neither Molière's position nor reputation was as secure at this time as they were later to become. It required a considerable courage on the part of Boileau to speak out so unequivocally for his beliefs.

The opening line of the poem refers to Molière as a "rare et fameux esprit." According to Boileau, Molière is such a master that rhyme seeks him out, rather than the reverse. Boileau would like Molière to teach him the secret of rhyming with facility. The poet describes himself in almost opposite terms—he has to work hard for every rhyme. Especially is he troubled with using proper names to make rhymes, often contrary to his intentions. For example, if he wants to mention an author without fault, his reason says *Virgil* but rhyme says *Quinault*. He has even sworn to stop writing, but when he is least expecting it, his poetic ardor reawakens and he takes up paper and pen to await patiently the appearance of a verse. If only his Muse would permit him to use a cold epithet, he would do like many other poets and always have a ready ending to tack on his lines. He then cites several clichés and stock epithets often used by contemporary poets for the sake of their rhyme. By the use of these clichés and by transposing subject and verb, he could write easily, without genius or art. But he is unable to permit an insipid phrase to fill up an empty space at the end of a line. So, beginning a poem for the twentieth time, he ends up erasing three words out of every four he writes.

Boileau curses the first person who invented poetry and, deciding to confine thoughts in the limits of verse, gave his words a narrow prison by chaining reason to rhyme. Without this fatal vocation, his days might be spent in leisure, singing, laughing, and drinking, as carefree as a fat canon who sleeps well at night and does nothing during the day. But some demon, jealous of his contentment, inspires him with the urge to write, and he spends his days nailed to his desk, writing, rewriting, erasing. How he envies those who, like Scudéry,[14] can give birth to a volume every month. Of course, Scudéry's works, artless and languishing, seem written in spite of common sense, but there will be someone to sell them and fools to read them. As long as the rhyme is found at the end, what difference does it make if the rest of the verse is turned backwards and upside-down? A fool writes everything with pleasure, is in love with what he writes, and admires himself, astonished at his own ability. But the spirit which aspires to the *sublime* is never able to reach it. Such a poet is perpetually discontent with what he has written, even though he may please others. Boileau ends the poem with an appeal to Molière either to teach him to find rhymes more easily or teach him not to write verse any more.

A lengthier discussion of Boileau's critical theories will be found in Chapter 4. However, it should be stated here, in connection with *Satire II*, that Boileau seems to have given us a fairly accurate, though obviously incomplete picture of his own creative process. He did not write with great facility, and was especially troubled with transitions and rhyme. Although he may be accused with some justification of occasionally forcing a rhyme or of using a proper name solely for the sake of rhyme, he is very seldom guilty of using the clichés and stock epithets which were so common among the second-rate poets of his day. Evidence is everywhere to be found of his constant rewriting of his poems, not only in manuscript but from one printed edition to the next. We may also suspect that, in spite of Molière's large production and his duties as actor and director of a troupe, he did not write with all the ease Boileau ascribes to him. However, for one like Boileau who had to work so assiduously over his verse, it must have seemed so. It is also interesting and enlightening to note that Boileau defends Molière not on the basis of his ideas—others were both defending and condemning these—but on the basis of his style.

Satire IX

Satire IX, A son Esprit, is generally considered to be Boileau's best effort in this genre. Written in 1667–68, it also marks the last of his early satires, before he settled down to the more serious *Epîtres,* the *Art poétique,* the *Lutrin,* and the translation of Longinus' *Traité du sublime* (*On the Sublime*). *Satire IX* already shows much of this more serious nature of the man. The poem takes the form of a reprimand addressed by the poet to his own spirit or mind (*esprit*). The capricious *esprit* has been playing the role of Cato the Censor toward the vices of the time, deciding the worth of writers, and trying to give lessons to the learned. The poet, who knows all the shortcomings of his own *esprit,* can only laugh to see it trying to reform the whole city of Paris. Although actually feeble and sterile, the *esprit* persists in bitter and biting satire. Boileau wonders what indiscretion, without the permission of the nine Muses, has made him a poet. Does the *esprit* feel the creative breath of genius; has Apollo smoothed the ascent to the height of Parnassus? Does it not realize that, in matters of poetry, whoever does not fly to the summit falls on the lowest slope; that there is no room for mediocrity?

If the poet cannot convince his *esprit* not to rhyme, it should at least try something worthwhile, such as singing the marvels of the reign of Louis XIV. In this way one can hope to see some fruit from one's labors, in the form of an annual pension. (Boileau was not yet on the royal pension list, drawn up by Colbert with the aid of Chapelain.) The *esprit*, however, will reply that it is incapable of the lofty inspiration required for such ventures. An insipid and foolishly flattering poem dishonors both the hero who is praised and the poet who flatters.

The poet then asks if it would not be better to lose oneself in the clouds, in a soaring but impossible attempt, than to enrich the booksellers by calling attention to the bad books that are being produced. Perhaps the *esprit* flatters itself that it will be able to reach immortality by the same path as the satirist Horace. Many writers are deceived by this vain hope. Their books are popular for a time but are soon relegated to collecting dust in the corner of a bookseller's shop. The ultimate fate of the worst books is to be used to wrap fish and groceries, after the booksellers sell them by the pound for wrapping paper. Even if this is not the case and a book survives to posterity, what use is it to be esteemed in the future if one is considered criminal by contemporaries? What demon forces the *esprit* to criticize? If a book displeases, who forces one to read it? A foolish author should be permitted to languish in obscurity, as many authors of contemporary epics are now doing. What harm has been done by all the poets whose names the satirist has used to fill up his verses? If they bore him, they have also bored the king and the court without an edict being handed down to punish them or suppress the writing of poetry. Anyone who desires, without breaking the law or offending custom, can take pen and paper and write whatever he wants, even to the extent of conducting a hero through ten volumes of adventures. Should the satirical *esprit*, more disgusted than others but without power or reputation, take on the task of executing Apollo's laws? How does the *esprit* think other people consider his own works and talk about them? Critics will perhaps say that he is a young fool who thinks he can get by with anything and that all he says has already been written, and better, by Horace or Juvenal. Moreover, readers will be afraid of him because they will see themselves in the pictures the satirist paints of others. How long will the *esprit* continue to stir up quarrels?

The *esprit*, Boileau's creative genius or *genie*, then answers. Is what it has been doing such a great crime? Has it been maligning or simply telling the truth? To blame harsh or languishing verse, to criticize an author who shocks our common sense—these have always been the rights of every reader. A fool at court has the right to prefer the base metal of a Tasso to the gold of a Virgil. A clerk has the right to buy his ticket and go to hiss the verse of Corneille. Every valet in Paris makes critical judgments of the authors of the day. As soon as a poet is published, he is the slave of whoever buys his book; he submits himself to others' caprices, and his poems alone may speak for him. This being the case, should Boileau's *esprit* be the only one who is not permitted to speak out? The authors he criticizes shouldn't complain. Without his satires, which call attention to them, their books would remain unread. Satire only affords them free advertisement.

Some will say, however, that the satirist should not name names. Boileau protests that he has always been careful to make a distinction between the man and his works. He is ready to join in praise of all Chapelain's admirable qualities of character, but cannot remain silent while his poems are set up as models of good style. Whatever a satirist may say against him, it does not prevent an author from continuing to write. If a book has true merit, a critic cannot succeed in taking anything away from it. The public and posterity will be the ultimate judge. Richelieu and the Academy found fault with *Le Cid*, but an obstinate public continues to admire it.

Satire, they say, is a wretched trade, and the satirist often has cause to regret and repent words written in haste. It may please some people, but it shocks most. The *esprit* should abandon the vain and fruitless pleasures of this genre. What, then, shall the satiric poet write—odes, eclogues, pastorals? These are contrary to his talent and he will leave them to others. Satire has many good qualities. It can mingle the pleasant and the utilitarian by pointing out the faults of the times. Fearlessly it attacks vice at its very source and defends reason against fools. This sort of satire is in the noble tradition of Horace, and Boileau has vowed to write in this way.

Nevertheless, if necessary the poet will try to change his style and will praise the poets he has been criticizing. It is no use, however, because they will still think he is making fun of them. Even if he praises the king, he will be accused of being lawless and faithless. But can these insults harm him? Can they keep him off a

pension list to which he does not aspire anyway? His tongue does
not need money to praise a king already praised by the whole
world. Without expecting any reward, the honor of praising Louis
XIV is reward enough in itself. Boileau then informs his *esprit*
that he believes in his good intentions, but fears the threats of the
authors whom he has angered. The satire ends as Boileau orders
the *esprit* to keep silent.

Satire IX is the most critical of Boileau's literary satires. Addressing himself to his creative *esprit*, he affirms the rights of the
satirist and catalogues his responsibilities to follow the paths of his
own individual talent, telling the truth as he sees it. He attacks by
name about twenty writers, of whom about a dozen had been
mentioned in his earlier writings. Chapelain alone is mentioned
nine times. The motives are sometimes personal, sometimes borrowed from friends, sometimes genuinely critical. Boileau's main
fault as a literary satirist is that he too often attacks writers on the
hearsay evidence of his friends and acquaintances, without actually having read their works. He has also been accused of being a
poor critic because he does not base his attacks on any critical
principles, and indeed most often gives no reasons why he condemns an author. He repeatedly prefers to use such vague terms
as *cold, harsh,* and *silly.* It must be remembered that Boileau is
writing satire rather than literary criticism. What he should have
done as a critic cannot be considered an omission as a satirist,
whose job is to get across his attack with wit and irony. To state
critical principles and then analyze on the basis of them would
have completely changed the genre of the poem. Detesting poorly
written books, Boileau lashed out against them in an almost instinctive reaction. It is important to remember that these critical
judgments were uncannily accurate. With very few exceptions,
those whom Boileau condemned were forgotten by posterity and
those whom he approved among his contemporaries have proved
to be among France's greatest writers. Rarely has there been such
a sure critical ability for judging one's contemporaries. As for Boileau's lack of critical principles in his satires, it should be borne in
mind that Boileau knew better how to write a satire than his detractors, either in the seventeenth century or since. The critical
value of *Satire IX* is admittedly weak, but this is not its intention.
Boileau wanted to point out to his readers that his basic talent and
gift was for satire, that he could not and would not change it, that

the satirist has rights and responsibilities to truth, that satire serves good and useful purposes, and that no amount of satire can damage a work which has real merit. These were items that, at the time, needed to be pointed out to those who were attacking Boileau so vehemently. Boileau here is correct in his analysis of his own basic talent—no matter what the genre he may use at a given time, he is *always* a satirist.

Epître IV

Epître IV, Au Roy, is usually referred to as the *Passage du Rhin* (*Crossing of the Rhine*). It is a poem in praise of Louis XIV and the exploits of the French army, but the martial trumpet was hardly suited to the nature of Boileau's genius. The crossing of the Rhine was a minor episode in the campaign of 1672 against the Netherlands. Militarily it was of little importance, but it had succeeded in capturing the imagination of the people because of several instances of bravado and even heroism on the part of some of the nobility who took part. Added glamor was furnished by the presence on the field of the King himself. Boileau's poem is full of enthusiasm, too warm in its praise to suit our taste, but not sufficiently so in the opinion of the poet's contemporaries. Even in a poem designed to praise the monarch, Boileau is unable to suppress his natural humor and mockery. The poem begins and ends as a sort of *tour de force* which pokes fun at the names of the Dutch cities or forts and the difficulty in finding rhymes for them.

In the opening lines Boileau states that he has tried in vain twenty times to praise Louis XIV and his conquest of Holland. Though the walls of the Dutch cities have been unable to resist, their strident and barbarous names are not so easy to overcome in verse. He cites such names as Issel, Tessel, Voerden, Heusden, which resist rhyme and destroy the harmony of his verse. These names are not only difficult to rhyme, but their harsh, Teutonic sounds grate on the ear and ruin the harmonious sound of the verse. It would be easier if Louis' exploits were less great and especially less rapid, so the poet would have more time to work on his verse. Boileau is still struggling with the name of one town while Louis has conquered another.

Now, however, the crossing of the Rhine has encouraged his zeal and he must at least attempt to write in praise of it. He calls upon the Muses to aid him in depicting an action so glorious that

everything about it is incredible. In praise of such an exploit poetry can use all its ornaments without exaggeration.

With this introduction then, and a reasonably smooth transition,
Boileau begins the poem proper. The Rhine, pictured as a mytho-
logical and anthropomorphic figure, the god or tutelary spirit of
the river, is sleeping tranquilly in the Alps where the river begins.
He is awakened by the terrified cries of his Naiads who have come
to report that a hero, led by Victory, is about to tarnish the river's
reputation, and is threatening to place the entire course of the
river under a conqueror's yoke. This hero, Louis XIV of course,
resembles Jupiter, and nothing so great has appeared on the
banks of the Rhine since Julius Caesar. Father Rhine shudders
and trembles at the news. Fire flashes from his eyes, and he vows
to oppose the crossing with all his strength.

Drying off his muddy beard, the Rhine assumes the shape of an
old warrior and, covered by a cloud, sets out for the fort of Skinq.
Here he observes his defenders, scattered in fright and waiting to
surrender. Delivering a harangue to bolster their courage, he
urges them either to defend the river or slink away like cowards,
to conquer or die. Taking heart from the Rhine's exhortation, the
soldiers march to the river bank, where Louis in person is making
preparations to cross. Armand de Grammont, comte de Guiche is
the first of the French to venture into the river, and others follow
immediately. Here Boileau includes a roster of the cream of the
French nobility of fighting age. All are animated by the courage
of Louis, whose position forces him to remain on the west bank
and not expose himself to danger. Under the personal direction of
the King, a pontoon bridge is begun. The Rhine threateningly ad-
vances with his forces and those attempting to cross are met by a
hail of lead. For a moment the outcome is in doubt, but Louis
seems able to influence destiny by his calm demeanor and soon
Mars and Bellona, the Roman god and goddess of war, join the
French. News that the prince de Condé and his son the duc
d'Enghien have successfully crossed succeeds in demoralizing the
river's defenders. They flee and the Rhine himself abandons his
banks and the victory to Louis.

The report of the victory strikes fear into the hearts of the soldiers and General Wurts in camp—Wurts, the hope of the nation
and the bulwark of her ramparts; Wurts. . . . And Boileau can
go no further. "Ah! what a name, great king, what a Hector is this

Wurts!" Without the appearance of this name, so terrible to the ears, the poet was going to write marvelous things, but the name of Wurts has put an end to his ardor. The poem must be ended or even worse names will be encountered, such as Arnheim and Hildesheim. If only heaven had located France closer to Asia, Louis could have furnished him pleasant-sounding names by the thousands. Every plain, however dry and sterile, would have abounded in rich and fertile names. How many cities there are whose names offer agreeable sounds! What a pleasure it would be to follow the King to the banks of the Scamandre and the poetic ruins of Ilion. But, Boileau reflects, there is no cause for dismay since there is no shore too distant for such a valorous king. Since Louis has taken forty fortified cities in two months, Boileau will meet him in two years on the shores of the Hellespont, sure that the King's exploits will furnish deeds worthy of praise, in a part of the world where the proper names are less barbarous.

Contemporaries did not particularly appreciate this blend of praise and foolishness, and it is true that Boileau was not at ease in praise or flattery. Boileau has, however, adopted a rather ingenious device by means of which he is able to pay homage to a king he sincerely admired, without departing too far from his characteristic mockery. The result is certainly more pleasing to read than some of the abjectly flattering verse and interminable encomiums composed by contemporaries. Boileau's figure of the Rhine god does not quite come off, simply because the poet did not have the epic genius required for the successful use of this device. The list of names of the first nobles to swim their horses across has only historical interest today, but had considerable actuality when composed. The praise of Louis is sufficiently warm but does not continue to the point of boredom. Here Boileau is closer to our taste than to that of his contemporaries. All things considered, the poem is a fairly good one, given the intention of a poem in praise of the monarch for an insignificant military exploit. If there is any doubt as to the wisdom of Boileau's choice of method here, one should read the *Ode sur la prise de Namur* (*Ode on the Capture of Namur*) to see the disastrous result of his utilization of a more conventional method of praise for the king through a military exploit. As is often the case, Boileau knew better than his critics the type of poem most suitable to his fundamental talent.

Epître VII

Epître VII, like *Satire II*, was written by Boileau in defense of a friend—Molière in the latter instance and Racine in the former. Composed in the spring of 1677, it was an encouragement and a comfort to Racine, who was certainly in need of such after the premiere of *Phèdre* on January 1, 1677 and a violent quarrel which accompanied it. Just as Boileau had boldly come to the defense of Molière when the comedian was persecuted or disdained, he shows the same courage toward the detractors of Racine. In this epistle Boileau is older and more sure of his critical faculty, calmly appealing to the judgment of posterity against the spitefulness and foolishness of his contemporaries.

The poem begins with praise of Racine's ability to move, astonish, and delight his audiences. The real Iphigenia sacrificed at Aulis did not cause such tears among the Greeks as La Champmeslé, the actress who created the title role of Iphigénie in Racine's play, has done in France. Racine should not expect, however, to win unanimous approval. As soon as a genius finds the way to success, *cabales* arise against him in every quarter. His rivals, who have now been obscured, cry out against him, and his friends, dazzled by his fame, become envious. Only death can calm injustice and envy, and posterity will weigh a writer's works on the balance of good sense, assigning his verse its proper worth. Before the death of Molière many of the qualities of his comedies, which are so vaunted today, were rejected by fools. Ignorance and Error, dressed like marquises and countesses, came to the theater to insult each new masterpiece, failing to understand the most beautiful parts of the play. Each had cavilling criticisms to offer. However, as soon as Molière was dead, the value of his Muse was recognized, and comedy has not yet recovered from his death.

Racine, then, who follows in the path of Sophocles and alone among so many tragic authors is able to console Paris for the decline of the aging Corneille, should not be surprised if envy and calumny pursue him. Even here an omniscient Providence demonstrates its profound wisdom; merit in repose tends to grow lazy, but genius, aroused and inspired by those who are envious, often attains the summit of its art because of this unintentional impetus. The more the envious try to weaken true genius, the more it increases and soars to the heights of creative power. Corneille's *Cinna,* considered his masterpiece by contemporaries, owed its birth to the persecutions received by *Le Cid.* Boileau himself, although not renowned enough to excite much envy, has made quite a number of useful enemies. He confesses that he owes more to their hatred than to his own feeble talent. It keeps him wary and helps prevent him from stumbling. He is able to correct his faults through their criticisms and thus turns their anger to his own profit. Racine should emulate Boileau and, as soon as a group of envious authors attacks him, he should profit from their hatred and laugh at their impotent cries of outrage. The French Parnassus, ennobled by Racine's poetry, will be able to support him against all plots of his rivals and will arouse in his behalf a more equitable posterity. Seeing the virtuous grief of a Phèdre perfidious and incestuous in spite of herself, and astonished by such a noble work, will not posterity bless the fortunate century which was able to produce a Racine? What does it matter whether or not we are admired by foolish and jealous contemporary authors, provided we please the people, the great, the provinces, the king, the prince de Condé, and others of refined taste and judgment? As for the gross crowd of frivolous spirits, zealous admirers of every insipid work of literature, let them go admire the wisdom of Pradon.[15]

In *Epître VII,* by means of a critical insight which borders on the prophetic, Boileau separates the immortals from the dross of their contemporaries, sure that he is pronouncing the judgment of the future. Without hesitation, almost haughtily, he proclaims the universal greatness of the seventeenth century's dramatic triumvirate—Racine, Corneille, and Molière. It is this innate ability to recognize the truly great among his contemporaries that never ceases to astound us.

Epître VIII

Epître VIII, Au roi (*To the King*), was probably written in its final form in late 1677 or early 1678, because of its allusions to Racine's retirement from the theater and the appointment of Boileau and Racine as royal historiographers in 1677. This epistle has traditionally been considered Boileau's thanks to the king for his pension, granted in 1674 and officially registered in 1676. However, rather than a poem of gratitude *Epître VIII* is a poem of regret, both for the poet's inability to praise the king as he deserves and because he has been forced, by the dignity and importance of his new position, to cease writing satire at the expense of bad authors.

In the opening lines, Boileau requests Louis XIV to stop his conquests or the poet will have to stop writing. His style was born for satire but his *esprit* wants to disavow this talent and devote itself to praise. Boileau thinks about writing an ode or even formulating an audacious plan for an epic, but each day he sees his poetic genius growing weaker. His verse in the eulogistic style is boring, and dishonors his pen without honoring his monarch. If only the king's valor would allow him a year's breathing space, perhaps the poet would be able to make up for lost time. But hardly have one or two cities been captured before it is necessary to sing of a victory over others. What Louis accomplishes in one day gives to poets action enough to rhyme for a whole year.

It is not only in war that Louis XIV is great. If he would return to Versailles for a time, Boileau could sing of other virtues that he admires even more. Bearing alone the burden of the throne, Louis is still able to cultivate the arts, distribute largesse, and even reward Boileau's critical Muse. Satiric poets, useful for pointing out the foolishness of the times, seem to be born to be dissatisfied. Their Muse, often sterile and lazy, needs to be angry in order to be inspired, and the satiric style languishes when it is time to render thanks. The satirist, however, can lament elegantly, which Boileau then proceeds to do. If only he had lived in the time of the do-nothing kings of old,[16] he could write poems to them easily and still continue his satire. But in the reign of Louis one is so dazzled and grateful that the satirist finds it difficult to have malicious thoughts about anyone. Nevertheless, bad books are still around and bad writers no longer fear the satirist's verse. Worst of all, the French stage is left to Pradon (after Racine's retirement), and Boileau, instead of exercising his pen on such subjects, is occupied with compiling a weighty volume of the king's history.

The king knows well that Boileau's ardor in praising him is not due to any selfish motivation. His zeal on Louis' behalf manifested itself before the king ever rewarded him, and the pleasure of praising his monarch led him to do so even in the midst of his satires. Since he has found favor with the king and has been rewarded with a pension, Boileau admits a legitimate remorse. It seems to him that, his praise now rewarded, it no longer has the same worth. He is afraid that the world may attribute his enthusiasm for the king to his gratitude.

Nonetheless, Boileau will be able to overcome this remorse, for if those who have received royal largesse refuse to praise the king's glorious deeds, there will be no one left to do so. Therefore the poet will redouble his efforts and will make up in zeal what he lacks in genius. After all, Horace was able to write both satire and poems in praise of Augustus, and Boileau can do no better than imitate his example. But Horace had many talents whereas Nature gave Boileau only a bizarre humor. His audacity surpasses that of Persius and Juvenal, but the worst poet in the kingdom is his equal in flattery. What can the poet respond to this accusation? In the face of such true reproach, he can only stop, wonder, and remain silent.

Epître VIII then reflects the poet's regrets. He thanks Louis XIV for his generosity, assures him of his desire to praise his king worthily and of his inability to do so, and regrets that he is no longer in a position to write satire, which was his natural talent and inclination. One may also detect a feeling that perhaps the king has erred in his choice of two poets as royal historiographers. Before the monumental task of compiling the history of Louis' reign Boileau always felt inadequate, and even more so after following the king on the campaign in Lorraine and Flanders in early 1678. Near the end of his life he sent his regrets to the king that the royal history had not been properly written by two poets who were so little fitted for the task by talent and personal inclination. To the modern reader, who no longer appreciates poetry of flattery nor understands the need for this sort of occasional verse, Boileau's verses to Louis XIV, in comparison to those of his contemporaries, are the least obsequious of the century.

Epître X

Epître X, A mes vers (To my Verses) is fundamentally a reply to the attacks against Boileau brought about by *Satire X, Contre les femmes.* Boileau here tries to vindicate himself by stating that he has consistently sought the truth in all his writings. He also reveals several petty confidences about himself and his family in order to protest his fundamental humility and to prove himself a good fellow. *Epître X* serves to illuminate Boileau's perpetual interest in the small, everyday, even banal facets of life. Written in 1694 or early 1695, the poem also prefigures the conflict with the Jesuits which was to occupy and, to a certain extent, embitter Boileau's latter years.

Having vainly tried to halt his verse, the poet now gives his permission for his poem to leave him. This farewell to his verse probably applies equally to *Epîtres XI* and *XII*, since all three were published together, along with a *Préface* which treats all three. Boileau feels that he is growing old, and so refers to the poem as "final fruit of my inspiration." These verses, vain and feeble children of his old age, hope to follow the footsteps of their elders, to charm the court, Paris, and the provinces, and perhaps even become proverbial. They should abandon such ambition, since the time is no more when the poet's Muse, in all her youthful force, was able to clothe her lessons in such rich colors. Gone are the days when Boileau's *esprit,* urged by legitimate anger, appeared before the tribunal of Reason to bring suit against Rhyme. In those days there was hardly a reader, no matter how unlettered, who did not borrow from Boileau's verses to enliven his conversation.

Now that old age has come to whiten his hair under his blond perruque, his verse should no longer presume to see readers hasten to buy such frigid rhymes. The public will now mock, and compare him to the most mediocre writers of the time. The people will ask what indiscretion had made the old warrior return to the lists with his pitiful verse and languishing style. This will be the signal for a thousand punctilious authors to commence their cavilling criticisms of the poet's style, hooting at metaphor and metonymy, which Pradon thinks are chemical terms. In vain will his verses long occupy a prominent place on the booksellers' shelves; soon they will be put in the storeroom to collect dust along with Pradon's plays, meditations of the Jesuits translated from Latin, and epic poems like the *Jonas* of Coras.[17]

If the verse still insists on being published, then let it at least appear in an edition along with the earlier poems. Perhaps the new epistles will be treated more kindly through honor to the older ones. And if some day a reader should turn his eyes upon them, they should paint a portrait of their author, taking care to remove the incorrect traits added by false critics. First of all they should show that the man painted in such dark colors was in reality a gentle and simple spirit who loved equity and sought only truth in his verse, often committing malice without being malicious. His candor alone was the source of all his vices. The verse should also say that Boileau knew how to distinguish the author from the person and, while criticizing poems, he never cast aspersions on their authors' characters. The poet should be painted as being free in his discourse but always reserved, weak in body but gentle in countenance, neither large nor small, not sensual, a friend of virtue rather than especially virtuous.

If someone should ask about his family, let him know that Boileau came from a family of magistrates, was an orphan in the cradle and lost his father at the age of sixteen. With the aid of his own creative spirit and his study of Persius and Horace, he managed to take his seat on Parnassus near that of Régnier. It should also be mentioned that the king chose him to record the exploits of his reign, that he was beloved by many of the great of his day, that Colbert took pleasure in his company, and that even now, retired from court but not forgotten, he is visited in his solitude by the heroes of the nation.

Above all, the reader should be made to see that, even though Boileau was the declared friend of many Jesuits, Arnauld, the great Arnauld, wrote a justification of his work. This fact will always have a place in the poet's memory and should be chiseled on his tomb in letters of gold. But he has delayed his verse long enough; the printer is at the door, so farewell for the last time.

Epître X is one of the most personally revealing poems Boileau ever wrote, not so much on account of the meager biographical details as that it shows us what Boileau thought of himself, his past literary production, and what things were important to him. He shows a certain justified pride in the popularity of his poems, in his selection by the king as royal historiographer, in his friendship with some of the leading noblemen, and especially in the esteem Arnauld had for him. His picture of himself as a gentle and simple spirit, always seeking the truth, is perhaps colored by the mellowness of age and his own idea of how he wanted to appear to posterity. His role as a virulent attacker of the authors of his time is certainly played down. Most important, from a critical viewpoint, is the fact that Boileau himself recognizes the real cause for the popularity of his verse, both in his own time and since. The outstanding single quality of his verse and one of the

ns for its lasting success is the proverbial quality Boi-
ons. His poems abound with lines, either singly or in
h are easily remembered, pithy, aphoristic, containing
osophical or literary wisdom. There is hardly a French
schoolboy who cannot quote many of these finely sculpted lines.
Much of Boileau's lasting popularity has been due to the quality
of what he says in these quotable lines, their ease of remem-
brance, and the nostalgic pleasure of encountering such familiar
old friends when rereading in later years.

Epître XI

In 1685 Boileau had purchased a house at Auteuil, at that time
a village near Paris but today a suburb within the city. He found
great pleasure in this retreat, where he spent most of his time in
the seasons of good weather. Friends often visited him there, and
he particularly liked to entertain with a light meal and a glass of
wine in his garden, which was tended by Antoine Riquié. Riquié
had been gardener for the previous owner, remained during the
years Boileau owned the house, and continued in his position after
Boileau sold the house to his friend Le Verrier in 1709. Epître XI
is addressed to this gardener (A mon jardinier) and compares the
difficulty of the respective tasks of the gardener and the poet, concluding that work is necessary for man and that the truly unhappy
man is the one who has no useful work to perform.

The opening lines of the poem refer to Antoine as the laborious
servant of a most easygoing master. If only the poet could remove
the thorns and weeds from his own spirit as Antoine removes
them from the garden! He then asks Antoine what he thinks,
while working among the flowers, on seeing his master dreamily
walking through the garden. Does he think the poet is possessed
by a demon like the cousin of the four sons of Aymon, whose
legend Antoine likes so much to read? [18] Probably not, for Antoine
has learned in the village that Boileau has been chosen royal historiographer and thinks he must be working on the history of the
deeds of a king greater than Charlemagne and the Twelve Peers.
What would the gardener say if he could know that the poet is
thinking about a poem in which he will convey his thoughts to his
gardener? Antoine would say that his master would not enjoy the
garden so much if he were responsible for working the soil, prun-

ing, watering, and all the other tasks necessary to make things grow.

Antoine believes that, of the two of them in the garden, he is the busier. How he would change his opinion if, for a couple of days, he were freed from gardening and became a poet! Then he would have to find a way to say in verse the most insignificant things without using an ignoble style. He would have to be able to give elegance and dignity to rustic discourse, maintaining the noble style. Then, tired and pale from his poetic effort, Antoine would realize that he prefers working the soil to wandering among the clouds in search of visions.

Work and fatigue are the common lot, and man is condemned to labor even in repose. The nine Muses deceitfully promise poets rest in the shady groves of Parnassus. Even there tyrannous Cadence, Rhyme, Caesura, and Measure fatigue the poet. But there is no weariness comparable to the bored leisure of a man who has nothing to do or think about. A willing slave of Indolence, never leaving his stupid torpor, such a person must endure the burden of having nothing to do. Far from the noisy throng he thinks he will find peace and quiet in the hateful calm of sloth. But shameful pleasures, children of Indolence, usurp an absolute power over his soul and torment him with desires. These pleasures indulged are followed by Remorse, and on her heels the scourges of the body—kidney stones, colic, gout. Their effect on the body is much worse than the fatigue of the hardest work. Antoine must then agree that a masculine, active, and vigilant Poverty is less tired from work and fundamentally happier than lazy Riches in the bosom of voluptuousness.

The poet will prove to the gardener two eternal truths: that work, which is necessary to man, causes him happiness rather than misery; and that there is no repose for the guilty. But the poet already sees Antoine's mouth hanging open, his eyes closed, his head hanging on his breast. Since the sermon has put him to sleep, it had best be ended. Moreover, Boileau sees the melons and flowers waiting and asking each other if there is some holiday in the village for a new saint, since they must wait so long for water.

Epître XI is both a literary and moral poem. It compares the difficulties of the work of the gardener and the poet, concluding that the latter is more arduous. From the moral viewpoint, Boileau's conclusion is that work is not only necessary to man but also is the principal source of his happiness. Both these ideas are, of course, commonplaces, as is often the case with the themes of Boileau's poetry. This does not mean, however, that they should necessarily be discussed in terms of derogation just because they are banal. It should be within the poet's right to discuss the commonplace if he does so in an original and pleasing manner, which Boileau succeeds in accomplishing in this epistle. To the classicists of the seventeenth century, originality of thought was not as highly prized as today. It was the common notion, best expressed by La Bruyère, that there were few if any ideas which had not been thought at some time by someone.[19] Originality consisted in the manner in which these thoughts were expressed. An epistle of Horace (I, 14) contains a conversation of the poet with his tenant farmer, but the only debt of Boileau to the Roman poet is a title and a couple of episodic motifs. Boileau's tone is completely different—gentle, cordial, sympathetic, and genial. Though certainly not a great poem nor even one of Boileau's best, *Epître XI* is a pleasant poem which reveals a side of Boileau's personality not often seen.

Le Lutrin (The Battle of the Books)

The *Lutrin*, which is primarily a satire of manners, has already been treated earlier in the chapter. The episode of the Battle of the Books, however, is definitely literary satire and so has been left for inclusion here. In Canto V the partisans of the Trésorier meet the followers of the Chantre between the Sainte Chapelle and the Palais de Justice. This area was the center of the bookselling trade at the time, as may be seen from Corneille's play, *La Galerie du Palais*. Small bookstores surrounded the Palais de Justice, utilizing rooms on the ground floor of this structure. It is in the shop of Barbin, leading bookdealer of the period, that Evrard seizes a volume of the *Grand Cyrus* of Mlle de Scudéry. *Artamène, ou le grand Cyrus,* was an adventure novel which appeared in ten volumes between 1648 and 1653 and was still fairly popular. Boileau chose it as an example of a genre he detested. He had already satirized it in the *Dialogue des Héros de romans* begun in 1665 but unpublished until the edition of 1713 after the death of Mlle de Scudéry. The damage done in the enemy ranks by this volume, which Boileau characterizes as "épouvantable" (dreadful, appalling), is the signal for the other combatants to enter the bookstore and seize books for missiles. Obscure writings and unknown books fill the air, drawn for the first time from their dusty storage. Boileau takes full opportunity to poke fun at the books and authors he considered mediocre, most of them forgotten today and justly so. The effect of the *Charlemagne* of Louis le Laboureur is to put its target to sleep from boredom! [20] The *Clélie* of Mlle de Scudéry is also fatal to several combatants. A copy of the works of Quinault is so soft and without vigor that it has no effect when hurled in the face of the Chantre. The Battle of the Books is finally brought to an end, as stated earlier, by the episcopal benediction of the Trésorier, which forces the enemy to kneel.

The episode of the Battle of the Books is a minor, though amusing, portion of *le Lutrin*. It serves little purpose in the over-all scheme of the poem other than a comic effect and an excuse for Boileau to indulge in some literary satire. A similar device was used by Jonathan Swift in *The Battle of the Books* and by Alexander Pope in *The Dunciad*, and both of these men were doubtlessly acquainted with Boileau's work.

Dialogue des Héros de romans

Boileau's satire of the adventure novels popular during the middle third of the century, the *Dialogue des Héros de romans* (*Dialogue of the Heroes of Novels*), was composed in the years between 1665 and 1671. It was published in an anthology in 1687–88, without Boileau's prior knowledge or permission, entitled *Dialogue des morts* (*Dialogue of the Dead*). In 1693 it was inserted in an edition of the *Oeuvres meslées* (*Selected Works*) of Saint-Evremond, again without Boileau's permission. Its first appearance in Boileau's works was in the *Oeuvres complètes* of 1713. It had been Boileau's intention not to publish it until after the death of Madeleine de Scudéry, most famous of the writers of adventure novels, who was a beloved and respected person. The dialogue was, of course, fairly well known in manuscript form and because of Boileau's readings. Boileau himself states in a letter to Brossette of April 10, 1704 that the dialogue had never been written down by him and that the manuscript which circulated and on which the printed editions were based probably came from Charles de Sévigné, son of the famous letter writer, who reconstructed it

from memory after having heard it. Although Boileau states that
he did not want to print the dialogue until after the death of Mlle
de Scudéry, she had died in 1701. In his letter to Brossette of 1704
Boileau still is unwilling to publish it for reasons that he says are
legitimate. These reasons remain unknown.

In the *Discours* which precedes, Boileau informs us that the dialogue was composed because of a "prodigieuse multitude" of
novels which had appeared toward the middle of the seventeenth
century. The popularity of the *Astrée* of Honoré d'Urfé, a pastoral adventure novel, gave rise to many imitators, among whom
Boileau points out Gomberville, la Calprenède, Desmarets,
Scudéry.[21] These imitators chose for their heroes the great captains
of antiquity whom they depicted like the shepherds of d'Urfé and
interested only in love. Whereas d'Urfé made heroes out of shepherds, his imitators have now made shepherds and even bourgeois
out of legitimate heroes. The most popular of these were the
Cyrus and the *Clélie* of Mlle de Scudéry, who turned the great
Cyrus of Persia into the lovesick Artamène. In *Clélie* she made the
heroes of the Roman republic, such as Horatius Cocles, Mucius
Scaevola, and Brutus even more amorous than Artamène, and
wasted her time tracing maps of the country of love (the famous
Carte du Tendre). In other words, she created characters nearly
opposite from the heroic gravity of the early Romans. Boileau
goes on to admit that, as he was young when most of these novels
were published, he read them with admiration, like everyone else,
and considered them masterpieces. His years and reason having
matured, his eyes were opened to the fundamental puerility of
these novels. He found himself unable to rest until he had composed this dialogue in the manner of Lucian.[22] His wish was to
attack not only their lack of solidity, but the affectation of language, their vague and frivolous conversations, the portraits in
which they abounded, and the endless verbiage of love. Now that
the authors are dead, Boileau has decided to permit the publication of his dialogue, but doubts if it will have the same piquant
effect since no one reads the novels any longer. Under the veil of
a fiction, in appearance extremely silly but actually completely
truthful and true-seeming, he is giving the reader what is perhaps
his least frivolous work.

The scene of the dialogue, following the model of traditional
dialogues of the dead, takes place in Hades. Minos, one of the

infernal judges, is irritated because he has just had to listen to a
newly arrived young man who talked only foolishness, which he
based on the authority of the ancients. Worse still, he cited the
ancients in tones of gallantry which is contrary to the way they
spoke when alive. Minos, in spite of every effort, was unable to
shut him up. Pluto, to whom Minos has been speaking, agrees that
the dead these days are more foolish than ever before in history.
The people trained in law are bad enough, but those called "men
of the world" are even worse. They speak a language called "gallantry," and when Pluto and Proserpina indicate that the language
is shocking to them, the men of the world treat the rulers of Hades
like bourgeois and accuse them of not being gallant. Pluto has
even been assured that this affectation of gallantry has infected
Hades and the Elysian Fields, to such an extent that the great
heroes and heroines who live there have become the silliest people
imaginable. Pluto cannot believe that Cyrus the Persian and Alexander the Great have become amorous fops. For this reason he
has ordered that the heroes and heroines from all sections of
Hades appear before him in the palace.

At that very moment Rhadamanthus brings news that the crimi-
nals of Tartarus, with Ixion, Sisyphus, Prometheus, and Tantalus
at their head, are in rebellion against the authority of Pluto. Pluto
takes appropriate defense measures and prepares to receive the
great heroes. Diogenes arrives to offer his assistance and informs
Pluto that the heroes and heroines are on their way, dressed as if
for a ball. Pluto believes it would be best to receive them one by
one, introduced by Diogenes. First to appear is the great Cyrus of
Persia, but Diogenes cautions Pluto not to call him Cyrus but
Artamène. Pluto has never heard this name and, to Diogenes' accusation that the lord of the underworld does not know Cyrus'
story, Pluto replies that he knows his Herodotus as well as anyone.
But, answers Diogenes, Herodotus does not say why Cyrus conquered half the known world. Pluto assumes it was because he
was an ambitious prince, but Diogenes assures him that it was in
order to save his princess Mandane, who had been abducted eight
times. Pluto has never heard of Mandane but concedes that she
certainly passed through a lot of hands. He decides to speak to
Cyrus and inform him that he has been chosen to command the
troops of Hades in the forthcoming battle. Cyrus does not answer
and acts as if he doesn't know where he is. Finally he manages to

sigh "Ah, divine Princesse! Ah, injuste Mandane!" Cyrus talks to himself about the necessity of forever loving an inexorable woman and refers to Mandane and himself in the most outrageous and affected language of stylish gallantry. Rather than command the infernal hosts, Cyrus prefers for someone to read to him a love story. Pluto is tired of Cyrus' sighing and weeping and, when Diogenes informs him that Cyrus still has nine volumes to go, Pluto throws him out.

Next in line is Thomyris, queen of the Massagetes, who had conquered Cyrus, beheaded him, and thrown his head in a vessel full of human blood. Pluto is sure such a woman will not weep and sigh, but all she can think about is the loss of her tablets, on which she had written a madrigal for Cyrus, whom she loves. Diogenes regrets the loss of the tablets, for he would like to have seen what a Massagetian madrigal looked like. Pluto does not understand why Thomyris would have beheaded the one she loved, but Diogenes ironically informs him that history, mistaken for twenty-five centuries, has been corrected during the last fourteen or fifteen years. Pluto dismisses Thomyris and asks about the owner of the robust voice he can hear singing. Diogenes informs him that it is Horatius Cocles who is singing an air he has composed in honor of Clélie. Pluto orders one-eyed Horatius to be brought in, still singing his song. To all of Pluto's questions as to why a great soldier, who was able to defend a bridge single-handed against an army, should become an amorous shepherd after his death, Horatius can only sing his song—"Even Phenice acknowledges that none is so fair as Clélie." Pluto sends him away, despairing of finding a single reasonable person among the heroes and heroines.

The next to appear is Clélie herself, most illustrious of Roman ladies, who fled from the camp of Porsena and swam the Tiber to safety. Pluto has often admired Clélie in his reading of Livy, but fears lest Livy has lied. Clélie wants to know if it is true that Hades is about to be invaded by a rebellious band from Tartarus. Pluto is delighted to see someone who appears to be reasonable, but Clélie goes on to inquire if the rebels have invaded the country of Tender, in the Land of Gallantry. Clélie wants to explain to Pluto the cartography of the country of Tender, which is divided into Tender through Esteem, Tender through Inclination, and Tender through Gratitude, but Pluto wants to hear none of it and suggests that the whole map shows the route to the madhouse. Clélie confesses that she too is in love, with the son of her enemy Lars Porsena of Clusium. Pluto, irritated, sends Clélie and her lover straight to the devil!

Space does not permit going into detail on each hero or heroine who appears before Pluto, nor is it necessary to do so in order to grasp Boileau's satiric device. The great heroes and heroines of former days, under the pernicious influence of the adventure novels, have become amorous fops, sighing for their sweethearts and only performing glorious deeds for the sake of love. The arrival of Lucretia and Brutus gives Boileau an opportunity to make fun of the *précieux* poetry contained in the love verse exchanged by the heroes and heroines, full of conceits and awkward transpositions, lines written in reverse, and so on. The appearance of Sappho (the salon sobriquet of Mlle de Scudéry herself) leads to a mocking of the genre of portraits, a favorite pastime of the salons and a literary device favored by Mlle de Scudéry and scattered throughout her novels. By means of gallant words and elegant, *précieux* ways of speaking, even one of the furies may be made to appear beautiful in these portraits. Boileau then has Sappho read a portrait of Tisiphone, one of the Erinyes, in the style of Mlle de Scudéry. The description is ridiculous in its exaggerated and affected language, replete with the adverbs which were favorites in the language of *préciosité*, such as *furieusement, terriblement, prodigieusement,* and so forth. Tisiphone, too tall, with small eyes, sunburned complexion, and sagging breasts, is made to sound passably lovely by means of the *précieux* device of never saying exactly what one really sees.

Pluto finally orders the heroes to appear before him en masse and is astonished to learn that there are many of them who are figments of authors' imaginations, who never existed. These also have vowed never to talk of any subject except love, since it is now love which is the cause of heroic deeds and virtues. Among this group is Astrate, who owes his existence to the fact that a Latin historian once wrote *Astratus vixit* (Astratus lived), and to a tragedy entitled *Astrate,* composed by Quinault, in which the audience is doubled up with laughter from the beginning of the play to the end. Ostorius, hero of a tragedy by the abbé de Pure,[23] was seen one time on the stage of the Hôtel de Bourgogne. Joan of Arc appears, heavy and awkward as Chapelain had painted her in his epic *La Pucelle,* and she speaks in verse extracted from that poem, stiff and harsh. Diogenes informs Pluto that Joan of Arc speaks in this fashion because she lived for forty years before publication with a poet who wrote that way. Pharamond, first king of the Franks, is seen as La Calprenède depicted him in a novel, *Pharamond,* begun in 1661 but completed by Vaumorière after La Calprenède's death. Pharamond is one of the most perfect lovers, since he had fallen in love with Rosemonde because of the description of her by one of his rivals, never having seen her himself.

Mercury, messenger of the gods, comes to announce to Pluto that when the rebels caught sight of the artillery sent by Jupiter, they became submissive again and are no longer in rebellion. Pluto wants to know how Mercury, god of Eloquence, can permit such language as he has just heard from the heroes. Mercury replies that he and Apollo are rarely invoked by writers these days. Moreover, a trick has been played on Pluto, for these persons he has seen are not the real heroes of old but a group of phantoms, copies of the ancient heroes. Their lives were short and now they wander on the banks of the Cocytus and the Styx. Mercury is surprised that Pluto has been taken in by their false rhetoric, so he has brought from the Elysian Fields a Frenchman who can recognize each of them for what he really is. The heroes and heroines are brought back in and divested of their finery and borrowed glory. When this is done, the Frenchman recognizes that the majority of them are bourgeois from his own section of Paris. Pluto orders the lot, along with their gallant letters, passionate verse, and numerous volumes, to be thrown headfirst into the river Lethe, so all may be forgotten.

The heroic novels of love and adventure, in the Graeco-Byzantine fashion, found readers in spite of the *Dialogue des Héros de romans,* and remained in considerable favor. In addition to its literary satire, the dialogue shows true critical talent, perhaps more so than any other work except the *Dissertation sur Joconde.* Boileau attacks the heroic novel of gallantry and amorous adventures, especially as illustrated in the works of Mlle de Scudéry. His criticism is based on *bienséance* (seemliness, propriety) and *vraisemblance* (verisimilitude), although he also attacks amorous verse and *La Pucelle* on stylistic grounds.

Boileau's main critical fault lies in the fact that he did not give Mlle de Scudéry credit for having recognized and admitted that her characters did not pretend to be faithful copies of the original heroes of antiquity, but were modeled on living persons of her acquaintance. Boileau's main objection to the genre of the novel as practiced in his day, was that it was contrary to truth and nature—and this is really the foundation of his whole esthetic. Plot, characterization, and language were all, according to Boileau, against truth and nature. This judgment reveals a fundamental weakness in Boileau's esthetic and indeed in that of French classicism in general, i.e., lack of appreciation for works of sheer imagination and pure delight for the reader. Boileau and many of the other "grands classiques" too often expected and insisted on some utilitarian purpose in literature. This conception had a baneful influence throughout the next century, and it is only with the advent of Romanticism that a literature designed to appeal to the imagination rather than the intellect reappears.

Boileau's criticism of the outrageously affected language and of the length of these novels, most of which ran to a dozen or so volumes, is valid. Indeed it is these two factors—length and language—which have resulted in a conspicuous lack of readers for these adventure novels today. There is nothing intrinsically wrong with adventures or love as a mainspring of action (witness the tragedies of Racine), but the fault lies in the excess, which becomes quite tiresome. This excess is a fundamental part of what Boileau considered contrary to nature. It should also be pointed out that these novels did not appear all at once, but a volume or two at a time, in serialized form. Thus they were not read from cover to cover in one or two sittings and perhaps did not seem as tedious to seventeenth-century readers. Boileau has been accused of wasting time in attacking the adventure novels and *préciosité,* both manifestations of a spirit that had passed from the literary scene. This is true only if one considers new novels produced, and the production was certainly in decline after 1665. However, there were still large numbers of readers and novels continued to be read, by latter-day *précieux* and *précieuses* especially, even after Boileau composed his *Dialogue des Héros de romans.*

III *Summary*

Throughout the latter half of this chapter we have been primarily interested in Boileau as a satirist of authors and works which he considered mediocre. Many of these works of literary satire also contain germs of literary criticism and theory, while many of those to be examined in Chapter 4 ("Boileau the Critic and Theorist") also exhibit traits of literary satire. As a satirist Boileau primarily makes fun of excess in any form—language, versification, lack of harmony, plot characterization, and bad imagery and metaphor. The affected language of *préciosité*, the harsh verse of Chapelain, the interminable adventures of the novels, the boredom of contemporary epic poetry, the insipidity of amorous verse, the abject flattery of occasional poetry, the ridiculousness of the burlesque—all these, to Boileau, were manifestations of one great fault, being contrary to nature and truth, by counterfeiting, exceeding, or falling short of the ideal of nature.

CHAPTER 3

Boileau the Moralist

BOILEAU was a man of upright character, stern in matters of morality. Far from prudish or ascetic in his personal life, he nevertheless had an intellectual and philosophical affinity for upright moral teachings. In the latter half of the seventeenth century people were very much interested in questions of theology and morality. Much salon conversation revolved around such topics, especially inspired by the continuing Jansenist/Jesuit controversy. Thus both from personal inclination and as a man of his time, Boileau was led to discuss matters of morality and theology. His subjects vary from such commonplaces as the origin and nature of true nobility and honor (*Satire* V) to questions of particularly contemporary interest, such as the necessity for loving God (*Epître XII*). Although, as stated previously, Boileau was primarily a satirist in all his works, the poems to be discussed in this chapter have been selected principally because they exhibit a more positive approach, are less satirical than instructive, or uphold a moral or theological ideal.

I Satire IV

Satire IV is addressed to the abbé François de la Mothe le Vayer and was composed in 1664, before the death of the abbé in September. There are additions, made in 1665–66. Le Vayer, son of the well-known free-thinker, was a friend of Molière and it is probably through the dramatist that Boileau first became acquainted with him. Tradition holds that Boileau's satire was dedicated to Le Vayer in gratitude for his praise of *Satire II* (*A Molière*). *Satire IV* is generally subtitled *On Human Folly*.

Boileau begins the poem wondering why the least wise man believes he alone has a share of wisdom, and why every fool is always ready to send his neighbor to the insane asylum. The pedant, full of useless knowledge and bloated with arrogance,

85

may have memorized a thousand authors but he is still only a fool. He believes a book counts for everything, and that reason and common sense are useless without the guidance of Aristotle. On the other hand a *galant,* who goes about boring society, thinks knowledge is worthless, criticizes every book, and considers his own ignorance a title to wit. The bigot, who vainly believes he can fool even God with his affected zeal, damns all mankind while hiding his own faults under a saintly appearance. The free-thinker, without religious faith, makes of his own pleasure a supreme law. He considers the flames of hell good only for frightening women and children, and believes every pious person is foolish. There are many other examples, says Boileau, which he does not choose to mention.

There is in this world no perfect wisdom. All men are fools, differing only in degree. Each man follows an uncertain route, according to how far his own error leads him astray. Every man wants to raise his own folly to the eminence of wisdom, and to make a virtue of his own fault. The wisest man then is the one who does not consider himself wise, who is lenient towards others and severe in self-criticism. But everyone tends to be indulgent of himself. The avaricious man sees poverty in the midst of abundance and considers his folly a form of prudence. His heart is only in his treasure, which is useless to him since the more he amasses the less he spends. On the other hand, the prodigal will consider greed a strange madness. Both are equally demented, according to the compulsive gambler who regards a throw of the dice as a life-or-death matter.

There are other follies which blind the reason. For example, Chapelain wants to rhyme—this is his folly. And even though his grating verse is hissed, he applauds himself and ranks himself higher than Virgil. What would he do if someone should make him see his verse as it really is—without strength or grace? He would curse the day when he was disabused of his error. Once upon a time there was a bigot who believed he heard the voices of spirits. When cured, he cursed his doctor for having made life unbearable by removing his illusions. Boileau approves of his anger, for man needs his illusions and often reason may be the worst of all our ills. It is reason which, in the midst of our pleasures, stifles desire with remorse. Reason, rigorous toward those who possess it, is omnipresent and scolds perpetually. In vain is reason dressed up like a queen by dreamers who want to make it sovereign over our senses and who think to attain happiness through reason. These thoughts are beautiful to read in a book, but in real life the poet finds that often it is the biggest fool and madman who is most self-satisfied.

This satire on human folly certainly contains nothing original except a pleasant turn of the phrases. The moral is a commonplace—everyone considers his own idiosyncracies wisdom and those of others foolishness. The man of reason is often the unhappiest of all. We must not believe, however, that Boileau, a man of reason himself, would want to exchange places with an unreasonable person, nor does he advocate the discarding of reason in favor of folly. He is simply making an ironic observation on human life as it exists. Most monomaniacs do seem happier or at least display a more unified personality because their thoughts and energies are all focused on their mania. The reasonable man, who sees the relativity of all things, is never self-satisfied, nor should he be.

II Satire V

Equally commonplace, even banal, is the subject of *Satire V, A Monsieur le marquis de Dangeau,* composed in 1664–65 and often called *Sur la noblesse* (*On Nobility*). In this poem Boileau discusses those elements which go to make up true nobility, and concludes that actions rather than birth are the sign of a real nobleman. The occasion for the composition of this satire may have been the initiation, in August 1664, of a verification of the titles of the French nobility. Dangeau, who had served for six years in the armies in Flanders and Spain, had been named lieutenant colonel of an infantry regiment composed of nobility. Louis XIV himself was the regimental colonel. Dangeau was from a family of recent and minor nobility, and the men in his regiment had been somewhat astonished at the honor given him. Boileau had probably heard of some remarks made by the noblemen in the regiment, and wrote *Satire V* to Dangeau as a gesture of assurance. He imitates fairly closely *Satire VIII* of Juvenal, managing to renew a commonplace which will have interest in any epoch where there is a sense of class-consciousness.

Nobility, states Boileau, is not just a fantastic notion when a man of outstanding family, inspired by the law of severe virtue, follows in the footsteps of his ancestors. But the poet cannot abide a fop who has nothing except a vain title and ornaments himself with the merit of his ancestors. Even if valor in his grandfathers furnished material for the old chronicles, what good does this useless glory do him now? If a man can offer nothing to the world but some old parchment relating his family history, it is a very small contribution. If his heart gives the lie to his elevated origin, if the only great thing about him is his haughty arrogance, if he is sunk in the slough of cowardly and indolent inaction, he is no true nobleman.

Among animals a courageous war horse is most esteemed by men, but this does not extend to his posterity who, if they turn out to be nags, are treated as such. Why then should one respect in men an honor which is no greater? Virtue is the hallmark of a noble heart. If one is descended from heroes, one should show the same ardor for honor and horror of vice. One should respect the law and avoid injustice. One should be willing to forget repose for the sake of glory in war. These are the marks of the nobleman. Then, from whatever illustrious warrior one may claim descent, no one will deny it. And, if one is not descended from famous ancestors, one deserves to be by one's actions. But even if descended from Hercules in direct line, if one demonstrates only an unworthy and ignoble baseness, it is an insult to one's ancestors and they bear witness against their own progeny. The brilliance of their glory serves to set off, by contrast, the fop's ignominy.

The poet then realizes that perhaps he is being carried away by his bitterness. Admitted then that the fop's ancestors were great men, who will guarantee that their grandmothers were always faithful? How can we be sure that some lusty young blade did not "interrupt" the course of the family, and who can vouchsafe the purity of this aristocratic blood? Cursed be the day when family vanity came to soil the purity of manners. In the golden age of mankind the sole claim to glory was innocence. Everyone lived happily under the same laws. Merit created nobility and kings, and a hero received his reputation from his own glorious deeds. Unfortunately, merit was debased by time, honor was considered plebeian, and vice was ennobled. Pride, bolstering its weakness with the false title of nobility, became the master of men. Then someone invented heraldry and its special language. Reason surrendered to vain folly, and honor, saddened and ashamed, was no longer the fashion. To sustain the new rank it became necessary to make a display of luxury and expenditure; one had to live in a palace and dress servants in distinctive livery. Soon, in order to subsist, nobility learned the art of borrowing without repaying. Finally the marquis, in prison because of lawsuits, saw the ruin of his house. The haughty nobleman, pressed by indigence, sought an alliance with the knave, marrying his daughter to him and thereby selling out his ancestors. This practice is nothing less than re-establishing "honor" at the price of infamy.

Nowadays, continues Boileau, the splendor of rank cannot compare with the glitter of gold. When a man is rich, even if he started as a lackey, the genealogists can find ancestors for him. Dangeau then, a man of merit and honor, who has saved his virtue from the pitfalls of life at court, should especially avoid leisure. If he wants legitimate fame, he should merit the esteem of the king by his deeds, and show that he is a worthy subject of so great a monarch.

The subject of *Satire V*, although commonplace, is ever popular simply because there are always people who indulge in ancestor-worship, thinking that the eminence of their family gives the right to special consideration. What Boileau says had been said often before, but needs to be said again to each succeeding generation. Boileau states it well. The material is brought up to date by the use of contemporary references, such as heraldry and the genealogists who can furnish ancestors and coats-of-arms, for a price.

III   Satire VIII

Satire VIII was first published in 1668. Composed in 1663–64 and retouched in 1667, it indicates progress since the earlier satires. Boileau has acquired more virtuosity and has profited by his experience. Subtitled *Sur l'homme* (*On Man*), the poem is a demonstration of the aphorism that man is the most foolish of all the animals. *Satire VIII* is satirically dedicated to a doctor in the Faculty of Theology of the Sorbonne, named Morel, whose nickname was *mâchoire d'âne* (Ass's jawbone). Morel was an adversary of Jansenism, and this is the reason for Boileau's irony. Not only did Morel's lantern jaw resemble that of an ass, but Boileau considered him one because of the attacks he had written against the Jansenists.

Of all the animals, Boileau states, man is the most foolish. The reader may be surprised that the poet believes even insects, worms, bulls, or goats have more common sense than man, but it is true. Man is indeed the master of all nature, and all things were created for his use. In addition, he is the only animal with the power of reason, and from his use of it the poet concludes that he is the most foolish. Morel may reply that such a statement is fine to amuse readers in a satire, but that it must be proved. Boileau agrees and proceeds to do so.

What is the definition of wisdom? It is an equanimity which nothing can upset and no desire enflame, which follows its own counsels with moderation. But man ceaselessly goes from one idea to another, his heart not knowing what it wants. What man may abhor one day is all he desires on the next. For example a certain *marquis* had sworn he would never marry a flirt. Two weeks later he was married, cited as an outstanding example of a good husband, and now believes that God created a faithful woman, just for his benefit, from some new rib. This is the way man is; he goes from one extreme to another and in the morning condemns his sentiments of the previous evening. Importunate to himself and incommodious to others, he shifts with the slightest breeze.

One may maintain that man is the master of the other animals, but even this may be debatable. Is the bear afraid of the passer-by, or the reverse? Can the shepherds of Nubia decree the exile of all lions from Libya? And this king of the animals, how many rulers does he have over him? Ambition, love, avarice, and hatred keep man's spirit in chains like a galley slave. Hardly has he fallen asleep at night when Avarice awakens him, to begin making more money than he can possibly need or want. Only his heirs will profit. If money is not attractive, then Ambition will rouse him from his repose. He will go out to fight and get himself killed just for the sake of glory. One may reply that ambition was always the greatest virtue of heroes. Does the poet consider Alexander the Great a fool? Yes, replies Boileau, for he might have been a good king in the small country where he was born, but insisted on running all over the known world, considering himself a god when he was only a bandit. It would have been best if his wise tutor (Aristotle), with the consent of his family, had had him committed to the Macedonian mental asylum.

Without bothering to discuss all man's possessions and passions, look at his best side. Man alone is civilized, dwelling in cities, living under honorable customs, with governors, magistrates, and kings, creating a policed society and obeying the law. But even without benefit of law and police, has one ever seen animals turn against their own kind in brigandage and war? The proudest animal respects other animals and lives quietly, without debates or lawsuits. None of the chicanery of the law courts is known by animals; man alone considers it an honor to slaughter his fellows. Not only has his hand mixed gunpowder and sharpened the sword—he must now seek to destroy other men by means of the Code and the Digest.

Man does indeed have his vices, but they are more than counterbalanced by his virtues. Has not man, through his knowledge, measured the heavens and discovered the secrets of nature? Do animals have universities with the four faculties (Letters, Law, Medicine, Theology), and do they have learned men who dress up in scarlet and ermine for academic processions? No, replies the poet, nor do they have doctors who poison the forests with their assassin's art. But without further discussion of man's vaunted knowledge, is a man considered worthy today because of this learning and wisdom? Far from it—all the knowledge man needs is a little arithmetic so he can make money. The ideal today is to get rich by whatever means possible, legitimate or not, and then a man will gain honors. Whoever is rich has everything and is wise without having any wisdom. The rich man has knowledge, wit, heart, merit, rank, virtue, valor, dignity, and breeding. Never did a wealthy man find a woman who was unresponsive, for gold lends beauty to ugliness, while everything is ugly in the midst of poverty.

If a learned doctor of theology should grow wan from study of the Bible, decipher its mysteries, confound both Luther and Calvin, solve all the old quarrels, bring light to the darkness of Biblical study, and, in his old age, offer the book of his labors to some wealthy knave, he will be lucky to receive a "Thank you." If he aspires to greater honors, he should leave the Sorbonne and take a position with a banker or notary. At least the ass, instructed by nature, has his instinct to guide him and doesn't try to compete with songbirds. Man alone, enlightened by reason, refuses to see in broad daylight. Guided by whim, there is neither reason nor sense in much that he does. Are animals, like man, afraid of superstitions they themselves have created? Did ever an animal make sacrifices to an idol and beg it for rain or fair weather? But beasts have seen man worship and adore a metal image, melted and molded by man, of a monkey or crocodile.

Morel may wonder what Egypt and her false animal gods have to do with the matter. Does the poet, by this example, seek to prove that man, that a doctor of theology, is beneath a donkey? The ass is the butt of jokes, a stupid animal, whose very name is a satire in itself. But, reflects the poet, if the ass could receive the gift of speech and express itself on human faults, what would he say about the ridiculous costumes worn in the streets of Paris, about a medical assassin in his robes on the way to a patient's home, about a squadron of pedants in procession followed by the rector of the faculty, about the law ceremoniously killing a man? What would the donkey say if he could hear and see what goes on inside the Palace of Justice? He would say without jealousy, seeing foolish men on all sides, that man is a beast like the rest.

Satire VIII probably indicates some influence of Montaigne, and also contains a trace of Pyrrhonism. In the section about Alexander the Great and his conquests, there is an implied criticism of Louis XIV's warlike policies. The same idea, expressed from the positive viewpoint as praise for the benefits of peace brought to the realm (temporarily indeed), may be found in *Epître I* (*Au roi*). Politically Boileau is a bourgeois with some republican tendencies, an admirer of the king but especially desirous of peace. Reference to writers indicates that even in a primarily moral poem Boileau cannot resist the temptation of literary satire. If Morel was aware of his own sobriquet, then Boileau's satire had an especially stinging irony because of his utilization of the symbol of the ass. Here, perhaps more than in any other poem, we see the skeptical and misanthropic side of Boileau's personality. *Satire VIII* is carefully composed as a defense against those critics who saw in his other poems only juvenile temerity and audacity instead of the rightful indignation he must surely have felt at the spectacle of society. It is designed to show his detractors that Boileau did indeed have a serious and moral side.

IV Epître I

Some of Boileau's critics, notably Desmarets de Saint-Sorlin,[1] remarked that *Epître I, Au roi* (*To the King*) was primarily a satire and that Boileau did not know how to address the king.

Only the first part of this criticism is true, since the epistle does contain some satire, both moral and literary. In *Epître I*, composed in 1669 and reworked in 1672, Boileau mentions that he had vowed to cease writing satire and devote himself to verse in praise of Louis XIV. However, he realizes his own limitations and the direction of his talent and decides to speak frankly and truthfully. Nor is he able to resist the temptation to satirize the *marquis* (in the original version, later deleted), the chicanery of the law courts, and some of the mediocre writers.

In spite of his vow to abjure satire and write only laudatory verse, says Boileau, as soon as he picks up his pen Apollo warns him of the perils he will encounter and his danger of shipwreck on an unknown sea. It is not a question of lack of ability; he can rhyme an insipid ode as well as anyone else, and he proceeds to dash off an illustrative rhyme or two. But to praise the king in a worthy manner, one must depart from the common fashion. This is especially true of Boileau, who has criticized so many mediocre authors for their insipid verse. His product must justify his audacity, and if he does not succeed then he furnishes ammunition to his critics. Those whom he has attacked will say that his verse is no better than theirs and therefore he has no right to set himself up as a model. It would be vain for him to be satisfied with the beauty of his verse and stupid to lament the ignorance of the public when it does not agree with his own opinion of his merit. It is distressing not to have readers, so up to now Boileau has refrained from writing in praise of his king.

Nevertheless, it is only with regret that he can remain silent. Should he remain only a silent spectator of the virtues of his monarch? Even if his Muse dares not follow Louis to war, at least peace presents the king in a calm and serene attitude. Boileau then calls upon Louis to abandon sieges and battles and let someone else break down the walls of cities. Why should Boileau's Muse arouse the king's valor, which is already too great? The nation should enjoy at leisure the fruits of Louis' deeds and the sweetness of peace. Boileau certainly does not approve of a do-nothing on the throne, but in spite of the vain laurels promised by war, one may be a hero without ravaging the earth. There is more than one kind of glory, and it is an error to give the first rank among kings to the conquerors. Among the great heroes they are the commonest, since every era produces them. But a king who is truly a king, wise in his projects and able to maintain his subjects in a happy calm; who has cemented his glory by public happiness —to find such a king one must seek throughout history.

But why should the poet look elsewhere for what may be found at home? He cites the example of Louis' restraint and love for peace in his consent to the arbitration by the English and Dutch after his conquest of Flanders (1677) and Franche-Comté (1668). By this prudent diplomacy the first of these conquests was assured while Franche-Comté was returned to Spain. (Boileau could not know, of course, that Louis was to reconquer Franche-Comté six years later.) Louis thus was able to limit his own victory and seek glory in peace. Others may follow him to war and frighten the universe with tales of the royal valor; Boileau, far from the tumult of battle, will extol the exploits of peace. He will paint the pleasures of the court *fêtes*, for example the *comédie-ballets* of Molière and Lully. The oppressors of the people are being brought to justice and famine is halted. Abuses are being reformed. Taxes are lower. Soldiers are restrained by discipline and are engaged in public works in peacetime. Artisans are once again industrious. Manufacture has been encouraged, to the dismay of neighbor nations, who are accustomed to exporting luxury items to France. Boileau describes the magnificent buildings erected by the king, and the canal being dug from the Mediterranean to the Atlantic. Chicanery has been frustrated by new laws. The generosity of Louis is such that indigence has disappeared, especially in the case of writers, who are now being given pensions. Boileau advises Louis to continue this generosity to authors and even to increase it, since it is they who assure the lasting renown of great heroes. Even Achilles and Aeneas would have been forgotten except for Homer and Virgil. This is not to say that Louis is making vain efforts to immortalize himself, but Apollo owes him the fame only poets can insure. Therefore Louis should open to Apollo his treasures and thereby fill the land with famous poets. An Augustus can easily create a Virgil.

As for Boileau, he dares not boast of the worth of his own verse. However, if some of his poems should survive to posterity they will be witness to the truth of Louis' greatness, because Boileau is well-known for his sincerity, truthfulness, and penchant for criticism. If he then praises the king, it must be as true as history itself.

Originally, as has been mentioned earlier, *Epître II*, the fable of the Litigants and the Oyster, was included at the end of *Epître I*. It should be evident that its removal is an improvement, for its inclusion here could only have detracted from the tone of the epistle. In a poem which may seem excessively flattering to us, but did not seem sufficiently so to his contemporaries, Boileau lauded the king for the peaceful accomplishments of his reign. His praise of the peace policy certainly did not displease Colbert, whose ideas currently had the king's ear. Nor did Louis XIV hold the advice against the poet later, when he reverted to war under the influence of Louvois, the minister of war, and of his own appetite for glory. Most of what Boileau has to say about the king's policies and accomplishments in peace are really to the credit of Colbert, but the minister could not act without the consent of the king. This epistle, together with *Epître IV, Le Passage du Rhin*, in 1672, led to Boileau's formal presentation at court and his pension of 2,000 *livres* per annum.

V Epître III

The theme of *Epître III, A Monsieur Arnauld, Docteur de Sorbonne*, is what Boileau refers to as *mauvaise honte*, which might best be translated as *fear of public opinion*. Often *mauvaise honte* is at the root of man's errors, because it prevents him from admitting them. This is perhaps the most abstract of Boileau's epistles, but is still full of reality and actuality. The poem is dedicated to *le grand Arnauld*, most illustrious of the Jansenist theologians, who had recently returned to Paris from the retreat provided him by the duchesse de Longueville. The "Peace of the Church," brought about by Pope Clement IX, had put a temporary end to the Jansenist quarrels. Boileau and Arnauld met for the first time at the home of Lamoignon and began a mutual friendship and esteem which was to last to the end of Arnauld's life. Boileau was very proud of this friendship with such a saintly man, and justly so. He always felt that one of his greatest glories was the fact that Arnauld defended him against Perrault's criticism of *Satire X, Contre les femmes*. Composed first in 1670 and rewritten in 1673, *Epître III* takes as its point of departure the culmination of a polemical battle between the Jansenists and the Protestants, led by Jean Claude, minister to the congregation at Charenton. As early as 1664 Nicole, an eminent Jansenist theologian, had written a *Perpetuity of the Faith* which was refuted by Claude in a *Response to the Perpetuity of the Faith* (1665). In 1669–70 Arnauld, as a token of the reconciliation of the Catholic factions, presented a volume called *Perpetuity of the Faith Concerning the Eucharist.* Arnauld himself wrote the dedicatory epistle, in Latin, to Clement IX, and the body of the work is a development by Nicole of his earlier *Perpetuity* and his response to Claude's refutation. Nicole's arguments were so strong that, according to rumor, Claude had agreed to convert to Catholicism but was prevented by his followers and fellow Huguenots. Boileau's epistle then begins with this Jansenist attempt to bring the Protestants back into the bosom of the Roman Church.

In spite of the fact that Arnauld (in reality Nicole) has uncovered the fraud and error of Claude and the innovators in matters of faith, what good is it to have opened their eyes if a rebellious reticence keeps them from the Mass? Claude, clever though he is at deceiving himself, realizes the strength of the arguments; but a demon enters him and reminds him of what people will say if he becomes converted. Thus because of fear of public opinion Claude is prevented from embracing the truth. At this point Boileau expands the poem and generalizes on the power of this *mauvaise honte* over mankind.

The most paralyzing factor in human personality is fear of public opinion, adroit enemy of the noblest virtues. Under its rigorous yoke our spirits become servile and we become wretched slaves of each other. Through fear of public opinion virtue becomes cowardly and timid. The free-thinker, who intrepidly preaches in public against the very God that he believes in in his soul, would rush to embrace the truth he can see, but for fear of the mockery of his false friends. This fear and shame before the opinions of others is the foundation of all our ills. Miserable playthings of our own vanity, the least we could do would be to admit our infirmity. Before Heaven abandons us to our errors, we should profit from the moment that divine grace gives us.

It is this fear of the opinion of others that caused the fall of Adam and brought the end of the Golden Age. Here Boileau brings in a description of this traditional tableau of the Golden Age of mankind, with the aid of Virgil, Horace, and Ovid, and along with it the usual contrast to the present age of iron. These references have become rather tiresome to the modern reader, but gave pleasure to contemporaries who liked to read familiar things and compare the treatment with other well-known instances. After the Fall, Boileau describes the advent of man's troubles, such as labor, pestilence, war, and famine. None, however, equals the rigors of *mauvaise honte,* from which all vices come. Honor and virtue no longer dared show their faces, and piety retreated to the deserts and the cloister. Since that day there has been no heart, however detached from the things of this world, which has not been subject to the sin of *mauvaise honte.* Even the poet who writes this epistle is guilty of it, since he is trembling at this very moment at the thought of what people are going to say about these verses.

Epître III may be conveniently divided into four movements. The introduction establishes the uselessness of the Jansenists' attempts to convert the Protestants, and ascribes this lack of success to *mauvaise honte.* At this point the poet generalizes that *mauvaise honte* is at the root of all our troubles. This thesis is then sustained by the historical example of the fall of Adam and the end of the Golden Age. Boileau then returns to an individualized treatment of his subject, using himself as his example. As a whole, the thought of the poem is weak and repetitive, and the analysis seems sometimes uncertain, especially when the poet makes *mauvaise honte* responsible for the Fall. The idea, however, is not as commonplace as those in many of Boileau's moral poems. In a technique which is common in Boileau's work, ideas are presented as personifications: *mauvaise honte* enters Claude as a demon; the free-thinker represents libertinism. As a good rhetorician, Boileau knew how to make the most of rhetorical devices, and he uses dialogue, allegory, and even the commonplace to advantage. Boileau's epistles are not as lacking in poetic qualities as has often been claimed. We must consider that our taste has been irrevocably changed since the advent of Romanticism. Commonplaces are often treated by Boileau in a fresh manner, and the picturesque portions are interesting, as are the personal confidences, often hidden by superannuated ornament. Whatever criticism we may make of Boileau's poetry, stemming from our post-Romantic conception of poetry as almost exclusively a personal and lyric genre, we must concede that he rarely bores us. Boileau has treated in a not unpleasant fashion a moral verity which cannot be too often repeated—many of mankind's difficulties are caused by excessive attention to the opinions of others.

VI Epître V

Epître V (1664) might well be subtitled "Know Thyself," for this is its basic theme. It is a natural sequel and development of line 30 of *Epître III* ("We seek outside ourselves our virtues and our vices."). If one is to find virtue and happiness within, then it follows that one must know oneself. There are some echoes of the *Pensées* of Pascal, where the great Jansenist speaks of *divertissements* (amusements) as a method of avoiding self-examination. The poem contains also passages (l. 108 to end) in which Boileau gives a few glimpses of his personal life and family. *Epître V* is dedicated to M. de Guilleragues, secretary of the *chambre et cabinet* of the king.

In the opening lines of the poem Boileau refers to Guilleragues as born for the court and master in the art of being pleasant, a man who knows when to speak and when to remain silent. He then asks Guilleragues whether the poet should be silent or speak out; in other words continue to make his reputation in satire or not. When he was younger and more irritable, he aspired less to a reputation for discretion and wisdom. Now that time has matured his desires, he prefers repose to fame with its accompanying inconveniences. As a satirist he was insulted by a thousand authors. Now, like an old lion, he is gentle and tractable. His irritability has passed with his youth; he no longer feels the old, bitter bile, and leaves frigid rhymsters alone.

Having become a philosopher, having submitted to reason, his faults are now his only enemies. He wishes to avoid error and love truth, seeking to know himself and looking for himself within himself. This is the only subject he wishes henceforth to study. Let others seek knowledge; Boileau seeks self-enlightenment. We all aspire to repose of the spirit, but this happy state must be sought within ourselves. What did Alexander the Great seek in the horror and tumult of war? Possessed by a boredom which he was powerless to overcome, he feared being alone with his thoughts and wanted to escape from himself.

Unfortunate authors of our own misery, we are perpetually being drawn outside ourselves. What is the use of seeking gold in the bosom of the New World? Happiness is to be found at home as well as anywhere else. Whoever can live happily with nothing possesses everything. But, ceaselessly ignorant of our true needs, we importune Heaven for those things we need least. An heir hopes for the death of his father-in-law so the money will make him happy. Death finally comes, but is the heir now satisfied? No, for now that he has become rich he aspires to become a nobleman. In the popular opinion, money is everything and without money everything, even virtue, is useless and sterile. As for the poet, who is not dazzled by money and for whom spirit and wisdom are important, he esteems indigence more than riches gained through the misfortunes of France. Boileau does not claim to be completely opposed to money, like the sage of antiquity who threw his wealth away in order to be free.[2] The poet's good sense is in better equilibrium. However, virtue can be satisfied with little.

Boileau himself has practiced what he preaches. His father worked hard for sixty years and at his death left him a small amount of money and his example to follow. Son, brother, cousin, uncle, and brother-in-law of clerks, Boileau decided to follow a nobler profession and left the Palace of Justice for Parnassus. The budding poet had to renounce riches and, unable to acquire much money, he learned to get along without it. Fearing base servitude, truth became his unique study. His fate has been better than might have been expected, since the king noticed him, found merit in his works, and increased his revenues by royal gifts. Neither the envy nor the complaints of his adversaries have been able to halt the king's generosity. His happiness has surpassed all his expectations. He feels that the benefits he has received ought to be deserved because of the composition of some immortal verse. If he can do this, praising adequately his benefactor and silencing his critics, then he will be content. Never will he obey the law of base self-interest nor seek happiness anywhere except within himself.

Here again we have an example of Boileau's treatment of a commonplace, though universal, theme—the necessity to know oneself and seek true happiness within. The theme is indeed trite, but evidently needed repeating to the society of the age, since the great moralists of the century—La Rochefoucauld, Pascal, La Bruyère, and others—are unanimous in their condemnation of

their contemporaries for spending so much time in vain amusement in order to avoid thinking about themselves and their
human condition. The immense popularity of gambling throughout the century bears witness to this ennui. As usual, Boileau's
poem contains actuality as well as generality. When he speaks of
the necessity to scorn riches, it is from his own heart and experience. Although he was well-off because of wise investments and
his pension, he never accepted money from the publication of his
literary production, and his generosity was proverbial. Nor was
he, as we have seen, quick to begin to draw his pension. Among
the many faults of which Boileau was accused by his enemies,
niggardliness or avarice were not to be found.

VII Epître VI

Boileau's only contribution to the genre of bucolic poetry is
Epître VI, and even here there is a flavor of both literary satire
and satire of manners. The peace and quiet of the country is con-
trasted with the importunities of city life. The epistle is dedicated
to Monsieur de Lamoignon, *avocat général* to the *Parlement de
Paris* and son of Guillaume de Lamoignon, *premier président* of
the same body, whose "academy" Boileau often attended. The
elder Lamoignon died in the autumn of 1677, the same year in
which *Epître VI* was composed. The place which inspired the
nature descriptions and from which Boileau is supposedly writing
was the hamlet of Hautisle, on a piece of property which belonged to Nicolas Dongois, the poet's nephew. Boileau had spent
there the better part of the summer of 1677, possibly in a sort of
"suggested exile" to allow things to cool off after the previous
spring's battles over the rival *Phèdres* of Racine and Pradon. Boileau had, of course, taken the side of Racine in this *cabale* which
became so violent that the two poets were threatened with a beat-
ing and had to be given the protection of the prince de Condé and
his son, the duc d'Enghien. It is hard to believe that Boileau, in
spite of what he says about the chagrins of the city, would have
voluntarily absented himself from his beloved Paris for so long a
time. In similar cases of discord among courtiers it was often suggested that a "retreat" to some country estate would be advisable
until things blew over. It is possible that Boileau found himself in
an analogous situation in the summer of 1677. That he had not
fallen from royal favor is evident from his nomination as royal

historiographer the following autumn, but some have seen in this sinecure an attempt to remove the two poets from controversy and keep them busy at other tasks. In any event, Boileau seems to have enjoyed his stay in the country just as he had often enjoyed visiting the country seat of the Lamoignon family at Bâville.

In the opening lines of the epistle, Boileau states that he has found the country to be his only refuge from the afflictions (*chagrins*) of the city. There follows a description of the village beside the Seine, the scenery and the rustic dwellings, the manor house of the *seigneur*. The poet then mentions what he does to occupy his time—solid pleasures at very little expense. Sometimes, book in hand, he dreamily wanders through the meadows. Seeking for an elusive rhyme, he often finds it in a remote corner of the woods. Fishing and hunting are also enjoyed and, on his return from sport, a pleasant and rustic meal, seasoned by appetite, is prepared. Why, asks the poet, can I not remain forever in this happy place and forget the rest of the world?

The second movement of the epistle begins with his description of what awaits him when, in spite of his wishes, he is torn from the cherished vales and returns to Paris. *Chagrins* are waiting for him on his entry to his house. A cousin, abusing his relationship, wants him to go solicit some judge before he even removes his riding boots or washes off the dust of the trip.[3] He is informed that he has been criticized in front of the king; a new book has been published against him; he has been condemned at court for a word used incorrectly; and the rumor is even circulating that he has been assassinated. A scandalous poem is making the rounds under his name. Since his first satire was published a dozen years past, truth is a feeble ally, and every silly satire from the provinces is attributed to him. In spite of his denials, everyone claims to recognize his style in every satirical poem that appears. Lamoignon may judge for himself if the poet is able to find time to pay court to the Muses. People, however, laugh at his excuses and believe Apollo will come to inspire him on demand. News comes of a great French victory, and people believe it is as easy to make verses as it is to capture cities.

The third and final movement returns to praise of the simple life of the country. Happy is the mortal, unknown to the world, who lives contentedly in some quiet corner! Fortunate is the man whom love of fame has never bothered, whose pleasure derives

from his liberty, and who accounts for his leisure to himself alone.
He does not have to suffer insults and injustice and can laugh at
the capriciousness of mankind. However, once admitted to a position of literary eminence, the poet becomes the slave of the disdainful reader, who expects him to add marvel to marvel. Nevertheless, everything eventually declines and Boileau feels that his
fire is burning low and needs silence and the shade of the forests
for inspiration. His Muse can no longer walk on the paved streets;
only in the woods does Apollo still sometimes deign to inspire
him.

Lamoignon should not, therefore, ask why he has remained so
long away from him and Paris. It is Lamoignon's duty to remain
in Paris to watch over the maintenance of the law, as befits someone of his birth, rank, merit, and eloquence. He owes all his efforts
to the well-being of his country; if he leaves, the orphan will cry
out, oppression will rear its audacious head. To see clearly, Themis
needs Lamoignon's eyes. As for Boileau, who can only furnish
Paris a useless dreamer anyway, he needs the repose of the meadows and forests. Lamoignon then must be patient until September, the month of harvest, when Boileau will rejoin him in Paris—
so the two of them can flee to Bâville! There they will ride horseback over the fields or sit on the soft grass near the fountain, discussing true virtue in their carefree state. They will talk about
such topics as true and false righteousness, whether knowledge or
virtue is the surest path to glory. Such conversations are what Boileau likes best about their friendship.

There is little likelihood that the reputations of Virgil or Theocritus will be eclipsed by the pastoral verse of Boileau. In *Epître VI*
Boileau seems less successful than elsewhere in treating a banal
theme with freshness. This is perhaps because the poem contains
less actuality than others, and also because Boileau was not a
lover of nature in the deepest sense of feeling a communion with
her. We do not, of course, expect the same sentiment of nature as
exhibited by Rousseau or the Romantic poets, but in comparison
with La Fontaine, a contemporary, Boileau's feeling for nature is
quite weak. In addition, the over-all impression of the poem is
marred by the stilted references to fishing and hunting, both of
which fall absolutely flat. One of Boileau's favorite critical theories was that much of the success in the minor poetic genres was
due to the ability to say things of a simple, everyday sort, even

"base" things, in such a way as to make them partake of the *style noble*. This idea might even be considered a sort of residue of the *préciosité* to which he had been exposed as a youth. At any event, he describes the simple sport of angling in the following terms: "Sometimes by means of the allure of a perfidious hook, I sportively inveigle the greedy fish." (*Quelquefois aux appas d'un hameçon perfide,/J'amorce en badinant le poisson trop avide;* ll. 29–30.) Hunting, another of his leisure amusements, is thus depicted: "Or with a lead shot which follows the aim of the eye and departs in a flash of light, I make war upon the inhabitants of the air." (*Ou d'un plomb qui suit l'oeil, et part avec l'éclair,/Je vais faire la guerre aux habitants de l'air;* ll. 31–32.) The verse, admittedly, loses something in the translation to English prose, but not much. In addition, the last line cited contains three internal assonances, which was considered poor prosody. These are probably the worst examples in all Boileau's poetry of the sometimes disastrous results which may come about when trying to say simple things other than simply. It is unfortunate for *Epître VI* that both are found here.

VIII   Epître XII

Boileau's last epistle, *Epître XII, Sur l'amour de Dieu* (*On Love for God*), was considered by most contemporaries as his masterpiece in the genre. Its publication was urged by the Archbishop of Paris, and it was heard and approved by no less an eminent person than Bossuet. Published for the first time in 1697, *Epître XII* ably demonstrates that the sexagenarian had lost few of the robust and vigorous qualities of his earlier days, especially when treating a theme so close to his heart. Boileau knew when the poem was composed that it would cause dissension with the Jesuits, even though the order was then under attack and seemed to be losing credit. Open strife between the Jesuits and Boileau finally did break out in 1703. In his *Préface* to an edition of the last three *Epîtres*, Boileau states that he sometimes wishes the epistle *Sur l'amour de Dieu* were the only one he had ever composed. In order to reassure readers who might have some doubts concerning his qualifications as a theologian, Boileau states that he has read it to a number of Sorbonne theologians, Oratorian fathers, and very celebrated Jesuits, all of whom have found the doctrine sane and pure. The Bishop of Meaux (Bossuet) read it several times and has approved. The poem has also been examined by the Cardinal de Noailles, Archbishop of Paris, who offered some advice, which the poet took, and gave his approval for its publication. For the benefit of those who claim the epistle is only a vain declamation, attacking nothing real, Boileau gives in the *Préface* the proposition he is combating, in the language in which it is upheld in several schools: *Attritio ex gehennae metu sufficit etiam sine ulla Dei dilectione, et sine ullo ad Deum offensum respectu; quia talis honesta et supernaturalis est.* (The attrition which comes from the fear of Hell is sufficient, even without any love for God, and without offense to God in any respect; because it is in the nature of something honorable and supernatural.) This proposition Boileau attacks and considers false, abominable, and more contrary to true religion than Lutheranism or Calvinism.

The controversy over the doctrines of attrition and contrition had been going on for some time before Boileau's epistle. Some of the Jesuits had claimed that, in penance, attrition because of the fear of eternal damnation was sufficient for absolution if accompanied by a desire to love God and an earnest attempt to refrain from sin. Their adversaries, mainly the Jansenists with Pascal chief among these, maintained that contrition, which included true love for God, was necessary before effective absolution. For the uncomplicated and upright spirit of Boileau, it was manifestly ridiculous that anyone could be exempted from loving God in any circumstances. Boileau was probably furnished theological ammunition by Pascal's *Lettres provinciales* and by theologian friends. We are also reminded of Pascal by the tone of righteous indignation and disbelief in a proposition so contrary to the teachings of the Gospel. In reading *Epître XII* one receives the impression that, perhaps more so than anywhere else, Boileau truly believes in what he is writing. The question had been on Boileau's mind for some time, since it is mentioned in Canto VI of *le Lutrin* in the 1683 edition: "A servile fear took the place of charity: the need to love God passed for heresy" (ll. 55–56). Further indication of Jansenist inspiration is afforded by the dedication, *A Monsieur l'abbé Renaudot.* Renaudot, grandson of the founder of the *Gazette de France*, eminent theologian, and member of the Academy, was at the time preparing a *Défense* of Nicole's *Perpetuity of the Faith.* The poem was not offensive to all the Jesuits; Boileau also showed it to Father de la Chaise, Jesuit confessor to the king. The priest explained to him the difference between affective and effective love, and Boileau assured him that he was not attacking the Society of Jesus but only wanted to defend the orthodox doctrine of love for God as necessary to salvation. He admitted his readiness to correct anything Father de la Chaise might find defective, and proceeded to read it, with all his art of recitation. Father de la Chaise's only reservation was that it was a delicate matter, especially in verse. Father Gaillard, rector of the Jesuits in Paris, also gave his approval.

The epistle opens with the statement, attributed to Renaudot, that man deludes himself if he thinks he can leave the state of sinfulness without love of God. The salutory fear of the torments of Hell does not necessarily indicate remorse. A useful fear often does penetrate us, coming from divine grace, which is ready to enter our hearts and takes this means of knocking at the door. If the sinner then, impelled by this holy impulse, recognizes his crime and aspires to the Sacrament, the Holy Spirit will return to dwell in his heart and convert servile fear into filial love. In this way the Supreme Wisdom often makes use of Satan to chase out Satan himself. But woe to the sinner who is obstinate in his malice, astounded at the horrors of the thought of Hell but, far from loving the Father, fears Him like a severe tyrant. Such a sinner finds no attraction in the good which God promises and in his heart wishes that God did not exist. In vain does fear make him run to confession. Forever a vile slave to the yoke of sin, he remains attached to the Devil whom he fears.

Love, which is essential to our penitence, should be the fruit of our repentance. In spite of what ignorance teaches, God never gives His grace to one who does not love Him. Fear disposes and aids us to seek Him, but He never comes unless love succeeds to fear. Ignorant confessors and seducers of souls imagine that they have a limitless power to justify every frightened sinner. They are full of error when they preach that one may be loved without loving God. Can a frightened Christian, who never served God but only the Devil, continue to travel the paths of evil and gain Paradise by formalities? Because of a few sacraments received without zeal, will God admit His enemy before the very eyes of the astonished saints? There are doctors of theology, even austere in their personal morality, who go about piously preaching such error and sapping the very foundations of piety. Their hearts infected with criminal error, they claim to be the true and pure faithful, and treat as impious and heretical anyone who dares declare himself for God and against them. In vain do true Christians groan at their audacity; the boldest grow weak and, seeing the Devil thus accredited against God, dare preach the truth only in a faltering fashion.

Fearlessly following in the path of Renaudot, the poet goes on to say to their faces "Open your eyes!" It would be less horrible to refuse to recognize a God who is master of the universe than to admit His existence and then dare say one may please Him without loving Him. Such a base, shameful, and false Christianity is not worth the enlightened paganism of Plato. To cherish true goodness without knowing the author of it is better than knowing the Creator without loving Him. By love for God, brought to the heart by fear, the poet does not mean the joyful paroxysm which, rarely experienced on earth, is the just recompense of the blessed. In ordinary mortals love for God does not always produce pleasurable sentiments of sensations. Often the heart which has this love doesn't know it. Some are afraid of not loving God when they do so sincerely, while others sincerely believe they are burning with ardor when they actually have hearts cold toward God. Sometimes an indolent mystic, a peaceful fanatic in the midst of sins, thinks he has the gift of perfect love while actually cradled in the arms of Satan.

If you would like to know if your faith is sincere, examine yourself. Do you pardon your enemies, combat the appeal of sensual things, overcome your weaknesses? Is God the object of your generosity to the poor? Do you obey God's commandments? If your reply is affirmative, then you love God. Boileau here paraphrases the Gospel of John, XIV, 21: "He that hath my commandments, and keepeth them, he it is that loveth me. . . ." Obey His commandments then and, certain that He wants to save all, don't be alarmed on account of a vain aversion often felt even by the holiest soul. Seek Him and you will find Him (Matthew VII, 7 and Luke XI, 9). The more He seems to stray from your heart, the more you should try to keep Him there by your virtuous acts. But never believe the horrible blasphemy that a sacrament, a priest, even God himself can excuse you from the love you owe.

Theologians may say that, since love for God then suffices to save us, of what use are the sacraments? Is not the promise to take the sacraments implicit in love for God? Can the converted pagan really be a Christian unless he aspires to baptism? Can the Christian be truly touched by divine love unless he desires to confess his sins in church? The sacrament alone has power to break the chains of the slavery in which we are held by Satan. Love aspires avidly to the sacrament and is also the foundation of the sacrament. When a repentant sinner seeks penitence through the prescribed forms, even if he cannot complete them God will be able to consider them accomplished. The sinner may not dispense with love for God. It is through love that grace bears fruit within us. Love alone joins us to God and, without love, faith, virtues, and sacraments are worth nothing.

The poet proposes a further argument to the theologians. When we receive absolution, is or is not the Holy Spirit present in us? If it is in us, can it be there except that love for God warms our hearts to receive His supreme love? If the Holy Spirit is not in us, then Satan is still in possession of our hearts. Admit then that love must be reborn within us, and do not give the name of love to the innate feeling of uneasiness which fear alone has created in the sinful heart. The love which justifies and which God sends to us, even though it may be disturbed and joyless, is the same ardor which burns in the hearts of the blessed in Paradise. In the fatal instant which marks the limit of our life, our soul must be filled with love for God. If He does not find it there, He is deaf to our cries and does not kindle it after our death. Give in then, theologians, to the clarity of these arguments and no longer claim, by means of confused sophisms, to hide the love of God from the faithful. Be informed that glory, to which Heaven calls us, will one day crown the zeal of the children of God, but not the cold remorse of a fearful slave.

Some haughty Scholastic will doubtlessly wonder where the poet received his theology degrees and if he can prove his arguments by extracts and citations from the learned authors of the church. To decide that the Christian is obliged to love the Author of all good, the God who nourishes us, who gave us life, who redeemed us by His death, does one need a theology degree? Did not God himself write it on every page of His Holy Book? And yet vain theologians dare make of it a doubtful problem! They dare treat as error the indispensable law to love God for Himself, and

by false dogma eliminate charity from the duties of a Christian! If
the least severe of them were consulted as to whether or not a son
should love his father, he would say there is no doubt of it. Yet if
one asks at the same time whether man, creation of a God alone
good and worthy of love, should love this true Father, the most
severe of them fears to chance too much by affirming it.

The poet cannot resist the temptation to repeat an illustration
he had used a few days earlier in an argument with a pair of
Jesuits who upheld the doctrine of attrition. They had insulted
Boileau because he dared affirm that, in order to be absolved of
confessed sin, it was necessary to have at least the beginning of a
love for God. Boileau then made an analogy, repeated here, of the
parable of the sheep and the goats (Matthew XXV, 33–end). On
the day of the Last Judgment, when God separates the sheep
from the goats and tells each what made them impure or just in
His eyes, Boileau will be a goat. He will be sent to burn in Hell
for maintaining that man should love God and keep the First
Commandment. The Jesuit will, however, be accounted a lamb
because he is an enemy of this dogma. He will enter Paradise
where, after having delivered man from the burden of having to
love his Creator, he may then undeceive the angels. If God were
capable of such an action, Boileau would say to Him that at least
the poet's mouth spoke the same words as his heart. After this
sermon, the Jesuit remained speechless and, muttering under his
breath, left the room.

Whether one appreciates or approves of poetry of this nature or
not, it must be recognized that Boileau is here speaking with sincerity. *Epître XII* is an important poem, and one for which Boileau
had an especial fondness. He was indignant at those who considered superfluous the movement of love which bears up a Christian
heart to its Creator. The poet-theologian demonstrates his beautiful convictions in poetic fashion, without using convincing argument for his proof. He showed considerable courage in attacking a
society which, although losing some credit in 1697, was still powerful. Events later in the poet's life were to prove that the Jesuits
had neither forgotten nor forgiven.

IX   Satire XI

Satire XI, Sur l'honneur (On Honor) was composed between
1698 and 1700, and was published in the edition of the *Oeuvres* in

1701. It is both a moral satire and a satire of manners, attacking
the casuists and religious hypocrisy. Boileau castigates all those
who would interpret religion in their own way and use God for
their own ends instead of allowing themselves to be used by Him.
Boileau's sympathy for the Jansenist cause in their opposition to
Jesuit casuistry is particularly indicated by the following two
lines: "Virtue then [under the reign of Saturn, the Golden Age]
was not subject to ostracism nor was it called Jansenism."

Much of the detail of the actuality and even the true theme of
this satire remain obscure. Boileau informed Brossette in a letter
(September 8, 1700) that he speaks in *Satire XI* of his suit concerning the nobility of the Boileau family. However, by the time
the satire was printed there is no longer any direct allusion to this
suit. A cousin of the poet, Gilles Boileau, had been condemned for
having falsely claimed patents of nobility. Nicolas and Jacques
Boileau, the doctor of theology, joined Gilles in an appeal of the
case, since they too were indirectly affected by the decision. The
Boileau family won the appeal in 1699, when the court upheld the
nobility of the family, dating back to Jean Boileau, who was ennobled in 1371, along with his descendants. The original letters patent had been based on Jean's descent as grandson of Etienne
Boileau who had been the provost of Paris about 1269 under Saint
Louis. The prosecutor of the case, Lacour de Beauval, was severely reprimanded by the appellate court, in the name of the
king. An aura of mystery has since continued to cling to the whole
affair, the idea often being advanced that the claim of Gilles was
upheld because of the esteem in which his cousin, the poet, was
held by the king. Boileau showed a degree of pride in this vindication of his family honor, but certainly did not try to trade on any
claim to nobility, either before or after. As far as *Satire XI* is concerned, the only indication of the affair may be an impression of
general irritation which permeates the poem.

A similarity may be noticed between *Satire XI* and *Satire VI* of
Régnier, but Boileau's fundamental idea was to distinguish true
from false honor. The idea is not, however, neatly developed. The
real subject seems to be hypocrisy of all sorts, in a society in which
Boileau now feels generally ill at ease. This uneasiness came from
his own personal affairs, his declining health, worsening affairs
of state, and the hypocrisy of society. The combination of the subject of true versus false honor, and a general idea of hypocrisy,

which the poet either could not or would not express clearly, may
contribute to the generally vague impression left by the poem.
Boileau also seems to feel the need of further defending the Jansenists, without knowing exactly how to go about it. *Epître XII*,
Satire XI, and *Satire XII* all seem to be written in the same general frame of mind, and the latter may be Boileau's resolution of
this state.

Satire XI is dedicated to Valincour, elected to the Academy to
the seat of Racine, and new associate with Boileau as royal historiographer. Honor, explains the poet, is everywhere cherished and
men have abundant words to exalt it. Even the convict sentenced
to the galleys laments honor condemned, in his person, to rowing.
If the general opinion is consulted, self-interest has no effect and
honor is the rule everywhere. Nevertheless, if one examines the
spirit which governs men, one perceives only foolish ambition,
weakness, iniquity, cheating, corruption, and self-idolatrous pride.
The world is like a great theater where each is deceived in public
by the other and often plays a role opposite from what he really
is. Every day the fool wears a false face to counterfeit the wise
man, the ignorant pretend to be learned, rogues feign virtue. In
vain does one mask oneself before the world; the public will inevitably learn the truth. In order to appear to be a gentleman, one
must be one. What is natural always comes out and one cannot
force it to remain hidden.

But the poet feels he is straying from his subject. Honor, he was
saying, is admired, but what is real honor? The ambitious conqueror thinks it lies in destruction, the miser believes it is in
money, the *miles gloriosus* in his frivolous prowess, the liar in
never keeping his word, the poet in putting ink on paper, the
marquis in defrauding his debtors, the free-thinker in breaking
the Lenten fast, the fool in defying honor itself. What then is
honor? Is it in seeing our eloquence vaunted, excelling in courage,
cleverness, prudence? Is it in seeing the world tremble at the sight
of us, in possessing many gifts and talents? Even with all these
qualities a king can remain infamous, like Herod or Tiberius.
Where may honor be found?

In this world, nothing is beautiful except equity. Without it
valor, strength, goodness and all other virtues are only baubles.
An unjust warrior who conquers the world is no more than a high-
wayman. If Caesar's like were delivered today to the Paris police,

he would lose his laurels on the scaffold. Greatness is measured by justice. Mithridates, Sylla, Tamerlane, Genseric, Attila and all the great conquerors, kings, princes, and captains are less great in the poet's eyes than Socrates, a bourgeois of Athens, who always sought to attain justice. Justice is the shining virtue in the world. Even if a popular person is unjust, it is the appearance of justice in him that attracts admiration. Equity is the only thing that truly attracts the human soul, and even an unjust person hates injustice in the abstract. There is no soul, however deeply sunk in vice, in which there does not remain some trace of justice. Even among such barbarous peoples as the Arabs and Scythians, it is justice which is the basis of the division of spoils.

The Gospel says nowhere to the Christian, "Be pious." It does say "Be simple, gentle, equitable." Often from the sanctimonious person to the veritable Christian there is twice as much distance as from one pole to another. By sanctimonious Boileau does not mean either an obvious hypocrite like Tartuffe, nor the Quietists, followers of Molinos.[4] He means a false Christian, badly instructed and guided, who believes in the Gospel but has never conceived of the spirit of it; a Christian who uses it to disculpate vice.[5] Confessors of this breed deceive the great and authorize their shameful weaknesses, believing sin can go to Heaven provided the sacraments are observed.

To place some limit on this vague subject, the poet concludes that the only solid honor is to take truth for one's guide in all things, to observe reason and the law, to be gentle to others and rigorous to oneself, to be just—this word includes all goodness. The poet doubts that the mass of humanity will easily support this discourse, so he begs indulgence to recount a fable. In the days of good King Saturn, friend of gentleness, Honor and her sister Equity enlightened the world with their wisdom, and reigned in profound peace. All was held in common in the world, and there were no enclosures or fenced fields. Virtue was not called Jansenism. Honor, beautiful without vain ornaments, had no need of gold or diamonds, and maintained the salutory rules of her sister Equity. But Honor was once called to heaven by the gods and remained away from earth for a long time. During her absence, Deceit, who resembled Honor, took her place and convinced man in the deception. He claimed that he came from heaven and that man should henceforth obey him. The world believed him. Innocent

Equity, shamefully banished, could scarcely find a desert to flee from ignominy. The impostor, decked in splendid clothes, mounted on a jeweled throne, surrounded by Haughtiness, Disdain, and Audacity, was crowned by Luxury and Pride. By his orders *mine* and *thine* brought about war and lawsuits; under the name of law they divided the earth. The law of the strongest was established; the new king triumphed and established a fantastic code of vain laws based on property and might. Vengeance was preached, men began to kill each other at the slightest affront and, their souls filled with remorse, they traced in letters of blood the commandment "Kill or be killed."

Then it was that the age of iron, under Jupiter, was begun. Brother took up arms against his brother; the son shed the blood of his father; thirst for rule gave birth to tyrants and conquerors; ambition passed for virtue; successful crime became no longer criminal; man lived on hate, division, envy, fright, tumult, horror, confusion. True Honor was finally advised of the troubles of earth and returned from heaven. But man could no longer bear the sight of her, since virtue was out of style. Honor herself was treated as a cheat and an impostor. Finally, unable to bear any more outrage, Honor delivered mankind over to his wretched slavery and fled to heaven with her sister Equity. Since that time, growing rich from the ruin of Honor and Equity, false honor has ruled mortals, governing all things and acting as the motivation of all actions, perhaps even these verses. But even if this were true, the poet concludes that true honor is to be found in God alone.

Again we have a commonplace subject treated by Boileau, but this time less successfully and more abstractly. We are tempted to see in *Satire XI* a decline in the poet's creative powers, and this is surely a factor in our feeling of disappointment, along with those other elements already mentioned. The poet is speaking sincerely, to be sure, from irritation at the society around him which he felt was in a decline from the glorious days of the period from 1660 to 1680. Boileau was right in many ways, as the following century and the Revolution were to demonstrate. In *Satire XI* he exhibits a vague uneasiness and irritability which will still be apparent in *Satire XII*, his last work.

X Satire XII

Boileau's last poem, as well as the last in a series of polemics concerning moral uprightness and pure Christianity, whose worst enemy, according to the poet, was Jesuit casuistry, is *Satire XII*. Composed in 1705–8, *Satire XII* is written under much the same inspiration as *Satire X, Epître X, Epître XII,* and *Satire XI*. The satire is subtitled *Sur l'équivoque (On Ambiguity)* and contains no dedication. In a *Discourse of the Author To Serve As an Apology for the Following Satire,* Boileau relates the circumstances of its composition. Intending to write a satire against the poor critics of the day, and having already composed several verses, he perceived that an ambiguity of language had occurred which he could not correct. Abandoning his original intention, the poet decided to write a satire against ambiguity itself. He realized immediately the difficulty in writing a satire on such a dry subject, the first of which would be which gender to make the word *équivoque,* since both were current. Boileau decided that it would be humorous to begin the poem with this very difficulty.

The occasion related by Boileau was undoubtedly only the most recent factor which influenced the composition, and perhaps the most immediate for the form. His state of mind was about the same, one of irritation, as when *Satire XI* was composed, with an additional cause for chagrin. The *Journal de Trévoux,* established and edited by the Jesuits, had attacked Boileau in 1703 on the occasion of an edition of his works which had appeared in Holland in 1701. The attack is not direct, but takes the form of an apparent eulogy by a Father Buffier. The article points out all the passages in which Boileau allegedly imitated Latin poets, in order to demonstrate that Boileau was absolutely right in having upheld the side of the ancients in the Quarrel of the Ancients and Moderns. Buffier even goes so far as to state that those portions of Boileau's verse most generally admired are also those most laden with borrowings from the ancients. He accuses the poet of having translated, nearly word for word, long series from Juvenal, but with such genius that they are the best passages in his work. In *Satire X (Contre les femmes)* and *Epître XII (Sur l'amour de Dieu),* however, there are hardly any lines imitated from the Latin. These were, of course, the poems of Boileau most detested by the Jesuits. Buffier leaves no doubt that he considers them inferior and insinuates that their poor quality is due to the fact that they lack a Latin model. The entire article, insidious, insinuating, and full of innuendo, is designed to take vengeance for the epistle *Sur l'amour de Dieu* which, in spite of the approval of some Jesuits, notably Father de la Chaise, had enraged the Society of Jesus as a whole.

Boileau was naturally sensitive and impatient toward criticism of his work, and he answered the article by a couple of biting epigrams, taking care not to embroil himself too much with such a powerful group in whose membership he counted several friends. He tried to distinguish the Society itself from certain injudicious critics among the membership. By 1704 peace had been arranged, but it was not to last. Boileau, because of his known admiration for Arnauld and in spite of his protests that he was not interested in theological hair-splitting, was intellectually and morally sympathetic toward Jansenism, a sympathy obvious to all. From now on the Jesuits would be watching him even more carefully, and Boileau often lacked prudence when inspired by his satiric Muse.

Satire XII, once the inspiration had shifted to ambiguity in all its forms, could not help but deal with practices of the Jesuit casuists. The poem was read in public or circulated in manuscript form, and it called the attention of the Society again to Boileau. The poet permitted himself to be so carried away by his ideas that not only did ambiguity become the source of belief in oracles and false honor but even of sin, idolatry, heresy, and casuistry, which is difficult to explain. The satire is directed toward the idea which obsessed Boileau—the enmity of casuistry to pure Christianity. As the poem became known by the poet's readings, his friends claimed it was a masterpiece. His enemies, in spite of Boileau's precaution to get approval of the Cardinal de Noailles, Archbishop of Paris, began to take steps against publication. In 1706 appeared a little book, *Boileau at Grips with the Jesuits*, which contained a satire attributed to Boileau which he did not write and was not worthy of him. Boileau immediately disavowed it. Inspired by a desire to set the public straight on his works and urged by the bookdealers, he decided to publish a new edition of his works.

Several corrections were made to *Satire XII* in order to attenuate any portions which might offend the Jesuits. The machinations of his enemies made him despair of ever seeing it in print before his death. Therefore he put it in writing, as he informs Brossette in a letter of June 16, 1708, so it would not be lost. Father de la Chaise had died in the interim and had been succeeded as royal confessor in 1709 by Father Tellier, who was violently opposed to Boileau. It was probably due to his influence that Boileau was issued a *privilége* only for those works which had already been seen by the king, and not including *Satire XII*. Tellier also insisted that Boileau deny in writing the authorship of the satire in *Boileau at Grips with the Jesuits*. Boileau had not, of course, written the piece, but the nature and tone of Tellier's insistence irritated him and his denial was imperious and disdainful. The *privilège* was still not extended to include *Satire XII*, and Boileau preferred to abandon plans for the edition rather than leave it out. The copy of *Satire XII* was turned over to the bookdealer Billiot, but it did not appear in Boileau's lifetime.

As stated in his preliminary discourse, Boileau begins *Satire XII* with the word *équivoque* itself, which he calls a hermaphrodite since it is used in both masculine and feminine genders. He then moves from the word itself to *équivoque* or ambiguity in language, which torments both writers and their readers. He has decided to write a last, useful satire against ambiguity. Would it be best to approach the problem from the point of view of the amusing misunderstandings which result from ambiguity? This is not the time for such things and the public would not be amused by frivolity on such a subject. Much wrong has been committed against literature by the vain attraction of ambiguity, but the poet will now speak of the evils spread throughout the world by ambiguity, source of all error.

To begin at the beginning, was it not ambiguity which, shortly after the Creation, deceived man with an apple and ambiguous words to the effect that he would be able to know all and make himself equal to God? Man tried the apple and all the knowledge he acquired was of his own nudity. He learned that he was a wretched creature, oppressed by hunger and thirst, who would come to death in sorrow and misery. (Boileau here refers to the passages in Genesis III, 5, 7: "Your eyes shall be opened, and ye shall be as gods, knowing good and evil; And the eyes of them both were opened. . . ." The ambiguity is in the word *opened*.) Thus the Fall of Man is the result of an *équivoque*.

Also a result of ambiguity was the rebellion of the giants, born from the union of the sons of God and the daughters of men (Genesis VI, 4). The Flood was sent by God to punish their au-, dacity, but ambiguity was saved from the deluge by one of Noah's sons and preserved in the ark in the form of a serpent. Pursuing its old ways, *équivoque* spread lies among men and filled their spirits with fables and dreams. God himself disappeared under the veil of ambiguity, leaving only ignorance and unlimited impiety. Then superstition, spreading idolatry and illusion, brought about the making of gods of gold, silver, and copper. The very artisan who made it prostrated himself before the metal image and asked for goods, health, and wisdom. Ambiguity is also behind the speaking of oracles, which were able to tell the truth while lying because of the double meanings provided by *équivoque*. In order to keep man in ignorance, ambiguity caused virtue to take on the appearance of vice, while vices were dressed in splendor and appeared to be virtues. Humility became baseness; candor became crudeness. On the other hand, blind and foolish ambition was called the passion of the great-hearted; impudence was considered noble pride; cheating became prudence. Audacity increased throughout the entire universe, and the only heroes were usurpers, tyrants, and conquerors.

Ambiguity's malice was especially directed toward the suborning of justice. Insinuating itself into the clearest laws, obscurity caused doubt in the wisest judges. The more one tried to understand, the less enlightened one became, and the text was often obscured by the gloss. Eloquence joined the ornamentation of words to ambiguity, and together they made the true pass for false, and right appear wrong. Man finally lost all enlightenment and, deceived into thinking he saw everything, actually saw nothing.

Under the guidance of God, however, there remained still a trace of reason in Judaea. Among men elsewhere, groaning under the yoke of *équivoque*, one might seek in vain for virtue and uprightness, for what is human wisdom apart from God? Even Socrates, the honor of pagan Greece, was only a mortal inclined to evil and, in spite of his apparent virtue, his friendship for Alcibiades caused it to appear ambiguous. In the pagan world, enslaved under *équivoque* and deprived of reason, humble and true equity was hardly glimpsed.

Finally, in order to save man from his extreme disorder, God

had to become man and come down from Heaven to dissipate the
deceitful dogmas of ambiguity. At the sight of God, the demons
disappeared and the oracles became silent. All felt the effect of his
coming: the lame walked and the blind opened their eyes. Soon,
however, even in the nation which had remained faithful, the audacity of ambiguity armed followers: priests, pharisees, kings,
pontiffs, theologians. Soon the Supreme Truth was accused by
them of lie and error. The God of Heaven was dragged before the
tribunal of men, and the Author of Life was condemned to die.
The furor of *équivoque* was frustrated at the Crucifixion, for from
the night of the tomb, God arose shining with light. His teachings,
soon borne over the world, were heard everywhere. Ambiguity's
ridiculous gods were thrown from their altars and the stones were
used for buildings. Nevertheless, *équivoque* was able to weather
even this storm. Losing faith in idolatry, ambiguity obtained new
cords from Satan in order to bind man more subtly.

To aid the frenzy of ambiguity, Heresy, daughter of *équivoque*
arrived on earth from her abode in Hell. This monster made error
look attractive, and all ran to drink of her mortal poison. Even the
church herself was hardly able to escape because of the heresy of
Arianism, which attacked both the Word and His Divinity. A holy
word, augmented by a single syllable, filled spirits with bitterness
and caused Christian blood to flow in rivers.[6] In more than one
church council falsehood seemed to conquer the true Gospel.

But what good is it here to recall from the depths of Hell these
heretics, raised up by Satan against Christianity, with God's permission so His truth might be brought to light? Let us limit ourselves to the fanaticism stirred up on earth by heresy. When Luther and Calvin, filled with the spirit of *équivoque* and claiming
to be chosen to reform the church, freed the priesthood from celi-
bacy, the results were pernicious. Admitting no more visible authority, each man became infallible judge of the law, and without
approval of the Roman clergy, every Protestant became a Pope,
Bible in hand. Of this error were born more sects than insects in
autumn or silly love poems in Paris. Everywhere there were mad
Anabaptists, proud Puritans, execrable Deists; every artisan had
his private dogmas, and each Christian obeyed a different law.
Discord unfurled her banners in the midst of these haughty sects,
and Heresy, calling ravage and fire to the aid of vain reasoning,
caused cities to be desolate, churches burned, and Europe to be-

come a field of massacre and horror. Orthodoxy even, blind in its furor, forgot the gentleness commanded to Christians, believing that, in order to avenge God on his enemies, every violence God had forbidden now became legitimate. The signal given for carnage, a hundred thousand zealots, swords in hand, attacked their relatives and friends, joyfully burying a Catholic dagger in a heretic's breast. What lion or tiger equals in cruelty an unjust rage, armed by Piety?

These excesses were abhorred by the church, but *équivoque* entered into the schools of theology, abusing theologians with the doctrine that an impious, unjust, abominable sentiment, reputed tenable by two or three theologians, became a probable opinion.[7] This doctrine of probable opinion gave security to a Christian who, even while condemning it, could conscientiously follow it. It is upon this principle that *équivoque* founded the most dangerous and terrible morality that Lucifer could ever have taught to novice demons. One even heard preached in Christian schools that a sinner under the yoke of vice could be admitted to Paradise without loving either God or virtue, just through fear and the Sacrament.

True zeal no longer being necessary for a Christian, ambiguity went one more step and developed the doctrine of direction of intention, which could remove all sin from a culpable action.[8] Soon perjuring oneself ceased to be perjury; usury and simony were practiced with impunity; the miser was excused from the duty of helping the poor. Then began the doctrine of mental reservation, which permitted one to lie out loud while saying the truth in a whisper.[9] A priest could sell the same Mass three times provided he personally took no part in it other than reading it. Even murder became permissible with proper direction of intention. Boileau then realizes that he is getting beyond the scope of his topic. There is no use rhyming the entire papal bull of Innocent XI, in 1679, which has condemned these practices. He also realizes the criticisms and even the danger to which he is exposing himself. He will be called heretic, criminal, traitor, buffoon, cheat, impostor, calumniator, copier of Pascal and Nicole, execrable Jansenist. Therefore, in order to prevent such treatment, he will stop writing, and he orders *équivoque* to leave the premises. Ending now his writing of satire, he has given to *équivoque* an allegorical setting. In order to seek new patrons, ambiguity will have to go elsewhere, preferably to Trévoux. There a clerical senate of new Midases, aided by Ignorance, the sister of *Équivoque,* holds monthly meetings to pass judgment on Apollo and poetry.

In *Satire XII* Boileau shows how *équivoque* or verbal ambiguity may lead to equivocation of thought, ambiguity of meaning, and finally to casuistry. In this satire he follows closely in the steps of Pascal in the *Lettres provinciales.* Even foreseeing the accusations that would be made against him, he does not hide his thoughts. Without taking a side on the theological questions which divided the Jansenists from the Society of Jesus, he condemns the adversaries of Port-Royal in their morality, which he considered lax, and in their persecution of other Christians. In an effort to answer in advance the expected attacks of the Jesuits, Boileau states in the *Discourse of the Author To Serve As an Apology for the Following Satire* that he condemns nothing which has not already been officially condemned by Rome. When Pontchartrain, the chancellor, revoked his *privilège* on January 30, 1711, the Cardinal de Noailles, Archbishop of Paris, offered to intervene with the king on Boileau's behalf. Discouraged but still proud, Boileau thanked him politely but refused. At the time of his death the following March, he was still in the midst of controversy. It is significant that his weapons were drawn from the arsenal of Pascal, whom Boileau considered the greatest of modern prose writers and the equal of his beloved ancients.

XI *Summary*

Critics often refuse to recognize Boileau as a moralist, comparing him unfavorably with Saint-Simon, La Bruyère, Molière, or Pascal. It is certain that Boileau had little original philosophy and was incapable of really penetrating to the depths of the human soul. As has been stated frequently in this chapter, his morality is composed of commonplaces; but, however banal it may seem, his morality is sincere. It shows both vigor and a strong character and gives us an accurate picture of this thoroughly Parisian bourgeois, who mistrusts all excess and sees some folly and unreasonableness everywhere. Boileau has his own individuality and also represents a certain milieu of the France of his own day as well as ours. Moreover, it may be debated whether a poetic theme necessarily has to be original. Can it not derive its originality as well from the turn of expression as from the originality of thought? Boileau's contemporaries would have said so. Granted that Boileau is not an original moralist, the equal of some of his contemporaries like La Bruyère or La Rochefoucauld, still he is vigorous and sincere, and often succeeds in giving new life to commonplaces which had become stale through the years.

CHAPTER 4

Boileau the Critic and Theorist

BOILEAU is less a systematic critic than a theorist of literature. It would be erroneous to state that he lacked critical
principles, but in his criticisms of contemporaries he often appears
not to be applying these principles. Nor does he inform us concerning his reasons for disapproval except in vague terms. Boileau's
literary criticism seems to be both instinctive and subjective. Yet
with two or three exceptions, such as his inability to appreciate
Ronsard and his excessive admiration of Voiture,[1] today we
would tend to condemn those whom Boileau condemned. Nor
was his critical ability entirely negative, for he was able to see
clearly the universality of his greatest contemporaries—Racine,
Molière, Corneille, Pascal, La Fontaine—and predicted accurately the eminent position they would be granted by posterity. In
view of Boileau's extraordinarily high percentage of correct critical evaluations, we must conclude that he possessed a solid foundation of theoretical principles, most of which are universally applicable, coupled with a critical instinct for imagery, harmony,
and structure. In many respects Boileau is similar to Malherbe in
his ability to spot immediately a ridiculous image or a harsh combination of sounds, while he is superior to Malherbe in the more
positive aspects of critical judgment—an uncanny ability to recognize not only the mediocre but the truly great poets of his day.
It shall be the purpose of this chapter first to deduce from the
body of Boileau's critical and theoretical work his primary guiding
principles, next to analyze these works for specific theoretical
components of his principles, and finally to arrive at some conclusions as to the universal validity of his principles as well as to
indicate faults or weaknesses peculiar to the man or to his time.

I *Concept of Beauty*

For Boileau, as should be the case for any critic or literary artist, beauty is at the summit of artistic creation—its purpose and its

result. Content, form, and structure should be directed toward and subordinated to the production of beauty. Neither Boileau nor his contemporaries were much interested in the philosophy of esthetics, but directed their attention primarily to the ends and means of poetry rather than its essence. A work of art should be beautiful and, if it is beautiful, it will give pleasure to its audience. For this reason, like Racine, Molière, La Fontaine, and the other *grands classiques,* Boileau places emphasis on the necessity for the artist to please his audience. Although they were just as consciously and conscientiously artistic as the later poets of the Parnassian and Symbolist groups, the idea of "Art for Art's Sake" was fundamentally foreign to their concept of artistic creation. Art, for them, could not exist except as a type of communication, and the public was necessary as a recipient. The worth of an artistic creation then is decided by the public—the cultivated and enlightened public of the court and the *haute bourgeoisie.* This public judged the merit of a work on several bases or combinations of bases: comparison with what had been done before; accepted ideas of beauty; what pleased them and was considered stylish; the taste of the king and court; political, social, economic, and religio-philosophical factors; the universal and the natural. Hopefully the latter would exert the greatest influence on public taste and judgment.

The contemporary public could, of course, be mistaken in judgment, but posterity ultimately could not. For this reason Boileau continually emphasizes not only the necessity of pleasing the contemporary public but also posterity, which would have the final word. There is a very considerable emphasis in Boileau's doctrine, both stated and implicit, on what might be called the classical distance. That is, only time can ultimately tell what will be of lasting artistic merit because too many factors may color the judgment of a contemporary public. In this matter, Boileau was fortunate to be guided by one of the surest tastes that ever directed a critic. In spite of errors in his evaluation of his predecessors, and in spite of the fact that he is sometimes guilty of admiring the right people for the wrong reasons, Boileau was never mistaken in important matters regarding his contemporaries. His taste has generally remained our taste. Posterity then, composed also of the enlightened and cultivated segment of the public, is the ultimate judge of artistic worth. The bases of posterity's judgment will be universality, nature, and the doctrine of universal consent. The latter doctrine states, briefly, that if the most quali- fied people over a long period of time have admired certain artis- tic works, it is because they are worthwhile. Therefore, since a thought is beautiful only insofar as it is true, and since the infalli- ble effect of Truth well stated is to strike men's attention, it fol- lows that what does not strike the attention is either not beautiful, not true, or poorly stated. Consequently a work which is not to the taste of the public is a poor work. The majority of men may, for some time, take the false for the true and admire unworthy things, but it is not possible in the long run for a good thing not to please the public. A person who cannot see this merit suffers from faulty taste, insufficient preparation to make a judgment, or both.

This same doctrine of universal consent is at the root of the admiration of Boileau and his fellow *classiques* for the ancients. The ancients are not deserving of praise, admiration, and emula- tion simply because they are ancients. Many of the ancients' works did not survive, perhaps deservedly so, and there are many others whose works have survived the ravages of time only to be completely neglected because of a lack of intrinsic merit. How- ever, the greatest of the ancients—Homer, Virgil, Pindar, the Greek dramatists, and others—have survived and are still read and admired because men for two thousand years have said that their works are great. These are the ancients to be emulated, and if there are those who are unable to appreciate their qualities, the ancients are not to blame.

Beauty of Content

Beauty is defined by Boileau only in terms of truth and nature. This is true to such an extent that the three terms become almost synonymous to him. When Boileau refers to truth and nature, he refers to content, form, and structure. There must be truth in what is said and there is a true and natural way to say it—the means varying, of course, with what is being said. Truth, then, is so fun- damental and necessary to beauty that beauty cannot exist inde- pendently from truth. If this be so, then the doctrine necessarily emphasizes either a rather restricted definition of beauty or a rather expanded conception of what is true. In Boileau's case, al- though he has often been accused of a narrow concept of truth, it should become apparent in the course of this chapter that he

tends more to the broad definition of truth, with certain faults and
limitations. The primary difficulty, then, is to define what is a true
thought in poetry. Since poetry is an art, then truth in poetry
should not be too different from truth in sculpture or painting. To
Boileau and most of his contemporaries, it is the truth of imitation
—conformity of the figured representation to the model. This doctrine would also hold true whether or not the model was an actual
object, but especially in literature where the only model exists in
the mind of the writer. In matters of poetic style, then, truth is
the equivalence of the word to the idea in the mind of the poet.
"Nothing is beautiful except the true," states Boileau in *Epître
IX*, and this is the basic axiom, completely positive, of Boileau's
literary theory and that of classicism in general.

Truth

Truth, in the classical doctrine, may take many and varied
forms: intellectual, psychological, emotional, religio-philosophical, and so on. This latitude in the definition and emphasis of truth
helps to explain the diversity of the works of the latter half of the
seventeenth century, where one seldom notices a feeling of sameness. The obvious danger in a too-restricted application of this
doctrine of truth is in the possible loss of individual, subjective
lyricism. Even when seemingly subjective, a poet may reveal to
us, through himself, latent depths of our own being of which we
were hitherto unaware. The subjective may be the vehicle of the
universal. Boileau was able to recognize this important aspect of
the artist as one who is able to express what other men have only
vaguely felt or thought. It must be admitted, however, that he
and most of his contemporaries had a vague and imperfect notion
of lyric poetry, and did not realize how universal emotions may
be. Truth then, for Boileau, must be universal and permanent or
it ceases, by definition, to be truth. The universal may sometimes
be carried to an extreme if one neglects the infinite variations of
the human spirit and all that is localized in time or space. The
general and universal live only in the particular, determined in
each epoch and in each man by a unique meeting of causes. Boileau's greatest weakness here is his imperfect knowledge of history. His method does, however, prevent the expression of insignificant peculiarities and exceptions.

Nature

Once having arrived at a working definition of truth, the poet is immediately confronted with the problem of how to recognize it and where it may be found. Here the idea of nature goes hand-in-hand with the doctrine of truth, for what may be found in nature is obviously truth by virtue of the fact that it exists. Nature, then, becomes a guide to the acquisition of truth, and nature is a key word in Boileau's theoretical structure. Under the abstract concepts of reason and truth, it is not a cold imagination nor a scientific dryness that Boileau advocates, but love of and respect for nature. Boileau's classicism might be considered a form of naturalism if this term had not already been pre-empted by literary historians to refer to the writings of Zola and his followers. Unlike the schools of Realism and Naturalism, Boileau does not advocate an integral imitation of reality but a selection and idealization of the model of nature. This does not, however, make his work, or those of the other classicists, less realistic. There is a distinction between an internal and an external realism, in which neither is more or less real than the other but simply real in a different sense. Thus the works of classicism may contain psychological or intellectual verities under an exterior which not only may no longer be realistic but was not even so at the time of composition. One might cite here the classical tragedies based on figures from Graeco-Roman mythology and legend, in which the externals are no longer realistic but the "internals" are universal. On the other hand, one may find extremes in the schools of Realism or Naturalism where the externals of daily life and environment may be meticulously depicted, even crudely so, but where the internal realism is almost completely lacking because the situation or case history being dissected is so uncommon as to lack any semblance of universality. This is, of course, an extreme, but it does serve to point out the distinction between what may be called internal and external realism.

Nature for Boileau, then, is selected and idealized, and the cruder elements are generally omitted. From such a concept of nature an unbalanced picture of life may result, since life does have its seamier side. However, it was generally believed that depiction of this coarser aspect of life was in bad taste and not fit for the consumption of the delicate ladies and refined gentlemen of the court of Louis XIV. What nature and truth lack in breadth in this treatment is more than compensated for by a gain in depth.

Selection in nature is also necessary because there are things that are true that may not be natural. Any event which has occurred is obviously true, but if it occurred only once it may not be natural. Thus, in order to depict truth one must select from nature those things that are more typical or, to use an unavoidable cliché, universal. As mentioned above, there is an inherent danger in making too narrow a selection—a pitfall usually avoided by the great classics but one in which their imitators too often fell. Boileau's doctrine, if followed completely, would avoid this restriction, because he states in the *Art poétique* that the unnatural should be avoided *unless it may be made to appear natural in the circumstances.* The monster in Racine's *Phèdre* affords an excellent illustration from a widely read play: the monster is surely unnatural but appears quite normal under the given circumstances. As in the case of truth, imitation of the ancients may be a guide to what might be considered natural, although it is certainly not an infallible rule. To return for a moment to Racine's seamonster, the same device had been used by both Euripides and Seneca and posterity had not found it unnatural under the circumstances. The question of what may be natural or acceptable in given circumstances has received its best-known discussion in Coleridge's statements on the "willing suspension of disbelief." [2] It was obvious to Boileau and his contemporaries that if posterity had been willing to suspend disbelief in certain cases found in the ancients, it would continue to do so if one took care to make the unnatural appear natural in the given circumstances.

Reasonableness

The word *raison,* along with truth and nature, is the third word of the triumvirate of key terms in Boileau's theoretical structure. *Reasonableness* is a preferable translation to *reason* since it avoids connotations of a cold and calculating logic and rationalism, often far from Boileau's understanding of the term as he uses it. The word *raison* may indicate *rationalism* in the eighteenth century, but most often *reasonableness* in the seventeenth. Here Boileau is closer to the root meaning of the Latin word *ratio,* among whose definitions are to be found *reasonableness, propriety, order,* along with the commoner *reason* and several others.

Reasonableness, then, is an important ingredient in the content, as well as the form and structure, of Boileau's theory. Two concepts which are integral parts of the idea of reasonableness to Boileau are *bienséance* (propriety) and *vraisemblance* (verisimilitude). *Bienséance,* as defined by René Bray,[3] had both external and internal connotations. External *bienséance* refers to those things which should not be mentioned or shown on stage because they might offend the dignity or sense of propriety of the audience, especially the ladies. The idea that no violence should be shown on stage stems partly from this concept of *bienséance.* Such a restriction would appear, at first glance, to be intolerable, and so it is to a dramatist devoted to the type of play Shakespeare wrote. To someone with the poetic gifts of Racine, however, the restriction proved a blessing in disguise because his poetic gifts could be fully brought to bear on a situation which had to be related on stage. The practice of using the *récit* on stage to describe to the audience and interested characters a death or horrible scene which has taken place offstage has received much unjust criticism, despite the fact that a violent display on stage has an instant shock value which tends to eliminate further elaboration or poetic evocation of feelings. The true poet will recognize the value of keeping such scenes as the death of Hippolytus in Racine's *Phèdre* off stage and developing the *récit* to suggest and evoke the full gamut of emotional and intellectual response. Such is the power of words.

Bienséance in its inner sense refers to a sense of propriety in which the characters in a book or play should conform to the audience's concept of them, even if this concept may not be historically accurate. This is particularly important in instances where characters from Graeco-Roman mythology or legend are used. The audience expects certain traits and qualities in the characters with which they are familiar, and any deviation from this commonly accepted notion will only tend to distract the attention of the audience, with a resultant loss of impact of the play's psychological focus. In a Racinian tragedy, where all elements are directed to the psychological conflict, any distraction of attention may be fatal. Thus, both internal and external *bienséance* are based on the idea of reasonableness, an agreement between the thing represented and the audience for whom it is represented.

Vraisemblance, or verisimilitude, is also based on reasonableness, and simply means that whatever is presented to the audience or reader must be true-seeming. What is true, because it may be too unusual or simply an isolated occurrence, may not be true-seeming. Boileau himself states that "Truth may sometimes not be true-seeming." (*Art poétique*, Canto III, l. 48.) Verisimilitude is thus a capital rule of literary creation to Boileau and is based both on reasonableness and the desire to please the audience. Verisimilitude is further implementation of the "willing suspension of disbelief" when what is not true may be made to be true-seeming. Just as an audience may refuse to believe what is true, it may also be led to believe what is not true but is *vraisemblable*. The important tenet of the doctrine is that whatever is presented must be true-seeming. The fault in this theory is that verisimilitude may be emphasized to the detriment of imagination and particularly of fantasy. Boileau seems to have been unaware that an audience will, in particular circumstances and genres, willingly suspend all disbelief in favor of the supernatural, magic, and make-believe. Perhaps this is a childlike trait which the mature Boileau could not grasp, but it is easily comprehensible to those familiar with the delightful mediaeval romances where enchanted princesses, magic rings and fountains, and the Celtic otherworld abound. The restriction of *vraisemblance* also led Boileau to a limited and actually unpoetic concept of the marvelous, which he considers only an ornament—a poetic procedure which has little or no support in the soul of either the creative artist or the reader. Because he had

this concept, it is not surprising that Boileau prefers the pagan marvelous, since to the modern writer it *is* little more than a storehouse of figures. Boileau is generally mistaken in his concept of the ancients' use of fable and mythology: that epic is allegorical and that mythology is either a means of making the abstract concrete, or a simple decoration. This excessively narrow concept of *vraisemblance* is perhaps Boileau's single greatest weakness as a critic and theorist.

Related both to nature and reasonableness is Boileau's insistence on no excess or exaggeration, either of which would be an unreasonable departure from nature. This departure from nature was condemned by Boileau in both directions—departures in the direction of an ornamenting of nature in *préciosité* and in the direction of a vulgarizing of nature in the burlesque. Both these tendencies of his time were attacked by Boileau with equal vigor.

Amorous conceits of both sentiment and language he regarded as a departure from nature and hence unreasonable. In the other direction, the frequent baseness of the burlesque, with its crude humor and degradation of the heroes and heroines of antiquity was equally unreasonable. It is perhaps in these areas that Boileau occupies his firmest critical ground, for both were excesses of which his century was especially guilty and both were very much alive during the period when Boileau wrote, though perhaps only waiting for his *coup de grâce*. Excess and exaggeration were, to Boileau, untrue, unnatural, and unreasonable, and thus violated all three of his basic critical tenets.

To please one's public and thereby assure oneself of readers and an audience was so intellectually sound to Boileau, as well as to Corneille, Molière, Racine, and La Fontaine, as to be obvious and paramount. Racine states in the *Préface* to *Bérénice* that "The principal rule is to please and touch: all the others are only set down in order to arrive at the first one." Other classical writers echo these sentiments. To the classicist a work of art necessarily implies a recipient, and the idea of art for its own sake or hermetic and obscurantist art would have been completely foreign to their esthetic philosophy. In addition, classical art is moral in nature, and there was a strong feeling that a work of art should also be utilitarian and instructive. This does not imply any tendency towards sermonizing, although the latter may be a result in the hands of a writer who is inferior. To Boileau and his great contemporaries, pleasing the audience and instructing them were, far from being incompatible, actually mutually complementary, for it was assumed that a reader received pleasure from learning when the lesson was beautifully presented.

Beauty of content then is composed of truth, nature, and reasonableness. It pleases the audience or reader both by the beauty of what is said and the usefulness of the information or lesson gained, with the former as the primary goal and the latter as a contributing factor.

II *Beauty of Form and Structure*

Many of Boileau's so-called rules deal with the mechanical aspects of the composition of poetry. However, he does give some general advice on form and structure. As in the case of content, so form and structure are directed toward the production of beauty

of a universal and permanent nature. In his criticisms of his contemporaries, it is in the area of form and structure rather than
content that Boileau is most severe in his condemnation. Except
for a stiffness, verbosity, or harshness of sounds, he seldom gives
any concrete criticism of the form of the works he condemns. The
reason is probably that one may tell a writer what faults prevent
him from being a good poet, but it is difficult to say what positive
items, especially in the matter of form and style, will improve his
production. When genius and inspiration are lacking, little else
matters.

Genius and Inspiration

Much adverse criticism has been directed against Boileau for
underestimating the importance of genius and inspiration. It is
true that Boileau does not dwell on the subject, but hardly because he did not understand its importance. Once having stated
the necessity for a writer to have the poetic gift, he deemed it
unnecessary to say more. At the very beginning of Canto I of the
Art poétique, he states the *sine qua non* of poetry: "In vain does a
rash author think to scale the height of the art of verse on Mt.
Parnassus if he does not feel within himself the secret, heavenly
power, if his star did not make him a poet at birth." He then
cautions novices not to take a love for rhyming for true poetic
genius. Even those who may have poetic genius must learn to
recognize the limitation of their talent and not attempt to write in
genres beyond their ability. After making this statement on genius
and inspiration, little remains to be said, since there are no rules
or processes which can provide them where lacking. Boileau thus
does not ignore the need for genius and inspiration, but simply
accepts them as something taken for granted, without which further discussion would be pointless.

Technique

In Canto IV of the *Art poétique,* Boileau admits the possibility
of breaking the prescribed rules and going beyond the limits of
accepted artistic technique: "Sometimes a vigorous spirit in its
course, too restricted by art, departs from the prescribed rules and
from Art itself learns how to go beyond their limitations" (il.
78–80). Here, however, Boileau is thinking of the exceptional
genius and even then such breaking of the rules should only be

permitted if an intelligent, critical friend has approved. Since rules are derived from the practice of writers of genius rather than legislated by critics and writers of arts of poetry, the true genius may sometimes create a new rule by breaking an old one. Boileau does recognize this possibility, but he everywhere advocates a careful and painstaking attention to technique and craftsmanship. The ideal result will be a feeling on the part of the reader that the poem was effortlessly made. Boileau makes a distinction between facile verse and verse which is facilely written. The former is the mark of the genius and craftsman; the latter is the sign of a mere rhymster. In this matter of technique Boileau is a man of his epoch, believing that there was little new to be said and that originality lay in how one said what most men must often have thought. Boileau himself stated that for every four words he wrote, he erased three and this is the advice he gives in the *Art poétique*—search for the *mot juste* (exact word), and constant polishing and rewriting. It is to this advice that the nineteenth-century Parnassian poets turned, and Théophile Gautier's "Sculpt, file, chisel" (*l'Art*) is a reiteration of Boileau's "Replace your work on the workbench twenty times" (Canto I, l. 171). Boileau believed firmly in the necessity of technical ability coupled with genius. Technical knowledge always enables genius to select the surest and most powerful modes of expression. This is why Boileau places so much emphasis on *métier* (craftsmanship) and gives an abundance of precepts on versification, style, and composition. The poet creates his work with words, and technique is primarily the manipulation of words.

Discipline

The question of technique leads naturally to that of discipline, for technique rarely exists without self-discipline on the part of the poet. Only self-discipline will enable the poet to seek the *mot juste* and not delude himself with self-satisfaction. Technique and discipline are cornerstones of the classical theory. In addition to improved technique, discipline tends to foster clarity of mind and logical force and aids in avoiding excess and extravagance. What may, on the initial writing, seem to be an inspired piece may, upon disciplined reexamination, turn out to be quite poor. Discipline is also required in the attainment of naturalness, for what may seem natural to a poet in a fit of "inspiration," may not seem so to a reader who has not followed his thought processes step by step. It is also discipline which will enable the author to accept criticism from intelligent and well-informed friends. Discipline is required to make the requisite choice from nature and to arrive at the universal and permanent. After genius and inspiration then, discipline is the most important requisite for the poet.

Reasonableness, Truth, and Nature

Truth and nature also apply to matters of form and structure. This is the basis of the doctrine of genres, the undesirability of mixing them, and the propriety of each for certain ends. Since the nature of a classical work is a selected nature, not intended to give an integral imitation of life, then a genre should be selected which best conveys or depicts that portion of nature selected. A classical tragedy of the seventeenth-century French style is designed to focus on a selected tragic moment or conflict, so any intrusive comic elements, given the purpose of the tragedy, would serve to distract attention from the primary and unique focus. One may quarrel with the concept of a selected portion of nature and truth but, once this is accepted as the artist's goal, there can be little argument concerning the means.

Reasonableness, as the means to arrive at truth and nature, is the basis for Boileau's insistence on the necessity for clarity, logic, and rules. The necessity for clarity, if one desires to reach an audience, should be obvious. Logic was necessary in an age imbued with the principles of Cartesianism and in which great store was set by the pleasures of the intellect. The very nature of the reading and theatergoing public of the salons, the upper bourgeoisie, and the court circles precluded any literature based solely on an emotional appeal. The emotions were something to be controlled rather than encouraged. Logic and reasonableness attracted the public, flattered the intelligence, and also aided in curbing the emotions.

The need for rules, especially the famous unities of time, place, and action, is more difficult to explain, but again one must consider primarily the goals and concepts. To understand the literature of the seventeenth century, one must accept the existence of certain *idées reçues,* or conventions. Once having accepted these conventions, the rules not only appear sensible but usually necessary. If one realizes that the prevalent concept of tragedy, as practiced by Racine, was to focus narrowly on a selected moment of tragic quintessence, then the rules of the unities are quite natural and reasonable. Because he held to this concept of tragedy so closely, Racine was never bothered by the rules, and one receives no impression of restriction in his plays but, rather, a heightened concentration and focus on the very essence of the tragic conflict. The necessity for unity of action has generally been admitted, although with sometimes wide latitude in its interpretation. Where concentration is the goal, this latitude must of necessity be restricted. Given the same intent toward focus and concentration on a single tragic moment, it becomes obvious that little time is available for the tragic *dénouement*. By further extension, if little time is available, there can be no travelling about the countryside —hence the unity of place. Given the necessity for unity of action in a concentrated moment, the unities of time and place follow naturally and inevitably. The desirability or restriction of the three unities may thus be argued only on the basis of the desired goal, but not as abstracts. For a Racine they were good; for a Hugo, writing plays of a different nature, they were restrictive. To Boileau and his contemporaries they were natural and reasonable.

The Sublime and the "Je ne sais quoi"

Because of his translation of Longinus' treatise *On the Sublime*, and because of his frequent references to a certain *"je ne sais quoi"* (I know not what) as true hallmarks of a work of genius, there has been much discussion on exactly what Boileau meant by these terms which are so positive and yet so ill-defined. It seems that the sublime and the *je ne sais quoi* are intimately related to each other and that both are closely connected to the concept of simplicity. The sublime indicates such a perfect adaptation and integration of expression to thought or image that no improvement is possible. And it usually comes about that the perfect integration is also exceedingly simple and noble. Lanson expresses the concept in this way:

If elegance and nobility consist essentially in giving to a poetic work an aesthetic and literary character, so that it is never vulgar, even when expressing the vulgarities of nature and life, then the sublime is the supreme degree of beauty. This degree is the expressive intensity of a word, of a turn of phrase, which realizes perfectly the effect desired and foreseen by the artist. It is the point beyond which art can do nothing, where our intelligence takes immediate and direct contact with nature and where interposition of another mind between us and the object is no longer realizable. Then a work is not just noble, or elegant, but sublime.[4]

Boileau's favorite illustration of the concept of the sublime, borrowed from Longinus, was the expression from Genesis: "And God said, Let there be light: and there was light." To Boileau this phrase itself partook to a certain extent of the very nature of Divinity, which could create simply by expressing the desire. It is an example of perfect relationship of expression to action, utterly simple, yet majestically noble, and incapable of improvement.

The sublime would certainly qualify as an example of the *je ne sais quoi*, but not every instance of *je ne sais quoi* would necessarily be sublime. If the latter is difficult of definition, the former is even more so. Boileau himself recognizes the difficulty of a precise definition when, after citing several forceful passages from La Fontaine's story in the *Dissertation sur Joconde*, he states: "I could point out to you many other instances of the same force, . . . These kinds of beauty are those one must feel and which cannot at all be proved. It is that *je ne sais quoi* which charms us and without which beauty itself would have neither grace nor beauty. But after all, it is a *je ne sais quoi; . . .*" (italics mine).

The definition is somewhat more detailed in the *Préface* to the 1701 edition of his *Oeuvres:*

In vain is a work of art approved by a small number of connoisseurs; unless it contains a certain attractiveness and a certain piquancy which will arouse the general taste it will never pass for a good work and at the end the connoisseurs themselves will have to admit that they made a mistake in giving it their approval. If one should ask me what this attractiveness and piquancy are, I should answer that it is a *je ne sais quoi* which is much more easily felt than described. Nevertheless, in my opinion it consists primarily in never offering to the reader anything except true thoughts and correct expression. The spirit of man is naturally full of an infinite number of confused ideas of Truth, of which he is often only half aware; and nothing is more pleasing to him than to be presented one of these ideas clearly expressed. What is a new, brilliant, or extraordinary thought? It is not, as the ignorant are convinced, a thought which no one ever had or could never have had. On the contrary, it is a thought which must have occurred to everyone but which someone undertook first to express. A well-turned expression is not such except insofar as it says what everyone thinks, but says it in a lively, clever, and new way.

In his concept of the sublime and the *je ne sais quoi*, Boileau recognizes the existence of certain qualities, not easily definable, which belong to the realm of pure genius and cannot be acquired through the application of any rules. The sublime moments are the exception, however, rather than the rule, and constitute a rule unto themselves. The truly great artist will still remain within the framework of the rules in the vast majority of instances and will depart from their limitation only for good reason. And this departure will have been confirmed by the opinion of the critical friends to whom he submits his production for their advice.

III L'Art poétique

The *Art poétique* (*Art of Poetry*) of Boileau is his single most important critical work. Boileau composed it at the urging of friends, because of the criticism of his enemies who accused him of having no positive principles, because of the example of Horace, and because of the needs of his career. His intention was not to compose a systematic treatise, as is obvious from the tone of the poem, its frequent lack of organization, its omissions, and the fact that it is in verse rather than in prose. He was actually composing a didactical and satirical poem, giving good precepts, citing bad examples, and justifying his own taste. The ideas found in the *Art poétique* are not new or original but a synthesis of the generally accepted critical theories on poetry. In these theories Boileau was in agreement with his contemporaries, even with Chapelain whom he attacked most vigorously elsewhere. His quarrel with this author was in the application of the theories. The remarks in the poem are of a general nature but prompted by specific details, and there is little in the way of an esthetic synthesis. The ideas are often poorly arranged and are connected by transitions which show how difficult this technique was for Boileau. Yet with all its faults, it is quite readable and remains, along with the *Préface* to the 1701 edition of his *Oeuvres* and *Epître IX*, the handbook of classical theory. The *Art poétique* is short, containing about 1100 lines arranged in four *Chants* (*Cantos*) of unequal length, Canto

iII being much the longest. <u>Canto I contains rather general liter-</u>
<u>ary advice: one must be inspired and have poetic genius; one</u>
<u>must know one's talent and limitations; submit to reasonableness;</u>
<u>avoid boring or displeasing; learn to write good verse and to com-</u>
<u>pose properly; choose an honest friend for a critic and censor.</u>
Canto II deals with the secondary genres, such as the eclogue,
elegy, ode, sonnet, epigram, *rondeau, ballade,* madrigal, satire,
vaudeville. <u>Canto III treats what were considered the major</u>
<u>genres: tragedy, epic, and comedy.</u> Canto IV again returns to
generalities, but this time of a more moral nature: again one
should reflect carefully before beginning to write; one should respect virtue and try to follow its teachings; one should live in society and not be a recluse. The entire poem is summed up by an
eulogy to Louis XIV, who is a protector of the arts.

Canto I

Canto I opens with the statement of the necessity for genius
and poetic inspiration. The would-be poet should reflect carefully
before undertaking to write verse, nor should he think a love for
writing rhymes is the equivalent of genius. Even when Nature
supplies genius, she divides talent differently among writers. Boileau cites a few writers who have excelled at various minor genres, such as Racan in the pastoral [5] and Malherbe in the ode.
<u>Often one will flatter oneself and not understand one's ability and</u>
<u>limitations.</u>

dan
Naturel
time

<u>Whatever the subject, common sense should be in accord with</u>
<u>rhyme, and the latter is a slave which must be forced to obey.</u>
<u>Rhyme must bend under the yoke of reasonableness and, with</u>
<u>experience and effort, the writer is able to find the proper rhyme</u>
<u>easily enough.</u> When rhyme and reasonableness are in agreement,
rhyme serves to enrich, but when rhyme is neglected, it becomes
rebellious. "Love then reasonableness. Let your writings borrow
from it alone all their lustre and worth" (ll. 37–38). Some poets
run to excess through fear of thinking what someone else has
thought before. Such excess should be avoided, and everything
should obey common sense. An author should avoid prolixity, especially in descriptions. Referring to an epic poem by Georges de
Scudéry, *Alaric* or *Rome sauvée,* Boileau mentions an extremely
lengthy description of a palace, which makes the reader want to
skip twenty pages just to arrive at the end. "Avoid the sterile

abundance of these authors, and do not clutter up your work with useless detail" (ll. 59–60). "Whoever cannot limit himself, cannot write" (l. 63).

If one seeks the approval of the public, one should avoid a monotonous style. No matter how brilliant it may be, if it is too uniform it will put the reader to sleep. A monotonous style sounds too much like psalm-chanting. Fortunate is the author who is able to make smooth transitions from the serious to the gentle, from the pleasant to the severe.

Whatever one may write, baseness should be avoided. The simple style has a nobility of its own. Boileau here condemns specifically the burlesque genre which, in spite of common sense, pleased some people because of its novelty. If a light, simple style is desired, the poet should "imitate Marot's elegant banter" (l. 96).

Neither should one employ the opposite tone from the burlesque—pompousness. "Be artfully simple, sublime without haughtiness, attractive without false decoration" (ll. 101–2).

The poet should offer to the reader only what will please him. He must have a severe ear for the cadence of verses; let the caesura mark the rest in the middle of the Alexandrine line; avoid hiatus; avoid juxtaposing words which have a harsh sound together. "The best made verse, the noblest thought cannot please the mind if the ear is offended" (ll. 111–12).

Boileau then offers a short history of French poetry up to his own day; this is the weakest part of the *Art poétique*. Boileau shared with most of his contemporaries ignorance of the poetry of the Middle Ages and scorn for the poetry of Ronsard. However, he was able to appreciate the poetry of Villon and Marot, even though for the wrong reasons in the former case. He accuses the earlier mediaeval poets of having only capriciousness for their law of versification and of using rhyme alone, without any consideration for measure. Nothing could be further from the truth. Measure was always a part of their prosody, even before they began to use rhyme and were simply writing in assonanced *laisses* (irregular stanzas). From the time of the *formes fixes* of Guillaume de Machault and Eustache Deschamps[6] to the extreme and often ridiculous attention to technique of the *grands rhétoriqueurs*,[7] the technical aspects of the art of poetry were well-known, practiced, and required. Villon, whom Boileau credits with being the first to untangle the confused art of the old poets, actually untangled nothing and invented nothing in the way of poetic technique, using only the standard forms of his generation.

Marot, according to Boileau, made the *ballade* flourish, turned *triolets*, rhymed *mascarades*, and forced *rondeaux* to regular refrains. Most of this statement is false; Marot did not write either *triolets* or *mascarades*. Boileau, rather than reading his poetry, was deceived by Marot's imitators, who did use these forms.

Of all the authors Boileau condemns, it is most difficult for us to understand his complete lack of appreciation for Ronsard, one of France's greatest poets. Boileau's criticism of Ronsard's excessive use of Greek and Latin, both words and mythology, is true to a certain extent. Ronsard himself had recognized this excess and set about correcting it before he was attacked by Malherbe, along with his even more guilty imitators. It was a fashion of the times to decry the poetry of Ronsard, and Boileau follows the taste and prejudice of the majority of his contemporaries. Even so, one is tempted to think that Boileau's reading of Ronsard was confined to the Pindaric and Anachreontic odes, Ronsard's least successful work. Surely Boileau could not have read the *Amours de Marie* and still not have a good word for Ronsard. Desportes and Bertaut are mentioned only as being more restrained as a result of Ronsard's excess, and the Protestant poets Du Bartas and especially Agrippa d'Aubigné are not even mentioned.[8]

"Finally came Malherbe, the first in France to put proper cadence in verse, to show the power of a word in its proper place, and to force the Muse to obey the rules" (ll. 131–34). These are the most famous lines of the *Art poétique,* memorized by generations of French schoolchildren. This book is not the place to engage in a lengthy discussion of Malherbe as either critic or poet. Boileau oversimplifies Malherbe's contribution to the history of French verse and overestimates him both as critic and poet. However, his judgment of the results of Malherbe's so-called reform is essentially correct, except for the statement that *all* recognized and obeyed his law. Boileau's advice then is to follow in Malherbe's footsteps, especially in matters of purity of language and clarity.

Obscurantist poetry, whether intentional or accidental, is condemned in the following lines: "If the meaning of your verse takes too long to understand, my mind immediately begins to get distracted and, quick to become detached from your vain discourse, does not follow an author it has to look for continually" (ll. 143–46). Unable to conceive of a poet being deliberately obscure, Boileau blames obscurity on unclear thought. "According to whether the idea is more or less obscure, the expression of it follows and is either less correct or more pure. Whatever is clearly conceived may be clearly expressed and words to say it come easily" (ll. 150–53).

Language should be sacred to the writer, even in the flood of inspiration. A melodious sound is useless if the term is improper or the language incorrect. Barbarisms and solecisms are to be avoided. The most divinely inspired author, without correct language, is a bad writer.

The writer should work at leisure, never priding himself on rapidity and facility of composition. A rapid style, which runs rhymingly along, shows lack of judgment. "Make haste slowly and, without losing heart, replace your work twenty times on the workbench; polish it ceaselessly and repolish it; add to it sometimes, but erase often" (ll. 170–73). In classical fashion, Boileau is concerned with the form and the unity of a work. It is not enough to begin writing what one thinks or feels, and simply stop when one has said it; there must be an organization of thought and a corresponding organization of the means of expression—the structure and architecture of the work. "Each thing must be put in its proper place and the beginning and end must conform to the middle; the assorted pieces, by means of a delicate art, should form a whole out of the diverse parts" (ll. 176–79).

The poet who fears the censorship of the public should be a severe critic to himself. He should cultivate friends who are willing and prompt to offer constructive criticism. With such friends he should divest himself of an author's arrogant pride, so as to benefit from their advice. He should also be able to discern a true friend from a flatterer: "Desire advice rather than praise" (l. 191). To an author, every word he writes is charming and divinely inspired, and the flatterer will play upon this weakness. A wise friend never lets one remain satisfied with faulty composition. So-called friends should also be wary, for often they are sought out by an author not for honest criticism but just to have someone to listen to him recite his verse. He wants only to be admired and he is sure to find someone to admire him: "Just as in foolish authors, our time is fertile in foolish admirers" (ll. 225–26). "And to end on a note of satire, a fool always can find a bigger fool to admire him" (ll. 231–32).

Canto II

Canto II, which deals with the minor genres, opens with Boileau's statement for the necessity of a humble style in the idyll. It should be simple and naïve and avoid any trace of presumption. It should be gentle to the ear and avoid long words. Boileau here equates the idyll with the eclogue, neither of which was pastoral poetry to the Greeks. In the genre of pastoral poetry one should avoid excesses of making the shepherds speak either too pompously or too basely. To find the golden mean between these extremes, the author should follow Theocritus and Virgil. From them one may learn how to descend to a simple subject without abasing oneself.

The plaintive elegy, according to Boileau, should be in a tone slightly higher than the pastoral, but not too lofty. This poem, a type of lament, should depict the joy and the sadness of lovers and should attempt to flatter, threaten, anger, or appease the beloved lady. To express these emotions it is not enough to be simply a poet—one must be in love. Boileau then launches into a satirical digression on his dislike for authors whose Muse is forced and who write about a love which is entirely cerebral. In the elegy the heart alone must speak.

The ode is a loftier genre and more ambitious. Its primary function is to sing the praises of heroes, athletes, or warriors. It may also be used for love poetry, but on a more noble stylistic level. The ode may be more impetuous and less obedient to the rules than other genres, mainly by virtue of the variety of its subject matter. Thinking of Pindar, whom he admired but could not imitate or really understand, Boileau writes: "Its impetuous style often moves along by chance. In the ode a beautiful disorder is the effect of art" (ll. 71–72). Especially irritating to Boileau are poets who are afraid of departing from a didactic and chronological presentation of the actions of a great hero. They never dare lose sight of the subject for a moment, and they fill the poem with useless detail of a historical and biographical nature.

Legend says, according to Boileau, that Apollo himself invented the sonnet and its rigorous laws to test rhymsters. No freedom is

permitted in this genre, as Apollo himself measures the count and
cadence; nor will he permit a weak verse or word repetition. In
exchange for these restrictions, the sonnet well done is of exceeding beauty. "A faultless sonnet alone is worth more than a long
poem" *which has faults* (l. 94). According to Boileau, French authors have tried in vain to attain the perfection of the sonnet;
among seventeenth-century writers there are only two or three
admirable sonnets among thousands.

The epigram is free in subject matter but more restricted because of the limitation of length. It is often little more than a
witticism adorned with two rhymes. In recent years the Italian
concetti entered French verse and infected all poetic genres, eventually spreading to prose and even the oratory of the law courts
and the pulpit. Outraged reasonableness finally chased them forever from serious discourse and outlawed them from all genres
except the epigram. Here they are permitted provided they are
apropos and depend on sense rather than on words alone. Even
so, play on words is still a favorite pastime among some of the
courtiers. One should avoid using these *concetti* to sharpen a silly
epigram.

Every type of poem has a beauty which is proper and suitable
to it alone. The *rondeau*, a native French genre, has value because
of its *naïveté*, while the *ballade* often owes its attraction to the
caprice of its rhymes. (Here Boileau is only partially correct.
While the *ballade* may be attractive because of its rhymes, these
are by no means capricious, since every rhyme of a *ballade* must
correspond to the same line in the other stanzas.) The madrigal is
simpler and more noble, and should depict sweetness, tenderness,
and love.

Satire does not come from a desire to slander but to speak the
truth. Lucilius was the first to write satire, showing to the Romans
their vices. Next came the gentle Horace, who censured with a
cheerful and sprightly touch. Persius, in his obscure but tightly
knit verse, wrote satire in few words but with much meaning.
Juvenal pushed his mordant hyperbole to excess, but his works,
full of frightful truths, nevertheless sparkle with sublime beauties. Mathurin Régnier alone among Frenchmen is a worthy disciple of these masters; there are many novel and graceful touches to
be found in his antiquated style. His only fault is a lack of modesty and restraint. The French reader wishes to be respected, and

the slightest idea of impurity outrages him unless the modesty of the words softens the image. Boileau also advocates a spirit of candor in satire.

The vaudeville, also a native French form, developed from the satire. Happily indiscreet and aided by music, the vaudeville spreads by word of mouth and the Gallic spirit is freely seen in this verse. However, even the liberty of this *esprit gaulois* does not admit God as the subject of a jesting poem. And even in songs one should employ common sense and artfulness. Wine and chance together, furnishing a couplet or two, do not produce a real poet.

Canto III

In the third canto of the *Art poétique*, Boileau deals with the three major genres: tragedy, epic, and comedy. His theory of tragedy, necessarily incomplete in a work of this scope, is fundamentally that of Aristotle, i.e., an imitation of nature which should inspire the emotions of fear and/or pity. The canto opens with the statement that even something inherently horrible may be pleasing through art. Thus tragedy, which deals primarily in bloodshed and murder, pleases an audience by making it weep. Whoever would be a writer of tragedies should seek the way to reach the heart and move it. Knowledge and erudition are insufficient unless the tragic author can fill us with a gentle terror and excite in the soul a *charmante* pity. (The word here is used in the primary sense of its etymon; *charmant < carmen*, an incantation or spell.) "The secret is first of all to please and to touch" (l. 25). This same rule is stated by others of the *grands classiques* and was one of the cornerstones of their doctrine. Seldom if ever, in the history of literature, have the greatest artists of an epoch been so concerned with their public.

NB ·   From the very first line the action should be prepared so as to facilitate the exposition. The audience does not want to be wearied right at the beginning by a lengthy and obscure exposition. "The exposition can never come too quickly" (l. 37). Let the place of the scene be fixed and marked once and for all (unity of place). Beyond the Pyrenees the dramatic authors may put on stage events that occur over a period of years, having the hero a child in the first act and an old man in the last, but this is bad practice on the French stage where reasonableness requires the rules of the three unities of time, place, and action. "Let one action, in one place and during one day, keep the theater filled until the performance ends" (ll. 45–46).

The rule of verisimilitude should also be strictly obeyed: "Never offer the spectator anything unbelievable. The truth can sometimes not be true-seeming" (ll. 47–48). The mind is not moved by what it cannot believe. The rule of *bienséance* (roughly translated propriety, but the matter is rather more complicated) is next invoked. What shouldn't be seen on stage, such as acts of violence, should be described. The eyes may grasp it better on seeing it, but there are objects which a discreet art should offer to the ears only. (Any poet will recognize the greater poetic value of description over the shock of showing a violent action on stage.) The action should progress smoothly from scene to scene, following a cause and effect principle, so that the *dénouement* is natural and well prepared. Use should be made of *peripeteia* and/or *anagnorisis* (reversal and discovery) so the mind of the audience will be pleasantly impressed. Boileau next proceeds to give a thumbnail sketch of tragedy, erroneous in some respects, mentioning the contributions of Thespis, Aeschylus, and Sophocles, but omitting mention of Euripides and Seneca. In a monumental error, Boileau states that the public of the Middle Ages abhorred the theater so that it was ignored for a long time in France until a group of pilgrims played in Paris a drama about saints, the Virgin, and God. This statement about the mediaeval theater could scarcely be further from the truth and reemphasizes Boileau's fundamental ignorance of French literature prior to the seventeenth century. Good sense, according to Boileau, finally eliminated these theatrical "preachers," and Hector, Andromache, and Ilion came to the stage. The actors did not use masks like the ancients, and violin accompaniment took the place of the chorus. (Here again Boileau is in error. Choruses were not infrequently used on the French stage during the latter sixteenth and early seventeenth centuries and Racine revived the practice in his biblical plays, *Esther* and *Athalie*.)

The sentiment of love soon took over the stage and eventually became the mainspring of French tragedy. A sensible depiction of love is the surest route to the heart, but heroes in love should not be like the shepherds of pastorals, singing sweet but silly love songs. "And let love, often opposed by remorse, appear a weakness and not a virtue" (ll. 101–2). Boileau follows the precept of

Aristotle which states that the hero should not be perfect, but for a different reason. Whereas Aristotle feels that the audience would be outraged at the fall of a perfect hero, Boileau believes the hero should have some weakness because it is more natural. The hero should also be depicted in such a way that his character is like his historical personality or as his historical personality is generally conceived (another form of *bienséance*). Some attention is given to the matter of local color and the difference between people in different nations and eras in the following statement: "Study the customs of the times and the countries. Climates often cause diverse spirits" (ll. 113–14). The dramatic author should thus avoid depicting his contemporaries as ancient Greeks or Romans. This may be excusable in a novel, but the stage exacts more reasonableness and adherence to *bienséance* and *vraisemblance*.

If a new character is invented, let him be consistent throughout the play. The language used should conform to the passions being expressed. Anger is haughty and requires lofty words, while self-abasement requires more humble expression. Declamation, especially in situations where it is out of place, should be assiduously avoided. "To draw tears from me, you must weep yourself. These high-sounding words which fill the actor's mouth do not come from a heart touched by misery" (ll. 142–44).

The theater in France is a dangerous field of endeavor because there are so many punctilious critics. Triumphs are not easy. The right to criticize is purchased with the price of admission, the author having the responsibility to please the audience.

Epic poetry should be written in an even more heroic tone than tragedy. It is the narration of a long action and requires fable and fiction. Personification is a prime requisite in the epic, where each virtue or quality becomes a divinity; Minerva is Wisdom, Venus is Beauty. In this notion of the nature of the epic poem may be found one of Boileau's most fundamental weaknesses as a critic. He believed that the epic was primarily an allegorical poem, in which mythology was a means of decoration and of making the abstract concrete. He seems to have had no concept of the religious nature of the epics of antiquity, in particular those of Homer. In spite of his genuine admiration for the ancients, he here makes of them a travesty. For Boileau fable and mythology were no more than a storehouse of figures and images, whose meanings were fixed, used only for embellishment and variety. From this concept results his stand in favor of pagan mythology, causing him to invoke pagan deities in a poem on the crossing of the Rhine by a French army. It is this mistaken idea which makes him deny that Christianity might have a place in the epic poem. Given this initial, though incorrect, opinion of mythology, it follows logically that something as sacred as Christianity should not be used as decoration. It is his narrow interpretation of the imitation of nature and his striving for the universal that cause this error, arrived at by working backward from a Christian to a pagan society. Because pagan mythology did not exist as a religion for him, he assumed that it never existed for Virgil or Homer and that, therefore, it was used by them as ornament and personification alone. By means of this line of reasoning Boileau was able to maintain the doctrine of imitation of the ancients. He does not realize that Homer and Virgil put the gods in their poems precisely because they were their national, popular gods. Studying the ancients only from the point of view of the universal, rather than in relation to the times and the historical development of peoples, it was inevitable that Boileau should make mistakes. It is true indeed that Boileau had not seen a decent Christian epic, in spite of the numerous efforts of his contemporaries. He was unable to appreciate the beauties of the *Gerusalemme Liberata* (*Jerusalem Delivered*) of Tasso. It is also ironical that, only seven years earlier, Milton had written a great Christian epic, *Paradise Lost*, which disproved by its very existence Boileau's theories on the Christian marvelous.

Aeneas and his companions driven to the African shore by a storm is only an ordinary adventure, says Boileau, but that the storm was caused by Juno, who persuaded Aeolus to unleash the winds to destroy the remnants of Troy—this is what surprises and strikes the reader. Without these ornaments the verse would be languorous and the poetry dead; the poet would be little more than a timid orator or a historian. Boileau certainly recognizes the components of the ancient epics which cause us wonder and delight, but he appreciates them, as is sometimes the case in his criticism, for the wrong reasons. Even though we know the pagan divinities are not real, we also know that they were real to the Greeks and Romans, and we read them in this spirit, participating in their belief. Mythology is indeed a decoration—not an ornament which is added but rather an integral part of the architecture of the poem. Boileau also feared that the use of fable in a Christian poem would run the danger of making even divine truths appear to be fables.

At this point Boileau takes a defensive position against those who would indiscriminately banish pagan mythology from all forms of poetry. In a non-Christian poem it would be vain scrupulousness and an attempt to please the reader without any attractive features, if nymphs, Pan, Charon, and the like were forbidden. The result would only be an irreparable loss of imagery and characters, to the impoverishment of poetry. Christians, then, may make use of fable, but not in connection with the true God. Moreover, the names in pagan mythology seem born for use in verse. With such happy sounds to use as Ulysses, Agamemnon, Orestes, Helen, Menelaus, Hector, Aeneas, why would one choose such a harsh sound as Childebrand? [9] Sometimes the harsh or bizarre sound of a single name can make a whole poem burlesque or barbarous.

If the epic poet wants to please, he should choose an interesting hero, dazzling in valor and magnificent in virtues. Let even his faults appear heroic. The subject should not be filled with incidents. "The wrath of Achilles alone, handled artfully, abundantly filled the whole *Iliad*. Often too much abundance impoverishes the material" (ll. 254–56). The epic should be rapid in narrations, rich and lofty in descriptions, for here is the place to display the elegance of verse. The poet should never present any base circumstances or anything which might smack of the burlesque. Let the beginning be simple and unaffected; if one begins with "I sing of the conqueror of the conquerors of the earth," [10] what can one possibly produce after that? Much better is the easy, simple, harmonious beginning of the *Aeneid*. Virgil's Muse, promising little, delivers much.

The epic should be enlivened with figures which present a smiling image to the eyes. Style can be elevated and pleasant at the same time, but a pompous tone soon tires. Boileau prefers Ariosto and his comic fables to his own too-serious contemporaries. He then praises Homer: "Then love his poems, but with a sincere love; it is sufficient profit to know how to enjoy oneself" (ll. 307–8). An excellent epic poem is not the result of caprice but of time, care, and organization.

After the success in Athens of the tragedy, ancient comedy was born. In comedy the Greek, born with a mocking spirit, loosed the poison of his slander in insolent and buffoonish joy. There was little good sense, intelligence, or honor. Aristophanes even made fun of merit when he depicted Socrates in *The Clouds*. Boileau obviously did not appreciate the foolishness and obscenities of Old Comedy. When the magistrates finally forbade the representation of persons by name or face, comedy learned to laugh without bitterness and venom. The plays of Menander were innocently pleasing and instructive. From individuals the representations shifted to types.

Nature should be the primary study of the author of comedy, and Boileau here means human nature. The comic dramatist should be able to penetrate to the inner man and know how to depict such types as the Prodigal, the Miser, the Fool. He should understand their characters and motivations and be able to make them come alive for us on the stage. Nature is fertile in bizarre characters, but not everyone can see them. Time, which changes all things, changes also our humors, making man behave differently in various ages of his life. The young man is always capricious, prompt to receive impressions, vain in his speech, fiery in his desires, restless under censure, and foolish in his pleasures. The mature man is wiser, likes to frequent people in high positions, engages in intrigue, tries to protect himself against bad luck, and looks to the future. The old man hangs on to his money, does everything slowly, laments the present and idealizes the past, and blames in youth the pleasures he himself is no longer capable of enjoying. Therefore the comic writer should pay strict attention to the age of his characters and not have a young man speak like a graybeard or vice versa. "Study the Court and know the city. Both are fertile in models" (ll. 391–92). Boileau here shows the limitations of his concept of comedy, since he mentions only the court at Versailles and the city of Paris as places to observe human nature. The restriction narrows the field of comedy to the nobility and upper bourgeoisie. If comedy were thus limited it would depict only what is most conventionalized and least human in man. (Fortunately, Molière had not restricted himself to such a narrow point of view.) Regarding Molière, Boileau criticizes him for having been too much a friend of the common people. Had Molière paid more attention to court and city, his comedies would have been more pleasing and sophisticated, with less buffoonery in them. In Molière's slapstick farces Boileau has difficulty recognizing the calibre of the author of *le Misanthrope*.

Comedy is no place for sighs and tears, not permitting any touch of the tragic. Nor is its function to amuse the populace of the village square with salacious words and scenes. Boileau did not care for vulgarity, in either satire or comedy, and made every effort to write words fit for the ears of ladies and modest gentlemen.

The plot of a comedy should be well organized and unfold easily. The action should be reasonable without useless and empty scenes. The style should be humble and gentle, full of witticisms and finely handled passions. The scenes should always be linked, i.e., the stage should never be empty, except between acts. One should avoid joking at the expense of common sense. The comic dramatist should not stray from nature, with Terence as a guide in remaining natural. Boileau is particularly fond of an author who is able to please the public through reasonable means, without insulting the intelligence or shocking the sensibilities. The gross and salacious writer should stay away from the theater and go amuse lackeys and the like with his foolishness.

Canto IV

Canto IV of the *Art poétique*, like Canto I, contains advice of a general nature, but more moral and less technical. Using as his example Claude Perrault, the famous doctor turned architect and brother of his enemy Charles Perrault, Boileau again warns the writer to be sure of his talent before embarking on a career of letters. This illustration also gives him an opportunity to insult Perrault, and this is the least true and most objectionable facet of the satire found in the *Art poétique*. It is better to be a mason, a useful worker in a necessary trade, than a poor poet. "In every other art there are different degrees, and one can fill the second places honorably. But in the dangerous art of writing, there are no ranks between mediocre and worst" (ll. 29–32). Boileau is, to say the least, exceedingly strict in this judgment. To eliminate all writers who do not attain the level of masters would not only obviate any possibility of comparison, but also rid the world of a lot of very pleasing poetry. From other remarks in various poems, and judging by some of the poets he appreciated who were less than great, we may assume that Boileau was not really as dogmatic as he sounds here. As is often the case, he takes the extreme viewpoint in order to illustrate better his thesis—that one without talent should not write. Boileau particularly attacks writers to whom he refers as "cold." "Whoever says 'cold' writer is saying detestable author" (l. 33). "A fool can at least make us laugh and amuse us, but a 'cold' writer knows only how to bore us" (ll. 37–38).

An author should pay no attention to the praise he may receive when reading his works aloud. Many poems sound fine to the ear but will not stand close scrutiny in print. Listen to everybody who may criticize, for even a fool may sometimes give a piece of important advice. The author should accept criticism and make corrections when the criticism is reasonable; he should not pay attention to a fool, either in praise or censure. (This is an apparent contradiction, but Boileau means that one *should* listen but not *follow* advice unless it is good.) Often an ignorant person, who is also vain, will give a destructive criticism of the most beautiful verse. His stubbornness in his poor judgment cannot be changed and his advice is to be avoided. The author should choose a censor who is enlightened by intelligence and common sense, and who will seek out the weak spots. He only can tell whether one is justified in departing from the rules. "Sometimes a vigorous spirit is too restricted by art and, departing from the prescribed rules, learns from Art itself how to go beyond their limits" (ll. 78–80). Such a critic is hard to find, for someone who may rhyme easily often has poor judgment.

An author who wants to be truly appreciated should add the useful to the artistic beauty of his works. The reader who is wise avoids vain amusement and wants to profit from his leisure. (It is this principle of utilitarianism in art which made the literature of classicism such a moral literature. Sermonizing may result when, in the writer's mind, instructing the public takes precedence over its pleasure.)

Boileau firmly believed that the morality of the author was important to the quality of his works—a concept which seems strange to readers of the post-Romantic era, who give artists the right to a rather more licentious behavior. Boileau insists that the author should offer to the public only noble images of himself. If this sounds like an extreme statement, it should be remembered that Boileau had a very high concept of the dignity of the poet's calling. Although he had a less elevated idea of the "mission of the poet" than Ronsard or Hugo, for example, he did feel that art was much more than an amusement for the idle. He had little patience for anyone whose primary goal in writing was to make money. In Boileau's opinion, authors who desert honor and make vice attractive are dangerous.

He then hastens to add that he does not go so far as some, who have even wanted to banish love from the stage. If expressed chastely, even the most dishonorable love does not excite in the audience any emotions which could cause shame. We condemn the sin of Dido, while sharing her tears. An author who is himself virtuous and whose verse is innocent does not corrupt the heart by titillating the senses. "Love then virtue and nourish your soul with it. In vain is the mind filled with a noble vigor, for the verse will always smack of the baseness of the heart" (ll. 108–10). (Boileau here defends the theater against those who, like Pascal and Bossuet, had attacked it on the grounds of its being dangerous to morality.)

Above all the author should avoid the petty jealousies indulged in by base spirits. A truly great author is never infected with this sort of thing; it is a vice which accompanies mediocrity. Envy is the cause of jealousy and tries to pull merit down to its own level. The author should never lower himself to take part in such intrigues nor try to attain a position of honor by dishonorable means.

Verse should not be the sole occupation of the writer or it will become a *pre*-occupation. The author should cultivate friends and try to be a gentleman. It is not enough to be agreeable and charming in a book—one must know how to converse and live in society.

The artist should work for the sake of glory and not for sordid gain. A writer may certainly, without shame or crime, draw from his work a legitimate financial reward (tribute, as Boileau puts it). But this should not be his primary aim. Especially does Boileau detest renowned authors who, tired of glory and hungry for fortune, put their Muse at the service of bookdealers and make a mercenary trade out of a divine art. Some may reply that the artist must make a living and that an author who is hungry cares little for sweet promenades on Mt. Helicon. Boileau replies that the disgraceful situation of a hungry poet rarely occurs in these times. In this century the fine arts enjoy the liberality of a great prince, who does not let merit go unrewarded. Boileau then calls upon the Muses and all the greatest writers to glorify the reign of Louis XIV, great as a patron of the arts and great as a conquering warrior. His glorious reign offers an unlimited number of subjects for poetic composition, and Boileau invites authors to redouble their efforts to become worthy of them. As for himself, primarily a writer of satire who does not dare attempt the martial trumpet or the lyre, he will give encouragement. He offers these lessons which his Muse learned from Horace (*Ars poetica*); he will second their efforts and their ardor, and will show them, from afar, the crown and the prize to be won. In exchange for this, they will pardon him if he continues to write satire and tries to separate the gold from the dross. He is a censor, more inclined to blame others than he is to accomplish great results himself. On this modest yet slightly threatening note the *Art poétique* closes.

IV Epître IX

Epître IX (1675) is dedicated to the Marquis de Seignelay, son of Colbert—an indirect way of praising the father who was averse to having poems dedicated to him. Along with the *Art poétique* and the *Préface* to the 1701 edition of his works, this epistle is one of Boileau's most important critical and theoretical documents. The opening lines refer to Seignelay as an enemy of flattery. In vain does a silly author try to flatter him, because he quickly rebels and avoids falling into such a trap. Throughout the poem Boileau tries to say that one cannot expect from a bourgeois poet, accustomed to satire, the same sort of praise and flattery one might receive from a courtier. This would be too much a change of personality for Boileau, and Seignelay would not appreciate it anyway. The literary theme of the epistle is that the author must please and be truthful.

Boileau does not oppose praise if it is offered in an artistic and delicate fashion. He does object to verses of eulogy which are ridiculously flattering, based on such far-fetched comparisons that they make the object of praise appear as silly as the author himself. Insincere praise is an insult to a sincere person. As an example Boileau refers to Colbert, who should be praised for the qualities he has—virtue, activity, ardor, vigilance, intelligence, constancy, love for the fine arts. If, instead of these qualities, an author should liken him to Alexander the Great or Mars, endowing him with warlike attributes, Colbert would recognize not himself but Louis XIV, and would force the poet to remain silent. (Boileau here very adroitly includes in the epistle several lines of praise, not only for Colbert but for the king as well.) The noble heart is satisfied with its own qualities and does not desire those of someone else. What use is praise which the recipient knows to be untrue? "Nothing is beautiful except truth. The true alone is desirable. It should reign everywhere, even in fables. The adroit falseness of all fiction only serves to make Truth shine before the eyes" (ll. 43–46).

If one would like to know why Boileau's verses are read and admired, states the author of himself, it is *not* because their sound is always agreeable to the ear, or because the meaning never interferes with the rhythm, or because the caesura is never misplaced. It is because in his verse Truth may be seen and grasped; because Good and Evil receive the treatment due them. "My heart, always leading my mind, never says anything to the reader that he has not often said to himself. My thought is exposed to the clarity of daylight, and my verse, well or badly, always says something" (ll. 57–60).

Boileau wonders if perhaps he is flattering himself. There is no one, however upright, who is not a bit false in some aspect of his personality. We all tend to mask ourselves and, departing from our own nature, are afraid to show ourselves as we really are. Quite often a person may try to appear exactly the opposite of what he really is, and we may finally dislike him simply because he tries too hard to please. "Simplicity pleases without the necessity of study or art" (l. 81). "The false is always insipid, boring, and tedious; but Nature is true and one feels the presence of Nature immediately. It is Nature alone that is admired and loved in everything" (ll. 85–87). Each person, taken as he really is, is agreeable, and a person is only displeasing when he appears to be what he is not. In so doing one may succeed in mutilating his real personality even while desiring self-improvement.

Boileau then returns to the theme of the poem—truthfulness. "I reiterate that nothing is beautiful except through truth. It is in truth alone that one may please and please for a long time. The mind tires easily if the heart is not sincere" (ll. 102–4). Virtue alone can stand the clear light of day, while vice must seek obscurity and be disguised before it can appear in public. It is vice which has banished frankness from contemporary manners.

Formerly, when man was busily occupied in earning his daily bread, he had no time for deceit nor was he deceived. Plenty brought laziness, which in turn encouraged false vanity. Vanity is the cause of most imposture, and poetry has had more than its share of impostors. From vanity proceeds also the mass of mercenary verses which extol and flatter. Boileau repeats that he has no desire to banish praise from verse but only wants it to be accurate. The qualities a poet praises must be those which the recipient actually possesses, and Boileau goes on to illustrate with some of the virtues of Seignelay, and particularly of his father, Colbert.

There is, as always, some element of satire in this poem, as well as a moral flavor in the plea for truth and for men to be themselves. It has been discussed among the theoretical works, however, because of its importance in understanding Boileau's ideas on truth in literature and his development of the concept that only the true is beautiful.

V Dissertation sur Joconde

The *Dissertation sur Joconde* (1665) is one of Boileau's earliest efforts in literary criticism and one of his best. It was composed at the same period in his life as the early *Satires* and the *Dialogue des Héros de romans*. The occasion for its composition was a controversy between partisans of two new translations of the tale of Astolfo and Gioconda, from the *Orlando furioso* (*Mad Roland*) of Ariosto. The first of these translations was by a poet of little ability, M. de Boüillon, who had formerly been secretary to the duc d'Orléans. The translation appeared in 1663 in an edition of the works of *feu* (the late) Monsieur de Boüillon, so the author was already dead when Boileau composed the *Dissertation*. The second translation was by La Fontaine and is contained in an edition of his *Nouvelles en vers, Tiré de Bocace et de l'Arioste* (*Tales in Verse, Taken from Boccaccio and Ariosto*). La Fontaine was not yet the famous author of fables, since the first book of *Fables* appeared only in 1668. In his treatment of Ariosto's tale, though, he already shows a superior talent.

The *Dissertation sur la Joconde* (*sic*) appeared for the first time in 1669 in a Dutch (Leyden) edition of La Fontaine's *Contes et*

Nouvelles en vers (*Verse Tales and Novellas*). The name of the
author is not given, and the dissertation is added at the end of
the volume as a defense of the Joconde. The Dutch editor himself
recognizes Boileau's worth as a critic: "Moreover, one will notice
in this dissertation a manner of criticism which is both astute and
witty; everything said carries its point and banter is agreeably
mingled with an inquiring and gentlemanly erudition." Boileau is
referred to as "one of the finest wits of the day."

Considerable sums had been wagered by partisans of Boüillon,
who had made an exact translation, and those of La Fontaine.
The latter was accused of having made changes from his original,
even in principal events. The *Dissertation sur Joconde* seems to
have grown out of these bets. Three judges were selected to decide on the merits of the translations. Among them was Molière
who, according to legend, refused to take part in the affair and
advised a friend, who had bet on Boüillon, to get out of it if he
could, for he was a sure loser.

There has been some dispute as to the authorship of the *Dissertation sur Joconde*, but René Bray seems to have established satis-
factory proof that Nicolas Boileau-Despréaux wrote it.[11] The
question had been posed because the *Dissertation* did not appear
in any of the editions of Boileau's *Oeuvres* during his lifetime. The
reason for this is probably given by Brossette in the 1716 edition
of Boileau's works he published—that Boileau did not think it
honorable to have used his pen to defend a work of the moral
character of *Joconde*, in which a husband is deceived by his wife
and her lover.

Even though Boileau was the natural opponent of Boüillon and
his circle of friends as well as a recent friend of La Fontaine, the
Dissertation sur Joconde is an objective work of literary criticism.
Boileau seems to have no definite critical method, but nevertheless the dogmatic foundation of the criticism is evident, as well as
considerable. Already Boileau knows the importance of reason
and the doctrine of universal consent in literary criticism. He believes in the concepts of *vraisemblance* and *bienséance* and op-
poses the mixing of genres or of the sacred with the profane. Naturalness, both of content and of expression, is essential to his
critical approach. Some degree of liberty is reserved for the creative genius by means of the doctrine of the *je ne sais quoi*. The

Dissertation sur Joconde already contains, then, many of the theories found later in the *Art poétique.*

In the opening paragraph of the *Dissertation,* Boileau states that the wager is amusing but not surprising, because poor works have always found supporters. There have even been cases where minor poets of no genius have been preferred to Homer, as if the commonly held opinion of men for several centuries were of no consequence. Thus the doctrine of universal consent is mentioned immediately as an important factor and foundation of critical judgment.

There can be, says Boileau, no comparison between the work of Boüillon and that of La Fontaine, since the former is a cold narrative and a dry translation. La Fontaine's version, however, is a pleasant and properly embellished invention. La Fontaine has taken his subject from Ariosto but has made it completely his own. Instead of making a copy from an original, he has created an original work based on an idea furnished him by Ariosto. This is the same way in which Virgil imitated Homer, Terence imitated Menander, Tasso imitated Virgil. Boüillon, on the contrary, has ruined what Ariosto furnished him, so that it is no longer either French or Italian in spirit.

Not only is La Fontaine's version incomparably better than that of Boüillon, it is even better than Ariosto's original. Boileau cannot agree that poetic license permits Ariosto to include a fable, an old wives' tale such as *Joconde,* in a serious, heroic poem. Boileau then paraphrases Horace (*Ars poetica,* ll. 6–13) on the inadvisability of combining in the same poem things which are basically incompatible. The *Orlando furioso* of Ariosto is guilty of this very error in its mixture of the serious and heroic with the base and foolish—and the story of Gioconda and Astolfo is one of the least serious in the poem. If such stories are permitted in a heroic poem, then common sense no longer has any jurisdiction over works of the mind, says Boileau, and it will henceforth be pointless to talk about art or rules. Ariosto's story is good, but out of place.

Boileau also criticizes Ariosto for telling the story in a serious manner, so that one would not only think it was true, but even a very serious and epic occurrence. It is as bad to recount a comic story in grave and serious language as it is to tell of a great deed in a base style. An exception may be permitted if the gravity is expressly affected in order to make something comic appear even more absurd. (This is exactly the procedure used by Boileau in the composition of *Le Lutrin,* which was begun seven years later, in 1672.) The secret in this procedure is to announce the subject to the reader in such a way as to make it clear to him that even the author does not believe what he is about to write. The reader thus laughs at the agreeable pleasantries of an author who is having fun, not speaking seriously. By following this procedure one can even say things contrary to reason, which are allowed to pass uncriticized because they excite laughter. In his version of the Joconde story, La Fontaine does not banter in a serious tone. He tells an extravagant tale, but announces it as such and hence is unconcerned with verisimilitude.

As an illustration, Boileau cites the methods used by Ariosto and La Fontaine to recount the husband's attitude and action when he discovers his wife in bed with his valet. In view of his character as hitherto depicted by Ariosto, a violent reaction would be expected. However, he does nothing because of his strong love for his wife. Such a reaction from a young man deeply in love is hard enough for Boileau to accept, but the reason given by Ariosto is completely *invraisemblable.* La Fontaine, on the other hand, realized the absurdity inherent in the circumstances and was careful not to make his character so extravagantly in love. Discovering the wife and valet sleeping together, he does nothing, either from pity or prudence, for in such circumstances the best action is to make as little fuss as possible. La Fontaine's solution thus gives a plausible explanation for the husband's refusal to resort to violence.

Ariosto's image of an honorable man betrayed by an ingrate whom he loves deeply is tragic and has no place in a comic tale. On the other hand, the picture of a husband who resolves to endure discreetly the affairs of his wife, as in La Fontaine's version, is pleasant and agreeable and is the usual subject of comedy.

Several other instances of violations of *vraisemblance* are indicated by Boileau, such as Astolfo's engaging the king to swear on the Holy Sacrament to keep the secret: where would he obtain a consecrated Host, and why would a king swear such a serious oath to a mere knight for such a frivolous cause? Again Boileau points out that such serious business had no place in a comic tale, and La Fontaine avoided it by having him simply cite to the king examples of great men of the past who had endured similar misfortunes with courage and equanimity. According to Boileau only Italian permissiveness would have allowed such impertinences, and similar silliness would not be endured either in French or Latin.

La Fontaine, Boileau feels, has been brought up in the taste of Virgil and Terence and would not be carried away by Italian extravagance, departing so far from common sense. Everything he says is simple and natural, and what Boileau likes about him is a certain *naïveté* of language which few people notice but which is the source of the attractiveness of his story. This same inimitable *naïveté* is what has long been admired in the writings of Horace and Terence, both of whom worked so hard to achieve it that they broke the measure of their verse to do so. La Fontaine has done the same thing in many places and has succeeded in acquiring the *molle et facetum* (grace and delicacy) which Horace attributes to Virgil. Boileau here shows his critical acumen, especially regarding sounds in poetry, and points out exactly the qualities that have made La Fontaine one of the world's great poets: the appearance of *naïveté*, ease, and simplicity through careful and painstaking effort.

Boileau states that there are many places of great force and beauty in La Fontaine's *Joconde*, but pointing them out would not convince anyone. "These sorts of beauties are the kind that must be felt, and which cannot be proved. It is a *je ne sais quoi* which charms us and without which beauty itself would have neither grace nor beauty. But after all, it is a *je ne sais quoi*; . . ."

Ariosto is also criticized for not making the expression suitable to the speaker—for having a mule driver talk like a lover from some adventure novel. La Fontaine is praised for the simplicity, even the bareness of his narrative, in which nothing is explained that might easily be supposed by the readers. This is a portion of the artifice of his story and, by not wasting precious time in useless words, he also frequently avoids absurd situations.

Boileau then states that he doesn't mean to infer that La Fontaine has eliminated all the absurdities of the original, for it would be unwise even to think of doing so, given the very nature of the story. However, wherever La Fontaine has departed from Ariosto, he has improved on the original. Credit for the invention of the story should be granted to Ariosto, who told it elegantly, neatly, and briefly. However, La Fontaine recounted more pleasantly a very good story and understood better the idea and character of the narrative.

As for the version of Boüillon, never was a style more full of faults nor so far removed from that of La Fontaine. La Fontaine is sometimes careless, but he does infinitely better than does Boüillon with his arid, crude, and forced style. Boileau then cites a passage from Boüillon and proceeds to analyze it in detail, pointing out every possible fault with minute care. He concludes that there is hardly a line that doesn't contain something which deserves to be condemned. Boileau feels shame for La Fontaine that he should even be compared with Boüillon.

As stated earlier, in the *Dissertation sur Joconde* Boileau demonstrates many of the same critical principles which were later to be found in the *Art poétique*. He also gives an excellent explanation and justification for the burlesque procedure he followed later in composing the *Lutrin*. The *Dissertation* also shows that, at least at this time, Boileau entertained a lively admiration for La Fontaine. The most important aspect of the literary doctrine set forth in the *Dissertation sur Joconde* is Boileau's recognition of the necessity for pleasing the audience. The seventeenth century is the period *par excellence* of accommodation between reason and the art of pleasing. This art of politeness, wit, finesse, delicacy, discernment, a natural good taste—all boils down to the *je ne sais quoi*, which must be felt and communicated but cannot be proved or demonstrated. Without this *je ne sais quoi*, a work of art could not please and, in order to please, it was the right and even the duty of the author to abandon the rules when they did not serve him—a right freely recognized and granted to authors of genius.

VI Traité du Sublime

Even though it is a translation, Boileau's version of Longinus' treatise *On the Sublime* must be given careful consideration, both because of its influence on the thought of Boileau and also because of the subsequent effect of Boileau's translation on European critical thought. Longinus' ideas may be observed whenever Boileau speaks of the sublime in literature, and much of the sublime enters into Boileau's concept of the *je ne sais quoi*. The translation seems a little too free today, but Boileau did try to be more faithful to his original than was usual in his time, to such an extent that his own natural style sometimes suffers from the attempt. There are some errors, but they do not cast serious doubt on Boileau's knowledge of Greek, which he knew better than most of his detractors.

Boileau's understanding of the sublime is not what we might at first expect from a man of the seventeenth century, since it has nothing to do with rhetoric, solemnity, or pomp. It comes fundamentally from the use, in the right place, of proper and simple terms of expression, exactly suited to the idea or emotion to be conveyed. The sublime is the supreme degree of beauty, which realizes perfectly the effect desired by the artist. It is the point beyond which art can accomplish no more because the receptive mind makes direct contact with the thought of the creative mind.

In addition to a personal preference, desire to be useful to the public influenced Boileau's undertaking of the translation. Although we do not really know who this Longinus was, or even if a Longinus is the true author, the treatise is, along with the works of Aristotle, Cicero, and Quintilian, one of the greatest works on rhetoric which has survived from antiquity. Boileau admired Longinus not only as a rhetorician but also as a philosopher and a gentleman. Longinus was enough of a philosopher to be able to enlarge the esthetic domain of taste and to demonstrate the relationship between the beautiful and the honorable—the principal reason for his attractiveness to Boileau. He maintained that the truly sublime comes from the noblest emotions of the human soul and that to attain the sublime one must be nurtured in the study of the noble and the good, both in ideas and passions. Longinus also had the imagination to be able to grasp rapports between diverse literatures. He was one of the first to understand the transformation wrought by the combination of Greek and Roman civilizations, mingled with the genius of the Orient. Longinus compares Demosthenes and Cicero, recognizing the contributions of each to the art of oratory. He goes even further in seeking an example of the sublime among the Jews, who were held in generally low esteem. As a matter of fact, it is Longinus' citation of the beginning of Genesis which struck Boileau most forcefully as an illustration of the sublime.

Boileau's translation was not long in producing effects, and with

its publication in 1674 Longinus enters European critical literature for the first time. In spite of earlier translations, most of them
into Latin from the original Greek, Longinus' influence did not
become perceptible until after Boileau's translation, the new
translations it inspired, and retranslations of Boileau's version.
This is not to say that Longinus was unknown before Boileau, but
he was known to only a few. After Boileau's translation, however,
he was familiar to everyone interested in literature and criticism.

Besides the intrinsic merit of Longinus' work and of Boileau's
translation, much of the credit for the success of the work must be
given to the prestige of Boileau and the extent of his reputation.
This brought the treatise to the attention of a public that might
not otherwise have taken note of it. Boileau had the general public in mind, not wanting to write a mere translation but a treatise
which would be useful to a large segment of his readers. Knowing
the scorn of the seventeenth-century reader for anything pedantic,
he takes an honest liberty with the original to direct it to the mundane audience of the day. Recognizing also his responsibility to a
more scholarly audience, he reserves the *Remarques* section for
the more specialized reader.

Contemporaries generally considered Boileau's translation a
masterpiece, more like an original work than a translation. Even
those who were occasionally critical on scholarly grounds did not
deny that Boileau's method was the only way of reaching a wide
public. Most of Boileau's departures from the Greek are deliber-
ate, either for clarity or esthetic reasons. The suppression of anything that might be considered pedantic and the attempt to impose some unity on a basically fragmentary work show that Boileau was not only a translator but also a propagandist, seeking a
vast public.

It should also be pointed out, as Brody has so well accomplished
in his excellent study, that Boileau had to seek out Longinus consciously and conscientiously.[12] One could hardly escape the influence of Horace's *Ars poetica*, which was part of the bread and
butter of the school system, or that of Aristotle, with his immense
prestige and hundreds of commentators. Boileau's seeking out of
Longinus revealed innate tendencies in the Frenchman. Brody
states the case nicely: "His eye blind to all but the heights of
literary excellence, he cut his way across differences of civilization, temperament, method, and orientation to the clearing where

he joined Longinus." [13] Longinus' greatest influence was exercised
on the Romantic poets, and this fact is interesting since it was
Boileau, of all the French Classicists, who was most severely attacked by the Romantics. Boileau had a deeper understanding of
Longinus than the Romantics, who misunderstood Longinus' attitude toward the emotion of the author as a source of the sublime.
To Longinus, as well as to the Classicists, the emotion evoked in
the audience is what is of paramount importance. The author's
own feeling is of little value unless he is able to evoke in his readers a corresponding emotion. Moreover, to both Longinus and
Boileau, the emotions were only one source of the sublime and
even then they had to be emotions of the highest type.

Boileau uses the doctrines of the sublime and the *je ne sais quoi*
to include those elements of art which are the intangibles, those
that cannot be forced to fit into any of the so-called rules. All the
rules set down by Boileau, in the *Art poétique* and elsewhere,
assume the prior existence of imagination, inspiration, poetic genius, and the qualities of the sublime and the *je ne sais quoi*. These
cannot be legislated but are an integral part of the very soul of the
poet. It is an injustice to Boileau and a misunderstanding of his
spirit to see in him only the "legislator of Parnassus," who believed
obedience to rules would insure a beautiful work of art. Boileau,
more than anyone of his time, realized, understood, and mentioned the necessity for the *sine qua non* of poetry, which he attempts to define by means of the sublime and the *je ne sais quoi*.

Emotion and even strong passion are not banned, either by
Longinus or Boileau. To them it is merely a question of using the
right amount at the right time. The statement points up one of the
basic esthetic principles of Classicism. To the Classicist, emotion
is an end and an effect rather than a means and a cause. Emotion
is not subjective in the mind of the artist, but an instrument to be
utilized, according to the nature of the subject, the time, and the
desired result. What is important is the feeling the artist is able to
convey or evoke, rather than the ability to express his own emotions. This does not mean that the classical artist must have no
emotions. On the contrary, he will be better able to express those
he has experienced. However, his primary concern will not be to
express his own experience, intact, to his audience, but to evoke or
suggest a corresponding emotional experience. In other words, to
the classicist, emotion may be an important condition of the de-

sired esthetic response but not of the creative process itself. It is at this point that craftsmanship enters the creative picture, for the artist must be a craftsman in order to know what expression and devices will most likely evoke the desired response. Quite often the most effective emotional response may be the result of the most sober calculation on the part of the artist.

Of course, this discussion of emotion as a part of the creative process in the artist or as a condition of the esthetic response goes back at least as far as Plato's *Ion,* where the poetic state is described as a divine madness, beyond the control of reason or of the creator. The discussion has probably been most lucidly stated in modern times by Nietzsche in *The Birth of Tragedy from the Spirit of Music,* where he sets forth the Apollonian and the Dionysian creative spirits. The controversy aroused a great deal of discussion in ancient times, and this discussion has continued unabated to the present. To both Longinus and Boileau the sublime depends upon place, circumstances, manner of expression, and motive. Longinus cites, as an example of the sublime, Demosthenes' oath sworn by the warriors who died at Marathon. He considers the ancient orator a master craftsman of language, through which he evokes the sentiment of the sublime in his hearers. Nothing is said about Demosthenes' subjective emotions or state of mind. The orator had carefully prepared his audience for the moment when the oath would be uttered with the most minute calculation and exquisite attention to every verbal detail.

The importance of place, circumstances, expression, motive, and the like is so great in the sublime that examples cited may often not appear sublime out of context. This importance of form and structure is also a classical trait. To the classical artist the principle of control is of paramount importance and inseparable from other creative principles or processes. There is a world of difference between the random use of literary or rhetorical devices and their right and effective application. In the *Préface* to his translation, Boileau adds an example of what he considers sublime in a modern author, the "Qu'il mourût" (Die!), uttered by old Horace in Corneille's *Horace.* Nothing could better illustrate the importance of context to the sublime, for Boileau is here impelled to explain the circumstances surrounding and leading up to the pronouncement. The sublime is rarely to be found in so-called purple patches which may be taken out of context and retain their beauty—such may be beautiful but are rarely sublime. As Brody states, sublimity depends upon the place and the manner and the circumstances and the motive. There must be, in addition to presence of mind and self-possession, an inner sense of appropriateness, an insight into the psychological limits of a situation, of which none but the greatest writers are aware.[14]

This concept of timeliness and relevance in artistic creativity necessarily assumes conscious, individual judgment and selection, and is thus antithetical to any notion of the creative process as either demonic possession or rigid formalism. It denotes the position of true Classicism between Romanticism and rigid neo-classicism. It is not without good reason that the French refer to the period of the reign of Louis XIV as *Classicism* rather then *neo-classicism*.

To Boileau and to Longinus, as Brody points out, nature is the original and vital principle of artistic creation.[15] Art will determine its limits and timeliness and also contribute to application and practice. Thus nature and art are subsumed in the idea of a trained instinct, of an "inner imperative" and "practised reflex" which join both elements of the nature-art dichotomy in a single notion of combined vitality and control. This explains why, in so many instances, Boileau seems to use the terms nature, beauty, art, and reasonableness as nearly synonymous.

Longinus attaches particular importance, in the ability to acquire the sublime, to the ability to form great and noble conceptions. This is why Boileau emphasizes the necessity for uprightness of character and greatness of soul in the writer. Only the great-souled person is able to form noble conceptions which may lead to the sublime.

The most clear and obvious impression gained from Boileau's discussions of the sublime and the *je ne sais quoi* is one of tentativeness. It is a concept which Boileau is unable to explain clearly, nor does he seem at all unwilling to leave it unexplained. As we have seen elsewhere, this attitude informs his criticism of literature in general and is especially evident in the *Dissertation sur Joconde* and the *Préface* to the 1701 edition of his works. From the beginning to the end of his long career, Boileau retains his position toward the mysteries of the creative process.

In the *Traité du Sublime* Boileau uses the word *esprit*, as Brody points out, almost synonymously with the word *nature* to express the creative ability or natural endowment.[16] Besides being a native gift, the innate genius, *esprit* also includes control through restraint, and an awareness of the proper time, place, and motive which may result in the production of the sublime. In his use of the term Boileau seems to mean a creative potential tempered and controlled by judgment and taste. In order to be great or sublime, the poet must possess, in addition to inspiration, the restraint, taste, and judgment necessary to insure poetic effectiveness. This concept is basically hostile to the concept of the divine *afflatus* and poetic frenzy derived by Renaissance theorists from Plato. However, to Boileau this control was not a case of energy restrained by any force or inertia. Control, as he saw it, was a positive force of creativity which should work together with genius and inspiration in the creative process. Man should contribute the restraint and control while heaven gives the inspiration of the creative process. The artist who does not possess this restraint and control is incomplete, and his creative process will accordingly be incomplete also. Boileau's use of the word *raison*, which we have usually translated reasonableness, is an integral part of his concept of artistic creation. It is not a negation of the process but a necessary, logical, and natural component. Reasonableness in the creative process comes to mean a controlled inspiration.

In our age it is all too easy to regard control of any kind as a denial of basic individualism. Much talk is heard about the freedom of the individual—to express himself, to find his identity, or whatever. Little expression is given, however, to the idea that the individual who does whatever he wants, thereby seemingly enjoying perfect liberty and individualism, is actually the least free of humans because he is in bondage to himself and his own basest passions and instincts—the worst master one could possibly have. The same analogy may be made in literature and has been best stated by André Gide: ". . . The triumph of individualism and the triumph of classicism are identical. The triumph of individualism is in the renunciation of individuality. There is not a single one of the qualities of the Classical style that is not purchased at the price of sacrificing some complacency." [17] This, then, is the freedom and individualism of Classicism in its truest definition. And this is why the writers of the Classical period were ultimately more individual than the Romantics: one will find more variety

and individualism among Corneille, Racine, Molière, La Fontaine, and Boileau than among the poets of Romanticism like La-
martine, Vigny, Hugo, and Musset.

Since *raison* is, for Boileau, not only the guide of rhyme but also
the *lustre* and *prix* (sum total of literary quality), the term must
be applied in the broadest possible sense or it loses all possible
relevance. It is this equation of *raison*, as Boileau uses the term,
with the rationalism of the eighteenth century that has led to
much adverse and basically unfair criticism of Boileau. Perhaps it
would be well to consider the Latin etymon of the word, which
has a much broader range of meanings than the word *raison* in
French. *Rătĭo* (*-ōnis*) means, among other things, *sum; relation,
respect to; regard, consideration, concern for; course, procedure;
method, plan, nature, kind;* ratio atque usus, *theory and practice;
judgment, understanding, reason; reasonableness, propriety,
order.* Thus, if we permit Boileau to use the word *raison* in the
sense of its etymon, the term immediately becomes broader and
more meaningful, removing many objections to the *Art poétique*
and other critical writings.

Raison is thus both means and end, the quality to be attained
and the method of attainment. Unless one is guided by reasonableness, one can hardly attain it. But instead of a vicious circle,
raison becomes, through perfection by experience, a reflex action.
It is as if Boileau's very vagueness in defining the term and the
method of conducting *raison* indicate that it is a sort of sixth
sense, having more to do with taste and sensitivity than with rational processes. As Brody astutely points out, *raison* as a creative
faculty has more to do with the expression *avoir raison* (to be
right) than with the verb *raisonner* (to reason).[18]

Boileau was himself poet enough to understand that, in poetry,
raison may still be followed in instances where logic seems to be
violated. What may outwardly seem to be disorder may, in poetry, be an inner logic or order. This is evident in Boileau's admiration for Pindar, in whom he saw an inner sense of rightness
which had to be felt rather than analyzed. Boileau is constantly
impatient with those who cannot see *raison* as he sees it, and he
refers to them as blind. It is as if *raison* were, to his mind, a sort of
enlightened judgment, perceived by the mind's eye. It is what we
would refer to as insight and intuition. As Brody states, esthetic

truths are immediately sensed and seized by this eye of the mind
with the same swift finality that impresses spiritual truth on the
enlightened soul.[19]

Boileau's own *raison* was what enabled him to understand the
originality and true meaning of Longinus' treatise. To invoke simplicity, as Longinus does and as Boileau emphasizes, was an inno-
vation. To Boileau simplicity was not only a characteristic of the
sublime but its very essence. He believed firmly in the ability of
an utterance to recapitulate or depict instantly the very essence of
truth. The most important essence and effect of simplicity is
speed. The language is instantly transformed into action or image,
the reader immediately grasping the affective meaning. The result
is a combination of both the grandeur of truth and the force and
rapidity of its impact. Boileau was always suspicious of an ornate
style, composed of fancy words which, on close examination,
often turn out to be merely hollow words—an attempt by the mediocre writer to dazzle his readers. The ornate style may often be
an attempt to pass off an external apparatus in the absence of any
real inner essence. Though the emotional effects of literature have
seldom been considered important in Boileau's critical thought, it
is evident from his appreciation of the sublime and his citations of
examples of it that he was most attracted to art which could evoke
the deepest and noblest feelings most quickly and sustain them
longest. Though the idea of the sublime is most often considered a
critical term of Romanticism and a contributor to the dissolution
of the classical esthetic, Boileau was perfectly at home with the
concept and felt no contradiction. The fault lies not in Boileau's
concept but in the Romantics' notion of sublimity, which came to
designate any astounding demonstration of power or energy.

The *Traité du sublime* reveals that Boileau was intensely interested in the emotion-invoking effects of literature. Seen in this
light, the *Art poétique* assumes the existence of the ideas in the
Traité du sublime. Once the nature and limitations of Boileau's
respect for the rules are recognized, it becomes apparent that
their role in his thought was to heighten and sustain emotional
effects. When Boileau invoked the rules it was not as abstract
principles but as means in the creative process. He was under no
delusions as to the rules' capacity to guarantee success, but he did
recognize their value as a precaution against failure. His interest
in the emotional effects of art is also at the heart of his concern for

unity of style and tone, and his notions on the purity of genres. Unity of style and refusal to mingle the serious with the frivolous lead to greater intensity of emotion. Shifting of tone results in an interruption of the primary esthetic experience, which must be unified and continuous in order to be fully, esthetically effective.

Viewed in the light of Boileau's ideas on the sublime, his belief in the unities in tragedy stems from the esthetic advantages of a plot which is unified in tone in order to produce the desired emotional effect, and a plot which does not hamper the audience's willingness to participate in the illusion of the theater. The rule of *bienséance* exists for the same fundamental reason—esthetic continuity.

It was Boileau who gave Longinus' treatise to the reading public, and his interpretation enriched the critical tradition. Even more importantly, it reveals to us another facet of Boileau's critical theories—a facet which would be difficult to observe without the treatise. The *Traité du sublime* shows us that Boileau, far from being a cold rationalist in matters of esthetics, was intensely interested in and committed to the emotive effects of art. Through the *Traité du sublime,* supplemented by the *Réflexions critiques* (*Critical Reflexions*), we are able to see behind the *Art poétique* to a whole body of thought, the existence of which the *Art poétique* assumes and mentions only at the beginning of Canto I. Longinus' sublime was, for Boileau, the supreme perfection of art. As Brody indicates, his concepts of genre and style, his insistence on naturalness and simplicity, his notion of tragedy—all were calculated to preserve this perfection and to keep the emotive effects of literature undisturbed, intense, and pure.[20]

CHAPTER 5

Boileau and the Quarrel of the Ancients and Moderns[1]

THE name "Quarrel of the Ancients and Moderns" was given to a literary wrangle which continued through the latter seventeenth and early eighteenth centuries. On the side of the Ancients were those who believed in the superiority or at least the permanent greatness of the leading writers of antiquity, and in the necessity for modern poets to draw inspiration from their Greek and Latin predecessors. On the side of the Moderns were those who upheld the theory of progress in all fields and felt that the modern artist should free himself from what had preceded. This statement is, of necessity, an oversimplification for the sake of discussion. Actually, the more intelligent of the Moderns recognized the greatness of Homer, Virgil, and the other leading authors of Graeco-Roman antiquity. Boileau himself, leader of the party of the Ancients, could see more clearly than anyone else the greatness of modern writers such as Racine, Molière, Corneille and was certain that posterity would give them a place equal to the greatest ancients. Rather than any basic disagreement on specific artists, the quarrel was an eruption of the fundamental conflict between the tendency to study ancient models and a tendency to work for one's own times. In an even broader sense, the quarrel was a part of the debate between humanism and rationalism, and was felt not only in literature but also in science, art, architecture, philosophy, and other disciplines.

I The Theory of Progress

The fundamental question underlying the quarrel was that of the theory of progress and, consciously or not, the participants either favored or opposed this notion. What seems obvious to us today, but was not always so at the time, is the fact that the theory of progress cannot be applied to creative works of art. The

168

Moderns were wrong in so doing, while the Ancients were equally wrong in permitting themselves to be drawn into an argument on this ground. The idea was not a new one, having been known in antiquity and the Renaissance. In antiquity it had taken the form of the idea of the Golden Age which, according to some, was the great heroic age of the past, while according to others it was in the future. In the latter concept, man would eventually attain the Golden Age through constant self-improvement. The Moderns were thus correct in their statement of the idea of progress as applied to those of man's accomplishments which progress by stages and build upon what has been done before, while they were wrong in applying the same doctrine to the fine arts. The Ancients were correct in refusing to apply the theory of progress equally to all areas of human endeavor, but wrong in their insistence on the superiority of the ancients and the necessity for imitation of them by modern artists. (This is perhaps least true in the case of Boileau, who admired the ancients not because they were ancients but because they had stood the test of time. He recognized that there were poor writers in antiquity who had not deserved to survive.) The quarrel was eventually won, in the eighteenth century, by the partisans of the Moderns because their argument had a broader base and hence was more widely true, and also because of the triumph of Cartesian rationalism over the humanistic ideal.

Actually, the Ancients were more nearly right concerning literature. When the quarrel began, there was no one yet known in France to balance Homer, Virgil, Sophocles, Euripides, Cicero, Demosthenes, Plato, Aristotle, Thucydides. The two greatest writers modern times had produced, Dante and Shakespeare, were virtually unknown in France. It is interesting to observe that the greatest modern writers of the latter half of the seventeenth century, such as Racine, La Fontaine, Boileau himself, were also the most vehement partisans of the Ancients, while themselves providing, by their works, the strongest arguments for the side of the Moderns. In addition, the extension of literature since the advent of printing, the increasing number of writers who could count on the royal bounty, the more numerous reading public—all these factors contributed to the opinion, shared by partisans of both sides, that they were living in a great epoch. During the latter third of the century there was a growing consciousness and awareness, often expressed, that the age of Louis XIV was comparable to Periclean Athens or the Rome of Augustus.

II *Early Phase of the Quarrel*

The seventeenth-century phase of the Quarrel of the Ancients and Moderns was actually begun by Desmarets de Saint-Sorlin, once a free-thinker but recently converted, with all the missionary zeal of the convert. He was indefatigable in upholding the cause of Christian inspiration in literature. In 1658, in the *Delights of the Mind,* he had maintained the poetic worth of the Bible as equal to the inspiration of pagan mythology. In 1669, in the preface to his epic poem *Marie-Madeleine,* Desmarets affirmed the superiority of the "marvelous" of Holy Scripture over the pagan "marvelous" of ancient fable and mythology. He also insisted that the French language is at least equal in expressiveness to Greek and Latin. He conceived of the development of mankind in the same way as that of individual man, antiquity being really the youth of the world, while modern times represent civilization's maturity. Since individual man is a being who constantly improves and corrects himself by means of past experience, Desmarets applied the same definition to mankind as a whole and thereby affirmed the superiority of modern civilization on the basis of having had more experience than the ancients—basically a theory of progress. Desmarets was also one of those who, like Perrault, criticized Homer, Virgil, and Ovid because they were not modern.

The quarrel continued over the question of whether to use a Latin or French inscription over a triumphal arch in honor of the king. The appearance of Boileau's *Art poétique* was a blow against the opponents of the Ancients. Open quarrel did not break out between Boileau and Desmarets, although it might have been expected. Yet before his death in 1676, Desmarets bequeathed the cause of the Moderns to Perrault. In an epistle entitled *Defense of French Poetry and Language,* Desmarets invited his friend Charles Perrault to help in the fight against the Latinizers and paganizers.

III *Perrault, Leader of the Moderns*

There were four Perrault brothers, all well-known: Nicolas, a doctor of theology in the Sorbonne; Pierre, *receveur des finances de l'université* (sort of treasurer/bursar); Claude, a naturalist, medical doctor, and architect who designed the colonnade of the Louvre; and Charles, *contrôleur des bâtiments* of the king, protégé of Colbert, member of the Academy, and author of the *Tales of Mother Goose*. It was the latter Perrault who succeeded to the leadership of the cause of the Moderns. Boileau had a natural animosity, the origin of which is obscure, toward the Perrault family. The story goes that he was poorly cared for by Claude when the latter was still practicing medicine. It is Claude whose ability as a doctor and architect Boileau insults in Canto IV of the *Art poétique*. Moreover, the Perraults were friends of Quinault and enemies of Racine. Friends also of Chapelain, they had intervened with Colbert on one occasion to have Boileau's *privilège* to print his works revoked. Boileau launched a series of epigrams against Claude Perrault, and the doctor or his brothers replied in a fable entitled *The Raven Cured by the Stock, or the Perfect Ingrate*. In 1674 Quinault's tragedy *Alceste* made Boileau and Racine indignant at what they considered a travesty of Euripides. Either Charles or Claude Perrault aided Quinault by an *Examen* of his play, to which Racine replied in his preface to *Iphigénie*. Boileau's *Epître IX* (1675) attacks Charles Perrault and his *Mirror of Love*.

Perrault was in the confidence of Colbert, having replaced Chapelain on the latter's death. He had an inventive mind and was a self-educated and self-made man. As is frequent with self-made men, he was overly self-assured and presumptuous, incapable of suspecting his own ignorance—more an amateur and dilettante than a gifted writer or critic. Both he and his brothers were interested in science and were quite popular in society. They were Moderns by temperament.

At first Charles Perrault did not seem inclined to take up Desmarets' quarrel, and the battle continued in epigrammatic skirmishes between his brothers and Boileau or Racine. In 1686 Charles wrote his epic *Saint Paulin*, with a preface in which he attacked Boileau's *Art poétique* on one of its weakest points, the criticism of the Christian marvelous. In 1687 Pierre Perrault translated the *Secchia rapita* (*Rape of the Bucket*) of Tassoni and in the foreword attacked Boileau and the Ancients. Nevertheless, the quarrel still did not break out into open warfare because it seems

that the Perraults lost Colbert's favor at the very moment when
Boileau gained it.

Soon a new champion of the Moderns entered the lists—Fontenelle, the nephew of Corneille. Besides his natural inclination
toward the side of the Moderns, it was also a matter of family
pride to defend his uncle, who was one of the greatest modern
writers. Fontenelle, interestingly, was probably closer to the truth
than anyone who participated in the quarrel. Upholding the theory of progress in science and technology, he recognized that it
was not equally applicable in the field of the fine arts. Thus the
moderns have no necessary superiority merely because they came
later. Nor are the ancients necessarily superior either—unless Nature is no longer as able to produce large trees or fecund minds as
once she was. Fontenelle, born in 1650, was only twenty-five
when his *Dialogues of the Dead* made his reputation as one who
had little respect for the ancients. He was also an indefatigable
collaborator on the *Mercure galant,* founded in 1672 by Donneau
de Visé for the reading of the mundane element of society, and
hence an organ of the Moderns. Fontenelle seems to have reawak-
ened the sleeping ardor of Charles Perrault.

IV *Quarrel Between Perrault and Boileau*

The immediate cause for open conflict between Boileau and
Perrault was the occasion of the reading, by the director of the
Academy, of Perrault's poem *Le Siècle de Louis le Grand* (*The
Age of Louis the Great*). This event occurred at a meeting of the
Académie française on January 27, 1687. In the poem Perrault
expressed the fundamental thesis of the Moderns. Protesting his
respect for the ancients, he declared that he did not bow before
them; they are great, but men like the rest of us, and the century
of Louis may be favorably compared to the century of Augustus.
Far from having the perfection generally and traditionally attributed to them, the ancients are not always good and sometimes
even bad. According to Perrault, Plato is sometimes boring,
Homer wanders, and Aristotle is less accurate in science even than
Herodotus in history. Perrault's verse was poor and his judgments
rash, although there are some good spots here and there. He was
correct in posing the principle of the perpetuity of the forces of
nature, and expressed it well. The partisans of the ancients, however, were unable to forgive him for his lack of appreciation of

Homer, in whom he found faults which he felt would not have been committed had Homer lived in the time of Louis XIV. This alone would have sufficed to arouse the ire of the Ancients, but they were even more incensed when Perrault opposed to antiquity the least estimable modern writers, carefully omitting both Racine and Boileau. He also praised contemporary art above ancient sculpture, architecture, and music. His basic thesis is that all art rests on the foundations of genius and technique. Since nature is unable to be worn out, the former remains constant throughout all eras. Technique, however, progresses with time and experience, and hence modern artists are superior.

Boileau became visibly incensed, according to the story, at this attack on names and works unsurpassed in his estimation. During the reading of the poem he twisted around in his seat with impatience and ill humor. Huet[2] attempted to silence him, but Boileau protested, right on the spot, that the reading of such a poem was a disgrace to the Academy. Racine maliciously congratulated Perrault on the success of such an agreeable joke and his ability at bringing it off. The Academy was generally favorable to Perrault's thesis, as were the women who presided over the leading salons. The latter could generally read little Latin and no Greek and the Moderns' position was complimentary to them.

The ancients were defended feebly by only a few partisans who were not even in agreement among themselves. The battle continued in fits and starts. Boileau was so angry he could at first only reply with rather vitriolic epigrams, but he eventually became the most active and vigorous of the Ancients and the acknowledged leader of their cause. La Fontaine, who had seemed distracted during the reading of Perrault's poem, took the side of the Ancients in his *Epître à Huet*. Huet himself was an erudite who fancied himself the protector of Homer and was jealous of Boileau who, he felt, was usurping his rightful function. Other partisans of the Ancients were Ménage and Dacier.[3]

Boileau began a campaign of epigrams against Charles and Claude Perrault, against the Academy, against Charpentier, the Perraults' friend and ally, and against the *Mercure galant*. However, put on the defensive, all he could do for the time was hurl insults, while his opponents exploited their initial success. Perrault was not an adversay without merit but an intelligent man, with a definite spirit of invention and a taste for novelty. To his efforts the

Academy owed their meeting place in the Louvre, the custom of election of members by secret ballot rather than the old method by voice vote, and the admission of the public to the reception of new members. The people of Paris owed to him their recent privilege of walking in the Tuileries gardens, hitherto reserved for members of the court. Basically, however, Perrault lacked much of the necessary mental equipment to sustain a struggle such as this with Boileau. His education was poor and undirected; this lacuna is at the root of many of the paradoxes in the *Siècle de Louis le Grand*. As a fervent Catholic, he was predisposed to be unfavorable toward the continued use of ancient mythology. Boileau is absolutely correct when he criticizes Perrault for condemning the ancients on the basis of Latin or French translations, since he could not read Greek. Perrault was, however, undaunted and probably did not even recognize or admit any of these deficiencies.

The Moderns were able to gain many recruits among the younger generation of writers most of whom, like Fontenelle, were witty and more ingenious than solid. In 1688 Perrault published *le Génie (Genius)*, a long poem dedicated to Fontenelle, and the first volume of his series of *Parallèles des Anciens et des Modernes*. Three other volumes of parallels were to follow, in 1690 and 1697. Fontenelle published in 1688 his *Digression sur les Anciens et les Modernes*. Lacking appreciation for the ancients and indeed for poetry in general, he took up Perrault's conception of the perpetuity of the forces of nature, developing it with wit and freedom. Fontenelle flattered the partisans of the ancients, who were also the best of the modern writers, and used them as proof of his own argument. He complimented Racine and Boileau and cited them among the finest of modern authors. This was surely doing justice to his opponents, but such was not Fontenelle's intention. Perrault's poem, *le Génie*, was read in a meeting of the Academy, and Fontenelle's reception into membership three years later (1691) was another day of triumph for the Moderns. Boileau and Racine had opposed this election, but to no avail. In his speech of thanks for his election, Fontenelle pointedly referred to his uncle, Pierre Corneille, as the greatest name in the French theater—with obvious intent to insult Racine. A reading of a fragment of Perrault's *Parallèles* and an exaggerated complimentary speech to Fontenelle, delivered by a friend of Perrault, completed the meeting. Boileau was not happy.

Finally realizing that insulting epigrams were not enough, Boileau decided to defend the ancients with more substantial arguments. In 1693 he presented to the public his *Ode sur la prise de Namur* (*Ode on the Capture of Namur*) in which his intention was to defend Pindar by composing an ode in the pindaric manner. The poem is a poor one and only serves to demonstrate that, even if Boileau appreciated Pindar, he was unable to imitate him. The ode was preceded by a *Discours* in which Boileau replied to the *Parallèles* of Perrault, especially to the third volume, which had appeared in 1692. Although Perrault had not named Boileau, it was clear that he had intended to displease him. He had praised those whom Boileau had condemned and had criticized Boileau's custom of naming names in his *Satires*. He had condemned *le Lutrin* as a reverse version of the very burlesque genre Boileau had so often attacked. In the *Discours*, Boileau reaffirmed his doctrine of imitation of the ancients and attempted to justify his admiration for antiquity. Perrault replied in a semi-apologetic *Letter to Monsieur Despréaux Concerning the Preface to His Ode* in which he pretends to pacify Boileau by praising his poetry and ranking him even above Horace as a satirist. To the public this concession seemed to put Perrault on the side of moderation. It also gave him the opportunity to rank another modern writer above the ancients. Praises given to him at the expense of his beloved Horace did not flatter Boileau's ego, however, nor was he vain enough to be disloyal to the ancients.

The next gun fired in the battle was Boileau's *Satire X, Against Women*. Although there were several women on the side of the Ancients, among them Mme de Sévigné, most were partisans of Perrault. Instead of trying to win them over, Boileau alienated them. Bossuet roundly attacked Boileau in his *Treatise on Concupiscence*, accusing him of having condemned marriage and of having sacrificed women's modesty to his desire for pretty verse. Regnard, the comic author whom Boileau had esteemed, defended women in a satire against husbands.[4] When Boileau complained of this new enemy, Regnard replied in a play, *The Tomb of Boileau*, in which he redoubles his insults. This estrangement was only temporary, however, for the two were reconciled in 1705.

Regnard dedicated to Boileau his play *Les Ménechmes* and declared himself a respectful disciple of Boileau.

In an *Apologie des femmes,* Perrault replied to Boileau's *Satire X* and attempted to defend and win over the ladies alienated by Boileau. It was preceded by a preface in which Perrault condemns *Satire X* in the name of morality and good taste. Perrault was particularly vicious in his picture of Boileau as a crabby old bachelor. La Bruyère, a partisan of the Ancients recently elected to the Academy (1693), denounced Perrault's outrageous judgment in the preface to his discourse of reception.

V Reflexions on Longinus

Finally, in 1694, appeared the *Réflexions sur Longin,* Boileau's main contribution to the quarrel. There are twelve of these *Réflexions,* but only the first nine deal with the Quarrel of the Ancients and Moderns and were published at this time. In the *Réflexions* Boileau's object is to show in how many places in the *Parallèles* Perrault is mistaken about the ancients, either from prejudice, ignorance, or a new type of pedantry—that of the man who considers worthless, in comparison with his own, the judgments of readers during a period of nearly two thousand years. He brings out the instances where Perrault had given inaccurate, unfaithful, or flat versions of Homer and other ancient writers, and Boileau's own translations, exact and elegant for the most part, point up the errors of his adversary. Boileau undertakes no reasoned or ordered defense or apology for the ancients; he professes no positive theory to oppose the idea of progress or the perpetuity of nature. Perhaps he had no positive doctrine to state or perhaps he deemed it sufficient defense to show that the greatest adversary of the ancients was so ignorant that he was unable to know and judge those whom he attacked. Not content with simply condemning Perrault for using poor Latin translations of Greek literature, Boileau criticizes him for putting this Latin into bad French, insinuating thereby that Perrault not only did not know Greek, but did not know Latin or even French very well. Boileau's style is harsh and sometimes insulting—an almost inevitable result of his method, which was to point out Perrault's errors in an essentially negative criticism. As a work of criticism, the *Réflexions sur Longin* are decidedly disappointing in their negativism and lack of positive defense of the ancients. Absent also is a systematic attack on the bases of the Moderns' doctrine. It remains a mystery why Boileau did not even get to the real heart of the matter, either in his defense of the ancients or in attacking the Moderns' theories. Perhaps it may be attributed to Boileau's essentially satirical and negative spirit and to the fact that he was in basic sympathy with much of what the Moderns believed, especially their exaltation of the century of Louis XIV.

VI *Arnauld's Defense of Boileau; Reconciliation*

Neither Perrault nor Boileau actually went to the heart of the question or debated the matter on principle. By now the main question had been shunted aside by the personal turn the dispute had taken. The general public had little to gain by a continuation of the quarrel, and hostilities were ended between Boileau and Perrault by the intervention of the Jansenist theologian Arnauld. Arnauld, now eighty-two years old and in exile in Brussels, received from Perrault a copy of the *Apologie des femmes*. Perrault had thought that Arnauld would share his opinions, but he was mistaken. Arnauld, far from being shocked at Boileau's attack on the vices of women, was of the same opinion. In May of 1694 Perrault received from Arnauld a long letter in Boileau's favor and in support of *Satire X*. Before Arnauld's exile, he and Boileau had met and formed a mutual attraction for each other. Boileau admired the vast intelligence and ascetic morality of the Jansenist leader, while Arnauld was favorably impressed by Boileau's support of Jansenism, his praise of Port-Royal and the virtues of an austere education, and his censure of novels and operas. Arnauld defended Boileau vigorously, finding the best parts of *Satire X* to be those most strongly blamed by Perrault. Arnauld saw in Boileau a staunch defender of public morality and honesty. The letter from Arnauld closed with a plea for reconciliation between the two, a reconciliation which finally came about.

Arnauld's defense filled Boileau with joy and assurance. It was a much-needed support in the midst of the attacks of the Moderns, but the principal satisfaction came from the profound esteem Boileau felt for Arnauld's virtue and upright character. He learned of Arnauld's letter in June 1694 and hastened to write a reply, thanking Arnauld for his defense in a beautiful letter, and manifesting his pride in their friendship. Boileau was willing to follow Arnauld's advice for a reconciliation and sent Racine and another friend to Perrault with an offer of peace. The offer does credit to Boileau's character and goodness of heart. Perrault, who harbored more bitterness and conceit, received the offer badly and, before agreeing to a reconciliation, demanded of Boileau an admiration of his works which Boileau in conscience could not promise. Nevertheless, Boileau declared that he was ready to do whatever Arnauld might want, with the condition that Arnauld's letter be published, so that he (Boileau) might not be deprived of the greatest honor of his life. The publication of the letter finally convinced Perrault to give in and, on August 4, 1694, they were reconciled—four days before the death of Arnauld, who never heard the news.

Perrault had asked Boileau to soften their differences in his next edition and, in the edition of 1701, he kept his promise. He removed from *Satire X* fourteen verses which particularly offended Perrault and published a *Lettre à Perrault* in which he attenuated somewhat his anti-modern thesis. Boileau remarked that neither he nor Perrault had changed his fundamental position, and compared their mutual compliments to those of Ajax and Hector in the *Iliad*. Boileau was willing to concede the superiority of modern France in many genres of fine arts and literature. He was never as much an opponent of the modern writers as he was a defender of the ancients, and he recognized the eminent position posterity would accord to some of his greatest contemporaries. Perrault, in the fourth volume of *Parallèles* (1697), was fairer toward the ancients and confined the discussion for the most part to science and philosophy rather than letters. This phase of the quarrel was now over, though it was to break out again in the eighteenth century with different adversaries. For the time being Boileau had fought a successful rear-guard action, but the Moderns were ultimately victorious because of popular opinion and the rationalistic spirit of the times, because they put forth a simple and logical argument and made fewer concessions, and because Boileau had not expressed clearly his reasons for admiration of the ancients—an admiration perhaps impossible to express.

VII *Summary*

Idea of Progress

The thesis of the Moderns is simple and vigorous, resting on three essential arguments: progress and the perpetuity of nature's creative force; Christianity; and the evolution of technique. According to the theory of progress, literature cannot escape the general law that civilization has progressed because of reason and experience. This universal reason, deductive and experimental, may discern in literature the rules and techniques which, when properly observed, result in masterpieces. (How much more really "modern" is Boileau than the Moderns in his recognition of the necessity for genius and imagination. And, in his ideas on the sublime, he realized that the rules are no sure method to reach perfection.) Since modern man has had more time to observe and examine the beautiful and has profited from the observations of others, he must consequently know beauty better and, of necessity, be able to write more beautifully. The flaw in the argument is apparent and was pointed out by Fontenelle: what is true of science and technology, which progress gradually and build upon what has been accomplished in the past, is not true of the arts. Beauty does not necessarily depend upon ideas and is not necessarily perfected with time. Perrault's paradox results from the fact that he insisted on judging the ancients from the point of view of the seventeenth century, rather than as one of their own intelligent contemporaries. Hence he felt that the poems of Homer lack unity, do not teach a moral lesson, lack the politeness and mundanity of the seventeenth century, do not obey the *bienséances,* and so forth. Today Perrault's error seems manifest to us and easily refutable. However, Boileau never thought of making a distinction between judging as a contemporary and as a contemporary of the author. He tried to show that Homer was just as much a man of the seventeenth century as anyone else, making the mistake of trying to argue with Perrault from the same point of view and using the same line of reasoning. This is one reason for the weakness of his arguments—a lack of historical perspective.

Christianity

The second part of the Moderns' thesis is based on Christianity and states that poetry inspired by a true religion is, by that very fact, superior to poetry which exploits pagan mythology. Boileau's answer to this argument, stated in several places in his critical and theoretical writings, was that the mysteries of the Christian religion are so sacred that they should not be debased by use in such frivolous pastime as poetry. If mingled with fictions of any kind, they run the risk of being disbelieved along with the apparent fiction. Both Perrault and Boileau are incorrect. In reading the ancient poets, we take into account the fact that, in most cases, the gods of Olympus represented to them true religion and not pagan mythology, and we read accordingly. Moreover, since Graeco-Roman mythology has become part and parcel of the heritage of Western civilization, poets who are Christian may still write poetry utilizing the ancient myths, which are a common treasury for metaphor, allegory, and classical allusions as well as beautiful legends in themselves. As for Boileau's argument, one need only call to mind Dante and Milton to show that poetry on a Christian subject may be both beautiful and completely free of danger to the faith. Boileau unfortunately did not know Milton's work and is more influenced in his ideas by Tasso and the French epic attempts of the seventeenth century than by Dante. If one reads some of the Christian epics produced by his contemporaries, Boileau's position becomes more understandable.

Evolution of Technique

The Moderns' doctrine of the evolution of technique states that the practical knowledge which constitutes the trade of the poet, painter, or sculptor never ceases to increase and improve and that, consequently, time will bring works of art closer to perfection. Perrault, in the fourth book of *Parallèles*, recognizes two types of beauties; one is universal and absolute, with mathematical or intellectual foundations, which satisfies reason; the other is individual and relative, of an artistic or literary order, which satisfies taste. Reason decrees that the ancients are inferior; taste cannot forever keep this viewpoint from prevailing. It is certainly true that technique may improve with knowledge and experience, just as techniques may also be lost. However, Perrault's argument is obviously faulty in not giving sufficient importance to factors such as genius and inspiration. We have only to observe that in tragedy, sculpture, and philosophy, to name only a few areas, the Greeks have never been equalled. Nor have the cathedrals and stained-glass windows of the Middle Ages been surpassed in spite of improved techniques.

Boileau's Position

The position of Boileau, as leader of the Ancients, was much less firm than Perrault's because he was not only an Ancient but modern himself and thought like the Moderns in many ways. He was an intellectual rationalist and had even fought against the authority of the ancients when this authority was contrary to reason and common sense (cf. *l'Arrêt burlesque*). He had no more use than Perrault for Latinizers or pedants and was a modern in the domain of language. Although he favored Latin as being less verbose and more sonorous for inscriptions and monuments, he ridiculed those pedants who composed Latin poetry, and he believed that no one could speak or write well in a dead language. Even in his translation of Longinus he modernized so that the text might be more understandable to the reader. Boileau enjoyed and appreciated the poetry of the ancients, and he felt, in a vague way, their poetic beauty which was foreign to his time and milieu. He felt it his duty to show that the Greek poets are noble, polished, and beautiful, that their works are clear and easily understood and contain qualities which a gentleman of the seventeenth century might admire. His taste was good and he had a correct feeling for poetry in general and for the poetry of antiquity in particular. He lacked, however, the historical perspective necessary to state exactly why the ancients are worthy of esteem. Boileau let himself be drawn into polemics and invective by the personal character of the dispute with Perrault and his own feeling of righteous indignation that his beloved ancients even required defense. There was too much animosity involved to favor a calm and rational discussion. Besides, Boileau's naturally satirical spirit dominates his arguments. Thus the *Reflexions sur Longin* are written in a journalistic and polemical style, and even the title is misleading, since Longinus serves only as a starting point and pretext for inveighing against Perrault's errors.

Perrault had logical reasoning on his side, but was incapable of appreciating poetry. On his side, Boileau had good taste and poetic sentiment. He too spoke much of reason, but also tried to maintain the rights of the artist and to bring into accord the true and the beautiful. As both rationalist and artist, Boileau was

hampered by his own inconsistencies, even though in his tendencies he was more right than the narrowly rationalistic and
fundamentally anti-poetical Perrault. Boileau was unable to conceive the problem clearly or to resolve it. He was incapable of
expressing his reasons, while those of Perrault were easily followed.

In summary, the whole argument, in the arts, is specious. Neither ancients nor moderns are superior to the other, *qua* ancient or
modern, but each artist should be judged on his own merit. In the
fine arts and literature all three bases of the Moderns' argument
are false. The Ancients should not have tried to prove the superiority of the artists of antiquity but that the modern writers were
not superior. The basic error of the Moderns' proofs, together
with the doctrine of universal consent, should have sufficed to resolve the Quarrel of the Ancients and Moderns in favor of the
former or at least in a draw, had the argument been stated in this
way. No one did so.

The best and most reasonable pages written during the entire
quarrel are those of Boileau in his letter to Perrault after their
reconciliation. In this letter Boileau, rising above pettiness and entirely negative criticism, looks at the whole question with a broad
and penetrating view. The truest admirers of antiquity are not the
pedants who read the ancients to make a parade of their learning,
but gentlemen of the world, even princes of the blood, whose
good taste is a matter of common knowledge. While unwilling to
admit that the century of *Louis le Grand* is greater than all others
combined, Boileau is ready to concede, even pleased to concede,
that it is greater than any other single period in the history of
civilization, including the century of Augustus. He then proceeds
to a parallel of his own, between the France of Louis XIV and the
Rome of Augustus, sometimes giving the advantage to the moderns and sometimes preferring the ancients, but with fairness to
both. With admirable accuracy, Boileau drew up the list, which is
still generally valid, of those seventeenth-century figures who
would best recommend their age to posterity. In a few pages Boileau spoke more truth than Perrault had done in four volumes of
Parallèles. In opposition to Perrault's theory of progress, Boileau
substituted the even more modern and reasonable theory of evolution of genres. Thus there is some rational explanation for the
beauty of works of art and for the richness of a certain genre in

one period and its decay and the substitution of another genre in a different period. The general movement of literature is made up of a number of individual movements of various genres, each moving at different speeds. Decadence in one genre, which often follows the near-perfect achievement of a genius, is accompanied by progress in another. Tragedy declined after Sophocles and Euripides until the time of Shakespeare. The seventeenth century in France was the heyday of the theater, while the nineteenth century saw the supremacy of the novel and of lyric poetry. Thus Boileau improved on Perrault's theory of progress, which violated the facts in its constant regularity. He advanced a more flexible literary and artistic principle and one which is much closer to the truth.

CHAPTER 6

Boileau the Artist

I N order to appreciate Boileau as an artist we must make every
effort to rid ourselves of the prejudice, evolved since the era
of Romanticism, which requires emotion in poetry. Many of our
judgments of Boileau have been unfairly colored by the criticism
of the nineteenth-century Romantics who attacked him as a way
of condemning their neo-classical contemporaries. These critics
tended to see Boileau's poetry as abstract and banal, monoto-
nously elegant without any real poetic expression. To them his
verse was nude and skeletal, always divided at the hemistich and
marching inexorably in Alexandrine rhymed couplets. We must
exercise care not to confound poetry with versification and style,
which are simply technical procedures. Today, having become
accustomed to the rich sonorities of Romantic verse, the chiseled
perfection of Parnassian verse, and the suggestive musicality of
Symbolist verse, we have a tendency to consider classical verse
rather poor and thin. La Fontaine is, of course, the exception.
However, the critic should always try to judge from the viewpoint
of an intelligent contemporary of his author. For this reason we
should not expect from Boileau a mode of poetic expression
which was simply not known in his time. Boileau selected the
mode of expression which was available to him, unaware of the
possibilties which would later accrue to the language. The stylistic procedures created in prose by Chateaubriand and continued
and perfected by the Romantic poets were unheard of and un-
imaginable to a poet of the seventeenth century. Boileau's style is
the least sensational and impressionistic imaginable.

I *Form: Rhyme and Rhythm*

While the poetry of Boileau has often been contested, it is impossible to deny that Boileau is an artist. Verse is for Boileau an
art, and one of the highest forms of art, with its own natural

beauty as well as the beauty inherent in translating the character of an idea into sensations for the ear. Much criticism has been directed against Boileau, especially from English speakers, long accustomed to blank verse, for the importance he attached to rhyme. To Boileau and his contemporaries, as well as his predecessors, rhyme was an absolutely necessary ingredient of poetry and, in spite of various literary movements which had as their goal the emancipation of poetry from the rules, the vast majority of French poetry since Boileau has been in rhyme. This aspect of French poetry has always been most difficult for an English speaker to understand, accustomed to a language in which every word has an accented syllable. Because of this combination of accented and unaccented syllables of each word, which roughly corresponds to the long and short syllables of Greek or Latin verse, English poetry may be scanned in a fashion similar to Latin, in feet of various types, such as iambs, trochees, and anapaests. In French, where the accent falls according to breath groups, with the accent always on the last syllable of the word at the end of the breath group, another system of prosody has, of necessity, evolved. In the absence of the traditional prosody of antiquity, it was felt until comparatively recent times that rhyme was a necessary quality of French poetry in order to mark the end of a poetic line. Given this attitude toward rhyme, it is easy to understand Boileau's concern with the accord of rhyme and reason. Boileau demonstrates his understanding of the function of rhyme in his condemnation of the use of facile and banal rhyme just to fill up the space at the end of a line with a sound like the end of the previous line. The accord of rhyme and reason was to him simply the invention of a form which would realize perfectly the idea being expressed.

In practice Boileau rarely uses the weak, the easy, the expected rhyme for which he criticized others. On the contrary, his rhyme is most often rich, expressive, and sometimes quite unexpected. Usually at least one of the two rhyming words is significant and quite often both. It was this refusal to utilize banal rhyme, together with the difficulty he experienced in making transitions from one idea or image to the next, that made composition so difficult for Boileau.

Boileau does indeed divide his verse at the hemistich, the fundamental form for him and his contemporaries and a characteris-

tic of the Alexandrine line. On the other hand, his Alexandrines
are far from being stiff or compassed. The displacement of the
caesura, *enjambement,* and all other methods of making verse
more supple were known and used by him, but with restraint, so
that when used the maximum effect is obtained.

II   *Harmony*

Boileau particularly excels in the expressive harmony of his
verse. Imitative harmony was, of course, known to every rhetorician and taught in every rhetoric textbook, but Boileau's imitative
harmony is not of the sort which has so often been ridiculously
abused. It is. the result of a very fine correspondence between the
character of the thought and the sound of the verse. Here are
examples, both taken from *le Lutrin,* of the sonority of Boileau's
imitative harmony:

> Les Cloches dans les airs de leurs voix argentines
> Appeloient à grand bruit les Chantres à Matines. (Canto IV,
>   ll. 1–2)

> (The bells through the air, with their silvery voices, called,
>   with loud sound, the choir to matins.)

> Sous les coups redoublez tous les bancs retentissent;
> Les murs en sont émûs; les voûtes en mugissent;
> Et l'Orgue mesme en pousse un long gemissement. (Canto III,
>   ll. 157–159)

> (Under the redoubled blows all the benches resound;
> The walls are moved by them and the vaulted ceiling moans;
> And even the organ sighs a long groan.)

It might be noted in passing that Boileau's imitative harmony is
accomplished without benefit of alliteration, which was frowned
upon in French prosody. He is one of the first to have made such a
happy use of imitative harmony.

One of our difficulties on reading Boileau's poetry is that we use
our eyes and minds too much, to the virtual exclusion of our ears.
His own practice should serve as our example, for he judged his
own verse by the sound to his ear. He read it aloud before publi-

cation—to himself, to close friends, and then in salon gatherings. Boileau had a reputation for his ability to read aloud, and he often did so with such liveliness and perfection as to win the enthusiasm of even the coolest listeners. He read as a poet, bringing out all the harmonious effects which escape the reader who does not hear the sound of what he reads. Words were most important to Boileau, not only as signs but primarily as sounds. It is especially to the ear that Boileau appeals for the detection of the sublime, where the sound and the thought are so unified as to become inseparable.

III *Visual Imagery; Realism*

Boileau is an excellent descriptive poet who uses visual imagery not only for objects but also for ideas. He saw things concretely and was able to recall visual images of them. Even if his poetic imagination was weak, he had recall of former scenes and sensations which turned to visual imagery in his mind. He was able to represent, with perfect exactitude, any place or event that he had seen. This is one of the secrets of his poetry—his ability to see and make his reader see. He does not have the epic, or the oratorical, or the lyric gift; he is primarily a realist. In the *Repas ridicule* (*Satire III*), the *Embarras de Paris* (*Satire VI*), the *Lutrin*, the *Satire contre les femmes* (*Satire X*), he may be compared with Villon and Baudelaire, two other great poets of the city of Paris. His realism is generally oriented toward small and insignificant things of daily life. He tried to describe, with elegance, the banal and petty and to bring them into the domain of polite poetry. The interest and merit of his verses is thus not in the subject or material but in the treatment. Boileau is a realist in the full strength and meaning of the term.

A creative imagination, able to give form to the ideal and the immaterial, was not present in Boileau. He is not a psychologist, like most of his great contemporaries, and he lacks a sense of the inner and invisible realities. Especially is he weak in the matter of sentiment, and this is why his poetry must be demonstrated rather than simply felt. His real poetry must be found especially in those works which are usually treated as insignificant—his descriptions of the ridiculous meal, of the city of Paris, of the quarrel in the Sainte Chapelle. He was born and reared in Paris and lived there all his life, so he is primarily a poet of the city. He loved the country whenever he went there, but with an affection completely different from the Romantic effusion of a later age, which often led to the pathetic fallacy. His enjoyment of nature had little intel-lectual or emotional value or result. He asked of nature only relax-ation and quiet beauty and did not possess the pantheistic imagi-nation required to grasp the soul of nature. Even had he been able to do so, he would not have been able to describe it, both because of his natural temperament and because the versification and language of his time were insufficient to accomplish it. He was poetically inspired by his garden at Auteuil, which was more suited to his personality than nature in the raw. It is an attitude common to his century, which is best exemplified by the formal gardens of Versailles. But Paris, with its throngs, its tumult, its traffic jams, its mud—this is what makes Boileau's poetry.

Boileau's best poetic qualities, as well as his worst, may be found in *le Lutrin*. The poem as a whole lacks action and the dialogue is far from sparkling. The subject is encumbered by too many cold allegories. The over-all invention is poor, but the ques-tion may well be posed whether Boileau ever really invented or whether he simply remembered, as Lanson states.[1] The events of *le Lutrin* are based on an actual event which Boileau either knew from first hand or from eyewitnesses. The use of books as missiles may have been suggested to him by a meeting of the Academy in which Tallemant and Charpentier allegedly threw dictionaries at each other's heads; he had surely heard of the time when Cardinal de Retz had made the furious prince de Condé bow under his episcopal benediction. All these memories make up part of a poem in which psychological and philosophical depth are surely lacking, but which is the most exact and living picture of the man-ners of a certain class of clergy which one could possibly find. The sketch contains an irresistible, mischievous gaiety, composed of a series of tableaux of picturesque description. What could be more realistically gay than Boileau's picture of the swollen-faced eccle-siastic sunk in slumber in his comfortable bed, or the eating and drinking of the clerics? Such a picture could only be equalled in a painting by Peter Brueghel the Elder, and indeed Boileau often appears to be more a painter than a poet. Wit is also found in what is offered to the ear as well as the eye, in the parody of the oratorical procedures of the contemporary epic. We may be sure that, in this reverse burlesque, Boileau was making fun of contemporary writers of Christian epics rather than Homer or Virgil, whom he adored too much to parody.

In *Satire X*, Boileau's realism approaches at times the brutal. He does not shrink from reality, even when it may be repugnant. His description of a woman's breath smelling of garlic and tobacco after a meal, of her cosmetic-produced beauty being wiped off at night, are sufficiently realistic to satisfy even a Zola. At almost every turn one may find these little tableaux of realistic color, even when Boileau is ostensibly moralizing. He had the knack of making these pictures immediately visible to the readers' eyes. There is seldom any lyricism, fantasy, or subjective element in Boileau's poetry, and for this very reason we have not done him justice. Boileau approaches the lyric only in his satirical enthusiasm or when dealing, as in *Epître XII* (*On Love for God*), with a favorite idea. (Even here he is animated also by a polemical spirit against the Jesuits.) The subjective element of his poetry is to be found in the ideas which, while not usually original, were nonetheless believed strongly.

We are accustomed, unfortunately perhaps, to seeing enthusiasm, passion, and subjectivity of emotions as the necessary ingredients of true poetry. We have difficulty appreciating a poet who is emotionally unmoved by nature except in its serene and restful aspect, who seems to have been unaware personally of the existence of love, who is not disgusted by the unwashed masses or the petty bourgeois nor an enemy of the society in which he must live. It is equally difficult for us to get away from the Romantic picture of the unappreciated poet, starving in his unheated garret, in order to appreciate a man who, like Boileau, was financially well-off and esteemed both by his king and the general reading public. However, one would deny Boileau the name of poet only at the risk of denying all realistic poetry. He must be judged on the basis of his time rather than in comparison with the beauties of Romanticism. Boileau has his beauties, but they are of a different kind.

IV *The Moralist*

It is as a moralist that Boileau has been most vehemently criticized, and this is perhaps the weakest aspect of his verse. Because of the society in which he lived and because of his education, he was prevented from following his own artistic originality. There are too few *Embarras de Paris* and *Lutrins* in his total production.

Obeying the taste of the age and his own admiration for the ancients, as well as his polemical nature and righteous indignation, Boileau wrote too many moral poems. As a moralist or original philosopher, Boileau is mediocre. He is seldom able to penetrate beyond externals or do much more than repeat commonplaces. We must avoid being too critical on this score, however, for again Boileau is the victim of a notion, current in the seventeenth century, that poetry should not be subjective, or at least not evidently so. Deprived of the benefit of recording his own experiences which, even if not particularly original, would at least have added color to the poems, there was little left in a moral discourse except to repeat commonplaces. And is there anything so wrong with this, provided the poet repeats them with taste, originality of expression, and brings them up to date for contemporaries to whom they were perhaps not so banal as they appear to us? Perhaps Boileau should be criticized rather for choosing to write moral discourses at all than for not writing them in a subjective style. However, for those who do not insist on the absolute originality of a poem in order to appreciate its originality of expression, Boileau's moral poems have much to offer. This is especially true of such works as *Epître XII*, which obviously proceeds from a deeply felt belief in the necessity for loving God.

V *Transitions; Uneven Style*

In spite of the richness of his rhymes, the elegant sonority of his verse, the verve of his satirical traits, we are constantly bothered in much of Boileau's poetry by the awkwardness of his transitions. Transitions gave Boileau a great deal of trouble, and he considered the art of making easy shifts from one idea or image to another the most difficult task of the poet. This difficulty is particularly felt by the piecemeal writer, who puts together his work from sections separately composed and then patiently brought together, somewhat in the fashion of a patchwork quilt with a definite pattern. Like a patchwork quilt, the different sections may be all to obvious and, frequently, too numerous. On the other hand, one may still appreciate the ensemble and its effect, as well as the individual sections, made in the same pattern but with differently colored material. The same is true of Boileau's poetry, especially the *Satires* and *Epîtres*, where the individual sections are often more pleasing than the whole poem. Neither Boileau nor his contemporaries could conceive of an impressionistic poetry, without continuity or connections except in the imagery or metaphor, or without a definite subject. Instead of presenting short pieces, in each of which there would appear, in reduced proportions, various aspects of common daily life, he felt obliged to join them into a whole and to give them unity where unity scarcely existed. Boileau is thus forced to use the form of satire or moral epistle when the intention of the various sections composing the poem is not necessarily moral or even satirical. Moral or satirical unity is thus imposed on picturesque fragments. In *Satire X*, for example, he has to imagine he is addressing himself to a friend who is contemplating marriage in order to impose unity on a series of studies of various types of women to be found in society. By the very joining of these fragments on women, he necessarily gives himself the appearance of a grouchy old bachelor—a picture which, in reality, could hardly be farther from the truth in one who was so popular in salon society.

Boileau also suffers, as an artist, from an inability to maintain his best style. The reasons for this may be found in his conviction that style should be varied and avoid sameness, as well as in the tendency towards abstraction and morality already mentioned. He consciously alters his style by the use of rhetorical devices and, subconsciously perhaps, changes an image into an abstraction and the concrete into analysis. The thinker, as Lanson puts it,[2] is often an obstacle to the painter. The idea drives out the sensation; the notion of truth or error, of good or evil interferes with a perception of form, color, and sound. Often the things he most compliments himself for, e.g., the ability to say the commonplace in noble terms, are actually farthest from his true genius and originality which was in describing the commonplace and the everyday just as he had seen and remembered it. We are less easily satisfied perhaps than his contemporaries, because we have seen more types of poetry, both excellent and execrable. The fact remains that what displeases us in his poetry pleased his contemporaries. The *Satires* and *Epîtres* were considered well thought out and well written in his century, and they were certainly masterpieces of their genres in comparison with what was being done.

VI *Enthusiasm in Satires*

When Boileau deals with literary satire, as opposed to moral satire, he is indeed a poet in the more modern sense. His material evoked his enthusiasm and the emotion of which he was capable, and this enthusiasm is catching. If we are used to thinking of poetry as coming from the heart, we must surely count his literary satire as true poetry, for literature was Boileau's passion. Even here, however, we see the same inability to sustain his inspiration, and his difficulty in giving continuity to fragments. Often the most fecund ideas of his criticism and theory, beautifully expressed in memorable lines, are found in the midst of a discourse on another subject entirely. For example, *Epître IX*, one of the most important of his critical works, is written to show that the great Colbert is exempt from flattery and that ease and luxury are responsible for false vanity and the corollary false praises. In *Satire IV* (*On Human Folly*) there are a number of conventional pictures of human types, such as the pedant, the bigot, the libertine, the miser, the spendthrift, the gallant—most of which are commonplace and lack relief. Suddenly the poet takes fire when he describes Chapelain in the serene fatuousness of the author content with everything he does. What there is of poetry in his satires has the same origin as the poetry of his realistic descriptive passages—what he remembers having seen or, in the case of literary satire, read. His passion and emotion, the subjective side of his nature, is found almost exclusively in his enthusiasm for literature.

As Lanson states,[3] Boileau's poetry is shut up in his works, often stifled. But this is no reason to deny it when it does make itself felt. And what is poor in his verse ought not to blind us to its originality and to what good it contains.

CHAPTER 7

Boileau's Subsequent Reputation

MANY writers in the history of literature have been more widely read than Boileau, but few bear so heavy a burden, for his works have often become pedagogical devices rather than objects of beauty. For two centuries, generations of French schoolboys studied, memorized, and explicated his poems and were nurtured on his legend as "législateur du Parnasse." The result, when not outright dislike, has often been the excessive familiarity which risks breeding contempt. As soon as French authors were admitted to study in the schools, Boileau was first to take his place, both as a model of sober and sane style and as a purveyor of morality. He became, for many French schoolboys, a creature of abstraction rather than a living person. Probably no other writer has suffered to such an extent from the dehumanizing process. Boileau deserves a better fate.

In France alone, during his own lifetime, there were more than one hundred and twenty-five editions of his works, of which over sixty were complete, i.e., all he had composed up to the time.[1] During the nineteenth century, when Boileau was least in favor with the public, there were over one hundred editions of his works, many of which were school text editions representing many more actual copies in circulation than a commercial edition. This count of editions is more than enough to establish both Boileau's popularity and his influence. The number of editions also indicates Boileau's pedagogical function, for, in general, he is not the sort of writer one reads in moments of idle leisure for pleasure, but for instruction, either voluntary or under the prodding of a schoolmaster.

I *Influence on Contemporaries*

In spite of Boileau's success among his contemporaries, we may see from Louis XIV's pension lists and from the results of elections to the Academy that Boileau's doctrines and taste were not accepted to the exclusion of all others. In general he reflects the spirit of the century, but this spirit was by no means unanimous, and the writers condemned by Boileau still had their partisans. There was also a considerable group of readers with a catholicity of tastes, who were able to appreciate all sorts of literature—the *précieux*, the burlesque, the *romanesque* (adventure novel) as well as the classical. As we have seen in Chapter 5 on the Quarrel of the Ancients and the Moderns, public opinion was generally either lukewarm or in favor of the Moderns through a natural inclination toward its own century. Since nearly everyone was of the same opinion on matters of doctrine and theory, even Boileau and Chapelain as René Bray has pointed out,[2] the basis of judgment in literature was talent. Here Boileau had the decided advantage over those he attacked and, as soon as personalities and literary quarrels were forgotten, it was recognized that Boileau had infinitely more talent.

II   *Influence in Eighteenth Century*

In the eighteenth century, up to the time of Rousseau, opinion of Boileau varied, depending on whether one belonged to the rationalist or the sentimentalist schools or, as was Voltaire's case, somewhat to both. He was condemned by the sentimentalists and praised by the rationalists. After 1760 opposition to Boileau became more vocal, developing into a *querelle Boileau* between critics who represented tradition, reason, the *bienséances*, and *vraisemblance* as opposed to the critics of the budding movement which would blossom into Romanticism. Voltaire and d'Alembert, among others, tried to bring about some accord between the two, but it was a rear-guard action which realized little success at the time and was doomed to eventual failure. Boileau was accused of having stifled and discouraged young talents with his rules, of lacking sentiment, and of being a pedant.

Perhaps Boileau's influence may best be seen by going outside France in the eighteenth century. All over Europe Boileau and especially the *Art poétique* were appreciated, not only for intrinsic merit but, perhaps more importantly, because Boileau was considered the most exact representative of the French spirit. Not since the late twelfth and thirteenth centuries had French language and mundanity enjoyed such universal acceptance and admiration, and Boileau profited from this pan-European attitude. Everywhere the *Art poétique* was read, esteemed, and invested with authority. In the England of the Augustan Age Boileau was influential, although not universally accepted as the final authority in literary matters. In England Boileau's precepts contributed to instilling in literature a discipline and restraint which it had often hitherto lacked. Although he was less influential perhaps in the Latin countries, he was known and appreciated. For example, the *Art poétique* was translated by Ericeyra into Portuguese during Boileau's own lifetime.

Especially did Boileau's example show that one could be a literary critic and theorist without being pedantic. His reputation and his verse, many lines of which had become literary proverbs, demonstrated that a theorist can have influence on literature or even create a new direction for it. Insisting on seeing Boileau as an innovator and the creator of a literary movement, European critics such as Dryden, Pope, Gottsched, Lessing, and others looked to his example and authority in attempting to create a national spirit in literature in their countries. Again one must exercise caution in separating the influence of Boileau from the pervading influence of the French spirit which he so well represented. It was not necessarily Boileau that foreigners sought, but the French taste, of which he was taken as the supreme arbiter.

III *Rationalists' Distortion of Boileau*

One cannot really understand the attitude toward Boileau of the nineteenth century without first comprehending what the eighteenth-century rationalists had done to his image. The attitude of the nineteenth century, and to a great extent of the twentieth, was based not on the real Boileau but on a remaking of him by the rationalists to suit their own ideas. They brought Boileau to their own level in order to use his authority. The rationalists of the eighteenth century, prosaic, limited in imagination and sentiment, hyperintellectual, devoted to thinking in generalities and abstractions, bereft of poetic spontaneity and devoted to form, realized their talent in other genres than poetry. Their intellectualism was best expressed in the discourse, the satirical letter, the treatise, the philosophical voyage. These rationalists accepted the *Art poétique* as gospel, ignoring Boileau's insistence on inspiration, the natural, the simple, and his ideas on the sublime and the *je ne sais quoi*.

Under the name and authority of Boileau, they attempted to glorify their own tastes and tendencies, and succeeded in abandoning Boileau at the point of his greatest originality—the balance between nature and esthetics which is the special beauty of classicism. The rationalists gave to Boileau's doctrine only the narrowest possible interpretation, and this interpretation was almost exclusively based on the *Art poétique*.

Both because of and in spite of the rhetorical education of the Jesuit secondary schools, as Lanson points out,[3] the rationalists had little true appreciation for the ancients, despite much talk of them. Nor did they have the true artistic sense in literature, and hence were unable to create an original poetry. The greatest poet of the century, André Chénier, was also the most thoroughly imbued with the ancients and perhaps the French poet above all others who best assimilated both the ancient form and spirit. He was the exception. In the early years of the century there is little poetry because of an absence of feeling and imagination. Later, when the sentimentalists brought back feeling and imagination, there was no accompanying sense of form because form had been so exalted, to the exclusion of other elements, that it had become atrophied. The truly poetic artists of the century—Marivaux, Buffon, Rousseau—generally abandoned verse in favor of a prose which they helped create and which would reach its culmination in the sonorous majesty of the poetic prose of Chateaubriand. Verse had fallen out of the hands of poets and into those of versifiers, who often reduced it to a mechanical process.

The rationalists did not understand what Boileau truly understood—the particular enjoyment of sounds and rhythm in poetry —nor did they bother with such esthetic questions as had concerned Boileau, such as the *je ne sais quoi* and the sublime. Boileau's insistence on truth and nature were forgotten in the search for form, verisimilitude, and propriety. The rules became an end instead of a means, and dry formalism was the inevitable result. Boileau himself had been able to admit that the rules might be put aside in order to attain the goals of true art, but when rules became the end rather than the means, there could be no exceptions. It is no wonder that the eighteenth century is a prosaic age and that its greatest monuments are intellectual rather than esthetic, in prose rather than in verse. There is little that may be said for any *positive* influence of Boileau in the France of the eighteenth century. His influence is primarily negative and often a denial of those very things he believed in most devotedly. By the end of the century, the neo-classicists were far removed from Boileau, the ancients, and the great artists of the century of Louis XIV.

IV *Nineteenth-Century Attitude Toward Boileau*

Thus Boileau's reputation was compromised by the rationalists of the eighteenth century. In the nineteenth century the neo-classicists took him as their authority and symbol, and the Romantics naturally attacked him as a way of condemning their adversaries. They might have done better to show the neo-classicists how far they had departed from Boileau's classicism, thereby turning against them their own symbol. Unfortunately, Boileau came out of the quarrel with an undeserved reputation as a pedant—a prejudice which still damages him. With the advent of Parnassianism in poetry and Realism in prose, the nineteenth century seemed to be drawing closer to the spirit of Boileau, for this movement was closer in its principles to Classicism than to Romanticism. Then came the Decadent poets and the Symbolists, who seemed again to be drawing away from Boileau in most respects except musicality. Yet they were nearer than the Romantics. In the twentieth century there are both poets and writers of prose, e.g., Valéry and Gide, whose artistic principles have been more like those of Boileau than of any other writer since his death.

In addition to his use in the schools and the distortion of his image by the rationalists, Boileau became a symbol—of correctness, reason, regularity—rather than a living poet. Blame lies with his own partisans and commentators, notably Brossette and Louis Racine,[4] and also with Boileau himself. As an old man, Boileau, the last of his contemporaries, the "grands classiques," tended to think of himself as their mentor and as a writer of moral and didactic poetry. Perhaps this is the image he wished to leave for posterity. In the edition of 1701, his favorite, chronology is abandoned and the poems are detached from their original inspiration in an attempt to give them a timeless and impersonal quality. It is not as much a question of Boileau intentionally falsifying his image as it is the forgetfulness of old age and the tendency to see bygone days in a rosy afterglow of idealism. Boileau truly thought of himself in this way and adopted the role which posterity would assign to him anyway. Teachers tended to forget the *Satires* and *Le Lutrin* and to concentrate on those works which were most pedagogically useful, the *Art poétique* and the moral *Epîtres,* thereby hiding the man under the theorist and moralist.

V *Twentieth-Century Rehumanization*

Scholars of the twentieth century have done signal service in destroying the tenacious legend of Boileau and revealing the real man, who was much more interesting than either the symbol or the theorist. His originality lay not as a legislator of Parnassus nor as an original theorist of literature but as a poet, with much talent and some genius, whose greatest gift was his ability to say, clearly, wittily, and forcefully, what most of his generation thought. Because of the works of such thorough scholars as Lanson, Bray, Mornet, Brody,[5] and others, we know that there was, behind his forbidding exterior, a real man, who lived, felt, struggled, and was thoroughly human. Eventually a real person will be substituted for the academic figure, and Boileau cannot help benefiting from the change.

Nevertheless, there is nearly as much inherent danger in the humanizing of Boileau as there was in the opposite process. If the real Boileau must be shown, it is equally important to realize that the legend also has much truth and, even when not true, has become part and parcel of our image of Boileau. In literature a writer not only is what he was but also what he has become. The extreme must be avoided in humanizing Boileau, so that the didactical moralist will not be wholly eliminated in favor of the satirist and his inspiration of actuality. The fact remains that Boileau wanted to be a moralist, a didactic poet, even a dogmatist. The real Boileau is to be found in both his legend and his actual life and momentary inspiration. He was conscious of posterity, particularly in later life, and was often guided by a desire to instruct. Even if the pedagogical Boileau has been carried to extremes of which he would never have dreamed, he is not entirely innocent.

VI *Summary and Conclusion*

In summary, one could hardly do better than to paraphrase and translate the conclusions of Mornet and Lanson.[6] After Boileau there have always been and will always be writers who are his disciples, consciously or otherwise, and others who want nothing to do with him. All those whose works keep a reflected equilibrium, the mean between the extremes, whose style is clear and sober, continue to follow the spirit of the classical ideal of which Boileau was the best spokesman. For two centuries of French literature what has been found to be healthy, solid, and lasting, and which has been saved from oblivion and the ravages of time, has basically conformed to the doctrines of Boileau. The intimate vices or apparent deformities which have made schools or works forgotten are in general what was condemned, implicitly or expressly, by Boileau. The French cannot get along without him. They have him in their very blood and marrow. They must have truth, clarity, precision. They cannot get along without rhetoric in the best sense of the word, qualities of composition and style which diminish the effort and increase the pleasure of the reader. They prefer to have the author come to them, rather than vice versa. The French are more positivists than metaphysicians or mystics. They want an author to speak to them about man and his humors. They want an author to try to regulate man's conduct. In other words, they want a literature which is psychological, moral, clear, precise, interesting, regular. This is what French taste demands, and this is why there will be for a long time yet something of Boileau in successful works written for the French. After so many years of French cultural influence in Western civilization, and even now in a period where France still remains in the artistic vanguard, what may be said of the French taste may also to a considerable degree be repeated for the Western man of Graeco-Roman and Judaeo-Christian heritage.

Notes and References

Chapter One

1. *Correspondance entre Boileau-Despréaux et Brossette*, ed. Auguste Laverdet (Paris: Techener, 1858), p. 7. Subsequent references to the Boileau-Brossette correspondence will be, by dates, to this edition.

2. Nicolas Boileau-Despréaux, *Lettres à Racine et à divers*, ed. Charles-H. Boudhors (Paris: Société les Belles Lettres, 1943). All references to Boileau's works will be to this edition, published in seven volumes, 1934–43.

3. Jansenism, founded by the Dutch theologian Cornelius Jansen, was a reform movement within the Roman Catholic Church, advocating a return to the ideas of St. Augustine. Jansenism ran afoul of the Church for its extreme predestinarianism, its discouragement of frequent communion, its doctrines on divine grace, and its attacks on the Jesuits and the new casuistry. Jansenism took strong root in France after 1643, where it early became involved with Gallicanism. The papal bull *Unigenitus* (1713) virtually put an end to organized Jansenism, but the movement continued as a tendency within the Church. The Jansenists were in perpetual conflict with the Jesuits in France in the latter half of the seventeenth century.

4. The *Parlement* in France is not a legislative body, like the English Parliament, but a judicial body, a sort of court of appeals.

5. Jean Chapelain (1594–1674) was a poet and critic, founding member of the Académie française, and in charge, under Colbert, of drawing up the annual royal pension lists.

6. René Bray, *La Formation de la doctrine classique en France* (Paris: Hachette, 1927; *reprinted:* Nizet, 1951), *passim.*

7. Daniel Mornet, *Nicolas Boileau* (Paris: Calmann-Lévy, 1941), p. 36.

8. Following are the most important works of scholarship dealing with the "quatre amis" problem, listed chronologically. Charles E. Revillout, *Essais de philologie et de littérature* (Montpellier: Hamelin,

1899), also found in the *Revue d'histoire littéraire de la France* (v. 34–38) in a series of articles; J. Demeure, "Les quatre amis de 'Psyché'," *Mercure de France* 201:331–66, Jan. 15, 1928, "Racine et son ennemi Boileau," *Mercure de France* 205:34–61, July 1, 1928, "L'Introuvable société des 'quatre amis'," *Revue d'histoire littéraire de la France* 36:161–80, 321–36, 1929; Antoine Adam, "L'Ecole de 1660; histoire ou légende?" *Revue d'histoire de la philosophie* ns 7:215–50, 1939.

9. This split occurred when Racine took his play *Alexandre* from Molière's troupe and gave it to the rival hôtel de Bourgogne actors.

10. The critical term *romanesque* in French has nothing to do with the architectural term nor with anything "Roman" but refers to items which might be expected in an adventure novel of the Graeco-Byzantine type, and is usually used derogatorily. The term comes from the French word for the novel, *roman.*

11. Madeline de Scudéry (1607?–1701) was prominent at the salon of Mme de Rambouillet and later established her own literary salon, one of the principal ones of Paris. Her two principal works, *Artamène; ou le grand Cyrus* and *Clélie,* are long, pseudo-historical novels, full of fashionable sentiment, gallantry, and preciosity.

12. See Chapter 4 for more on the *je ne sais quoi.*

13. Letter from Boileau to Racine, from Bourbon, August 19, 1687 (Boudhors edition, p. 31).

14. Nicolas Boileau-Despréaux, *Oeuvres de Mr Boileau-Despréaux, avec des éclaircissements historiques donnés par lui-même,* ed. Claude Brossette (Geneva: Fabri and Barrillot, 1716).

15. Many anecdotes concerning Boileau may be found in the *Bolaeana, ou Bons mots de M. Boileau . . .* published by J. Losme de Montchesnay (Amsterdam: Lhonoré, 1742). The *Bolaeana* may also be found in the edition of Boileau's *Oeuvres* by Lefèvre de Saint-Marc (Paris: David, 1747) and the Chéron edition of 1885. These anecdotes should be taken with extreme caution, as they are the source of some erroneous legends.

Chapter Two

1. Mathurin Régnier (1573–1613) was the nephew of Desportes and opposed the "reform" of Malherbe. He wrote sixteen satires, published in 1613, which are vigorous, realistic, and sometimes licentious.

2. Philippe Quinault (1635–88) was a writer of inferior tragedies and comedies, but the charm and delicacy of his style were well suited to the opera librettos which he wrote in collaboration with Lully. The abbé Charles Cotin (1604–82) was a preacher and writer, butt of the satire of Molière as well as that of Boileau. He was elected to the Academy in 1655.

3. Michel Lambert (1610–96) was the father-in-law of Lully and well-known for promising to be a guest and then never putting in an appearance.

4. Jean Puget de la Serre (1600–65) was royal historiographer and librarian to Monsieur, the king's brother. His name was a symbol of mediocrity.

5. Vincent Voiture (1597–1648) was a leading figure in the hôtel de Rambouillet and a poet in the precious manner. He was not really a bad poet, but Boileau admired him more than he deserved.

6. Mellin de Saint-Gelais (c. 1490–1558) was a poet, longtime resident in Italy, who helped introduce the Italian sonnet form and the spirit of the Renaissance into France.

7. Jean Baptiste Lully (1632–87) was a Florentine who went to France in 1646, entered the service of Louis XIV in 1652. He became chamber composer and conductor of one of the king's orchestras, and composed ballets, many in collaboration with Molière. In 1672 he obtained a patent for the production of opera and established the Académie royale de musique, holding a virtual monopoly of the French operatic stage. Shrewd and unscrupulous, he made a fortune producing his operas, for which Quinault wrote most of the librettos. He established the form of the French overture and set the style for French opera until the advent of Gluck.

8. The *directeurs de conscience* were spiritual advisers for the families in which they lived. The custom probably derived from the practice among the highest nobility of having a confessor and/or almoner attached to the household. The *directeurs de conscience* could be either unattached priests or laymen. Molière's *Tartuffe* is the most violent satire against the *directeur de conscience* who is self-seeking, but there were undoubtedly many sincere and devout men among them.

9. François Payot, chevalier de Lignières (1628–1704), was originally a friend of the Boileau family and then took Nicolas' side against Gilles. The reasons for their break are not clear. He was the drunkard for whom Cyrano fought a hundred men, in Rostand's *Cyrano de Bergerac*.

10. Stagyra was the birthplace of Aristotle, and the Lyceum was his school at Athens.

11. All were well-known philosophers of the seventeenth century.

12. William Harvey (1578–1657) was the first to demonstrate the function of the heart and the complete circulation of the blood. Acceptance of his theories was slow, especially in France.

13. John Duns Scotus (1274–1307) was known as the "subtle doctor" and led the school of philosophy opposed to St. Thomas Aquinas, the "angelic doctor."

14. Georges de Scudéry (1601–67) was brother of Madeline de Scudéry and a secondary collaborator on her novels. He wrote plays and other works and was active in attacking *le Cid* of Corneille.

15. Nicolas Pradon (1632–98) was a mediocre author of tragedies, best known for entering into competition with Racine's *Phèdre*, an action which alone sufficed to rouse Boileau's ire.

16. The *rois fainéants*, from Thierry III (675) to Childéric III (752) were the last of the Merovingian dynasty, who left all authority in the hands of the mayors of the palace.

17. Jacques Coras, besides collaborating on an *Iphigénie* with Le Clerc to compete with Racine's play of the same name, was author of four Biblical epics, *Jonas, Josué, Samson,* and *David*. He was a member of a literary faction opposed to Racine and Boileau.

18. *Renaus de Montauban,* or the *Quatre fils Aymon,* was long one of the most popular of the Old French epics. The oldest existing version dates from the end of the twelfth century. The poem belongs to the cycle of Doön de Mayence or the rebellious vassal cycle.

19. Jean de la Bruyère, *Les Caractères,* "Des Ouvrages de l'esprit" (I, 1).

20. Louis Le Laboureur (1615–79) was also attacked by Boileau in *Epître IX*.

21. Honoré d'Urfé (1567–1625) was the author of the principal French pastoral novel, which, although in an artificially learned style, became the embodiment of courtly manners and conversation, and contains a discriminating analysis of the nobler sentiments. *L'Astrée* had much influence in literature. Marin Le Roy de Gomberville (1600–1674) was the author of *Polexandre, La Caritée,* and *La Cythérée,* all novels of adventure imitated from d'Urfé. Gautier de Costes de la Calprenède (1610–63) was the author of *Cassandre, Cléopâtre,* and *Faramond ou L'Histoire de France,* as well as several plays. Jean Desmarets de Saint-Sorlin (1596–1676) was a protégé of Richelieu, and a founding member of the Academy. A poet and dramatist (*les Visionnaires,* 1637) as well as a novelist, Boileau here mentions him as author of *l'Ariane, l'Aspasie,* and *la Rosane*—adventure novels. A violent adversary of the Jansenists, he also precipitated the Quarrel of the Ancients and Moderns (see Chapter 5).

22. Lucian (c. 125–after 180) is best known for his Greek prose *Dialogues of the Dead,* which became the model for the genre.

23. The abbé Michel de Pure was a preacher and writer, best known because Boileau ridiculed him. His *Ostorius,* which failed at the hôtel de Bourgogne in 1659, was taken from Tacitus (*Annals* XVI, 14–15).

Chapter Three

1. For Desmarets, see note 21, Chapter 2 and also Chapter 5 on the Quarrel of the Ancients and Moderns.

2. Either Crates of Thebes or Aristippus of Cyrene.

3. Since judges purchased their position, it was through the custom of receiving gifts before trial that they made their salaries. This custom was followed by both defendants and plaintiffs and was not generally considered unethical at the time.

4. Quietism, founded by the Spanish priest Miguel de Molinos and spread in France by Mme Guyon, was a heretical form of religious mysticism condemned by Pope Innocent XI in 1687. The essence of quietism is that perfection lies in the complete passivity of the soul before God and the absorption of the individual in the divine love, to the point of annihilation not only of the will but of all effort or desire for effort. Its most famous convert in France was Fénelon, Archbishop of Cambrai, who was opposed by Bossuct. In 1699 Fénelon's book *Les Maximes des saints* was condemned by Innocent XII and Fénelon recanted.

5. Boileau here refers to the *directeurs de conscience*. See note 8, Chapter 2.

6. The words to which Boileau refers are the Greek *homoousia* (consubstantial) and *homoiousia* (similar in substance). The single syllable is formed by the addition of the *iota*.

7. Cf. Pascal, *Lettres provinciales, cinquième lettre, sixième lettre*.

8. Cf. Pascal, *Lettres provinciales, septième lettre*.

9. Cf. Pascal, *Lettres provinciales, neuvième lettre* on the doctrine of mental reservation or restriction.

Chapter Four

1. On Voiture, see note 5, Chapter 2.

2. *Biographia Literaria*, Chapter XIV.

3. *Op. cit.*, pp. 215–30 especially.

4. *Boileau*, 2nd ed. (Paris: Hachette, 1900), p. 155.

5. Honorat de Bueil, seigneur de Racan (1589–1670) was a disciple of Malherbe and author of the pastoral drama, *Les Bergeries* (performed in 1619 and published in 1625).

6. Guillaume de Machault (c.1300–1377) was a poet as well as the greatest French musician of the fourteenth century. Together with his disciple Eustache Deschamps (1340–early 1400's) he contributed most to the establishment of regularity in prosody by means of the *formes fixes*.

7. The *grands rhétoriqueurs*, popular around 1500, were mediocre poets who set much store by poetic technique and virtuosity. They

remained popular until after the middle of the century and the advent of the Pléiade. Jean Marot, father of the better known Clément Marot, was one of their number.

8. Philippe Desportes (1546–1606) was a favorite of Charles IX and Henri III. He was an imitator of the Italians and was especially attacked by Malherbe in his *Commentaires* on Desportes' works. Jean Bertaut (1552–1611) was a contemporary of Ronsard and Desportes and author of melancholy and graceful poetry. Guillaume Du Bartas (1544–90) was a poet and soldier in the Huguenot army of Henri IV. He is known chiefly for his epic poem *La Sepmaine; ou création du monde.* Agrippa d'Aubigné (1552–1630), poet and Huguenot soldier, was the author of *Les Tragiques* (1616) and grandfather of Mme de Maintenon.

9. *Childebrand ou les Sarrasins chassez de France* (1666) was written by Carel de Ste-Garde (1620–84).

10. The beginning lines of George de Scudéry's epic *Alaric.*

11. "*La Dissertation sur Joconde* est-elle de Boileau?" *Revue d'histoire littéraire de la France* 38:337–54, 497–517, 1931.

12. Jules Brody, *Boileau and Longinus* (Geneva: Droz, 1958), pp. 32–33.

13. P. 34.

14. Pp. 40–41.

15. P. 44.

16. P. 58.

17. André Gide, *Billets à Angèle, I* from *Incidences* (Paris: Gallimard, 1924). First published in the *Nouvelle Revue Française,* Vol. XVI (March 1, 1921). Contained in *French Classicism: A Critical Miscellany,* ed. Jules Brody (Englewood Cliffs, New Jersey: Prentice-Hall, 1966), p. 65.

18. P. 74.

19. P. 85.

20. P. 142.

Chapter Five

1. The standard reference on the Quarrel of the Ancients and Moderns is still Hippolyte Rigault, *Histoire de la Querelle des Anciens et des Modernes* (Paris: Hachette, 1856).

2. Pierre-Daniel Huet (1630–1721) was bishop of Avranches and a member of the Academy. An erudite partisan of the ancients, it was Huet to whom La Fontaine addressed his *Epître à Huet.*

3. Gilles Ménage (1613–92) was especially interested in etymology and the rules of language. He was the teacher of Mme de Sévigné and other ladies interested in learning and is made fun of in Molière's *Femmes savantes.* André Dacier (1651–1722) was also a philologist

and best known through his wife, the famous Mme Dacier, who translated the *Iliad*, the *Odyssey*, Aristophanes, and others, and took part in the latter part of the Quarrel of the Ancients and Moderns, defending Homer against Lamotte-Houdar.

4. Jean-François Régnard (1655–1709) was best known for *Le Légataire universel*. Inferior, of course, to Molière, he was nevertheless a good comic dramatist.

Chapter Six

1. *Boileau*, 2nd ed. (Paris: Hachette, 1900), p. 59.

2. P. 68.

3. P. 72. (This entire chapter is especially indebted to Lanson's work and his appreciations, still the best to be found, may be observed throughout.)

Chapter Seven

1. Emile Magne, *Bibliographie générale des oeuvres de Nicolas Boileau-Despréaux* . . . 2 vols. (Paris: Giraud-Badin, 1929).

2. *La Formation de la doctrine classique en France* (Paris: Hachette, 1927), *passim*.

3. *Op. cit.*, p. 190.

4. *Mémoires*, to be found in the *Oeuvres complètes* of Racine, edited by Raymond Picard for the Bibliothèque de la Pléiade (Paris: Gallimard, 1951–52) in two volumes.

5. All of whom have been cited in the text. Their works will be found in the *Selected Bibliography*.

6. Lanson, pp. 204–6; Mornet, *Nicolas Boileau* (Paris: Calmann-Lévy, 1941), pp. 198–99.

Selected Bibliography

Bibliography:

Magne, Emile. *Bibliographie générale des oeuvres de Nicolas Boileau-Despréaux, et de Gilles et Jacques Boileau, suivie des Luttes de Boileau.* . . . 2 vols. Paris: Giraud-Badin, 1929. Indispensable; meticulous scholarship. Introduction and the *Luttes de Boileau* contains much information on Boileau's life, friends, enemies. Also contains some hitherto unpublished documents. Does not include biographical or critical studies on Boileau.

PRIMARY SOURCES

Editions:

Complete Works

Boileau-Despréaux, Nicolas. *Oeuvres diverses du Sr Boileau Despréaux* . . . Nouv. éd. rev. et augm. Paris: Thierry, 1701. Boileau's favorite edition and last one revised by him. Text usually adopted as basic for modern editions.

——. *Oeuvres de Nicolas Boileau-Despréaux.* Nouv. éd. rev. et augm. Paris: Billiot, 1713. First posthumous edition by man who, according to Boileau's will, was to be his accredited publisher.

——. *Oeuvres de Mr Boileau-Despréaux, avec des éclaircissements historiques donnés par lui-même.* 2 vols. (also 4 vols. in-8) Geneva: Fabri and Barrillot, 1716. This is the Brossette edition, important because it contains Brossette's commentary from material supplied by Boileau.

——. *Oeuvres.* . . . Nouv. éd., avec des éclaircissements historiques donnés par lui-même et rédigés par M. Brossette.* . . . Ed. by Charles H. Lefèvre de Saint-Marc. 5 vols. Paris: David, 1747. Includes Montchesnay's *Bolaeana* and excellent notes and prefatory material to *Traité du sublime.*

——. *Oeuvres.* . . . Ed. by Berriat-Saint-Prix. 4 vols. Paris: Langlois, 1830. Now rare and still excellent edition, richly annotated with generous quotations from previous commentators. Still considered the definitive edition by some and should certainly be used along with any other edition.

————. *Oeuvres complètes.* . . . Ed. by A. Charles Gidel. 4 vols. Paris: Garnier, 1870–73. Not as good as Berriat-Saint-Prix but best and most generally available edition before Boudhors edition. Contains all of Boileau's letters, although those to Racine are not originals but as revised by Boileau for publication.

————. *Oeuvres classiques disposées d'après l'ordre chronologique.* . . . Ed. by Charles M. Desgranges. Paris: Hatier, 1914. Helpful presentation because of the chronological order; containing extensive commentary.

————. *Oeuvres.* . . . Ed. by Pierre Clarac. Paris: Mellottée [1936?]. Excellent edition, following a chronological order, of selected works.

————. *Oeuvres complètes.* . . . Ed. by Charles H. Boudhors. 7 vols. Paris: Belles Lettres, 1934–43. Nearest approach, since Berriat-Saint-Prix to a definitive critical edition of the complete works. Notes are scholarly, copious, yet fresh in style. No full-length biography. Lacks index of proper names, which is especially inconvenient since Boileau uses so many. Indispensable, but should be used with Gidel or preferably Berriat-Saint-Prix.

————. *Oeuvres poétiques.* . . . Ed. by F. Brunetière. Paris: Hachette, 1893. Convenient edition in one volume, almost complete. Contains important *Notice* and numerous *Préfaces,* Cotin's *Satire des Satires* (abridged), Voltaire's *Epître à Boileau,* Sainte-Beuve's *Fontaine de Boileau.*

Individual and Selected Works

————. *L'Art poétique.* Ed. by D. Nichol Smith. Cambridge: University Press, 1898. Excellent English edition with good introduction and notes.

————. *L'Art poétique de Boileau, commenté par Boileau et ses contemporains.* Ed. by V. Delaporte. 3 vols. Lille: Société de Saint-Augustin, Desclée, de Brouwer, 1888. Gives, verse by verse, all commentaries and criticisms since seventeenth century.

————. *Bolaeana, ou Bons mots de M. Boileau . . . publié par J. Losme de Montchesnay.* Amsterdam: Lhonoré, 1742. Collection of anecdotes about Boileau and remarks attributed to him. To be used with caution.

————. *Correspondance entre Boileau-Despréaux et Brossette.* . . . Ed. by Auguste Laverdet. Paris: Techener, 1858. Contains Boileau's letters to Brossette and the latter's letters to Boileau, as well as interesting material from Brossette's papers and selections from Brossette's *Mémoires*.

————. *Les Satires de Boileau, commentées par lui-même et publiés avec des notes par Frédéric Lachèvre. Reproduction du Commentaire inédit de Pierre Le Verrier avec les corrections autographes de Despréaux.* Paris: Le Vésinet et Courmenil, 1906. A most important contribution to Boileau scholarship, comparable only to Brossette's commentary. Le Verrier was a friend of Boileau and made his notes on the basis of remarks made by Boileau in his presence, supplemented by Boileau's autograph revisions of these notes, published for first time from the original manuscript.

SECONDARY SOURCES

General Studies of Life and Works:

Bray, René. *Boileau, l'homme et l'oeuvre.* Paris: Boivin, 1942. Excellent recent study, accurate and readable. Contains useful bibliographical guide of editions and studies. Indispensable.

Lanson, Gustave. *Boileau.* Paris: Hachette, 1892 (2nd ed. 1900). One of best general studies, clear and basically sound, masterpiece of critical insight. Dated in some areas of factual information but still the best appreciation of Boileau. Indispensable.

Mornet, Daniel. *Nicolas Boileau.* Paris: Calmann-Lévy, 1941. Excellent and very readable study which attempts to arrive at the real Boileau. Goes a bit too far in seeing Boileau as simply a writer who said what everyone was thinking. Not as balanced as Bray.

Sainte-Beuve, Charles-Augustin. "Boileau," in *Portraits littéraires*, I, 3–22. 3 vols. Paris: Garnier, 1864–83. Writes of Boileau as a passé figure.

————. "La Fontaine de Boileau," in *Portraits littéraires*, I, 23–28. 3 vols. Paris: Garnier, 1864–83. Verse criticism beginning, as his romantic enthusiasm lessens, his series of "rétractions" or "retouches."

————. "Boileau," in *Causeries du lundi*, vol. 6, 494–513. 3rd ed. 15 vols. Paris: Garnier [1850–65]. Pays eloquent tribute to Boileau, yearning for similar discipline among his Romantic contemporaries. Excellent psychological and literary insight. Did much to further now discredited view that Boileau was mentor of his greater contemporaries.

————. *Port-Royal.* . . . Ed. by René L. Doyon and Charles Marchesné. 10 vols. Paris: La Connaissance, 1926–32. Vol. 8, pp. 264–94 and *passim*. Devoted especially to the moralist of later years.

Special Studies:

Adam, Antoine. "L'Ecole de 1660; histoire ou légende?" *Revue d'histoire de la philosophie* ns 7:215–50, 1939. New evidence introduced to show that Racine and Boileau, as well as Boileau and La Fontaine knew each other earlier than conclusions of Demeure would show. Does not try to rehabilitate legend of "quatre amis."

Bonnefon, P. "Charles Perrault, littérateur et académicien. L'opposition à Boileau," *Revue d'histoire littéraire de la France* 12:549–610, 1905. Careful study of the quarrel between Boileau and Perrault.

Borgerhoff, Elbert B. O. "Boileau Satirist animi gratia," *Romanic Review* 43:241–55, 1952. Boileau's use of satire form as means of free expression in an age of restrictions.

———. *The Freedom of French Classicism.* Princeton: Princeton University Press, 1950. Pp. 200–212. Good statement of the role of the sublime in Boileau's thought. Whole book is indispensable for study of classicism.

Bray, René. "La *Dissertation sur Joconde* est-elle de Boileau?" *Revue d'historie littéraire de la France* 38:337–54, 497–517, 1931. Weighty evidence in support of Boileau's authorship, but questioned by Demeure.

———. *La Formation de la doctrine classique en France.* Paris: Hachette, 1927. *Reprinted:* Nizet, 1951. Indispensable for any seventeenth-century study. Shows that the classical theories were generally accepted and not original or unusual with Boileau.

Brody, Jules. *Boileau and Longinus.* Geneva: Droz, 1958. Very important study of Boileau's version of Longinus, showing that Boileau and Longinus are kindred spirits, preoccupied with the emotional impact of literature on the reader. Indispensable study and excellent appreciation of Boileau.

Brunetière, Ferdinand. "Boileau-Despréaux, 1665–1685," in *L'Evolution des genres dans l'histoire de la littérature,* pp. 87–110, 5th ed. Paris: Hachette, 1910. Boileau contributed to bringing the *esprit bourgeois* into an aristocratic literature. Originality of Boileau is in his attempt to justify the ancients' rules by showing them to be in conformity to nature and reason. Has now outmoded concept of Boileau as "législateur du Parnasse."

———. "L'Esthétique de Boileau." *Revue des deux mondes* 69 (3rd per. 93): 662–85, June 1889. Also in his *Études critiques sur l'histoire de la littérature française.* 8 vols. Paris: Hachette, 1896–1907, vol. 6, pp. 153–91. Exposition of what Brunetière thinks is Boileau's contribution to critical theory.

Clark, Alexander F. B. *Boileau and the French Classical Critics in England* (1660–1830). Paris: Champion, 1925. Excellent treatment of Boileau's influence.

Demeure, J. "Les quatre amis de Psyché," *Mercure de France* 201: 331–66, Jan. 15, 1928.

——. "Racine et son ennemi Boileau," *Mercure de France* 205:34–61, July 1, 1928.

——. "L'Introuvable société des 'quatre amis'," *Revue d'histoire littéraire de la France* 36:161–80, 321–36, 1929. Series of learned but caustic articles which did more than anyone since Revillout to demolish the legend of the "quatre amis." Indispensable study though conclusions perhaps go too far in some respects.

Fidao-Justiniani, Joseph E. *Qu'est-ce qu'un classique? Essai d'histoire et de critique positive; le héros, ou Du génie.* Paris: Firmon-Didot, 1930. Brilliant but should be used with caution. Sees Boileau as representative of a heroic, epic, and passionate age, the admirer of genius and the sublime. Represents one modern school of thought and has greatly influenced Boudhors' edition. Completely lacking in notes and references.

Gillot, Hubert. *La Querelle des anciens et des modernes en France de La Défense et illustration de la langue française aux Parallèles des anciens et des modernes.* Paris: Champion, 1914. Basis, with Rigault, of any study dealing with this subject. Gives broader French background, but not as good as Rigault for the Boileau-Perrault portion of the quarrel.

Haley, Marie Philip, Sister. *Racine and the Art poétique of Boileau.* Baltimore: Johns Hopkins University Press, 1938 (Diss., Minnesota). Good study of poets' knowledge of ancient drama and dramatic criticism. Comparative study of their theories of tragedy, showing Racine had more influence on Boileau. Good study of Boileau's knowledge of Aristotle's *Poetics.*

Hémon, Félix. "Boileau," in his *Cours de littérature,* VIII, Paris: Delagrave, 1892. Best introduction to Boileau as literary artist.

Hervier, Marcel. *L'Art poétique de Boileau; étude et analyse.* Paris: Mellottée, 1938. Study of origins, critical analysis of contents, history of reputation. Useful for student and teacher.

Monk, Samuel H. *The Sublime, a Study of Critical Theories in XVIIIth-Century England.* New York: MLA, 1935. Sees Boileau's influence as dual: neo-classic through the *Art poétique* and pre-Romantic through interpretations of Longinus known through Boileau's translation. Boileau first to see difference between the Sublime and the rhetorical sublime style.

Noss, Mary T. *La Sensibilité de Boileau.* Paris: Gamber, 1932 (Diss., Paris). Study of various types of sensibility to show that Boileau was not completely without it.

Pélissier, L. G. "Les correspondants du duc de Noailles," *Revue d'histoire littéraire de la France* 6:621–36, 1899; 7:624–44, 1900;

9:133–47, 284–311, 1902; 10:671–89, 1903; 11:140–55, 1904; 12:469–95; 1905. Unpublished letters giving information on Boileau's circle of friends at Auteuil, his relations with the Jesuits, and his difficulties with the publication of *Satire XII.*

Revillout, Charles E. "La Légende de Boileau," *Revue d'histoire littéraire de la France* (vols. 34–38 of complete set) 4th ser. 4:449–502, 1890; 5:548–96, 1891; 6:524–72, 1892; 7:59–114, 149–81, 191–215, 374–82, 443–56, 552–65, 1893–94; 8:75–83, 127–34, 221–31, 255–68, 316–29, 1895. Also in his *Essais de philologie et de littérature.* Montpellier: Hamelin, 1899. Very important in Boileau research, first important challenge to legend of Boileau as leader and founder of French classicism, literary mentor of Molière, La Fontaine, and Racine. Indispensable.

Rigault, Hippolyte. *Histoire de la querelle des anciens et des modernes.* Paris: Hachette, 1856. Standard work on the Quarrel and especially good for Boileau's part in it.

Scaglione, A. "Nicola Boileau come fulcro nella fortuna del 'sublime'," *Convivium* 1950, pp. 161–87.

———. "La responsabilità di Boileau per la fortuna del 'sublime' nel settecento," *Convivium* 1952, pp. 166–95. Both articles contain excellent analyses of Boileau's interpretation of Longinus. Points out that pseudo-classicism of the eighteenth century was not due to Boileau but the rationalists, while pre-Romantics used Longinus, with Boileau's translation as intermediary. Supplements Monk, *supra.*

Souriau, Maurice. "Boileau," in his *Evolution du vers français au dix-septième siècle,* pp. 359–401. Paris: Hachette, 1893.

Zdrojewska, Vera. *Boileau.* Brescia: La Scuola, 1948. Excellent study of the real Boileau which deserves more attention than hitherto received.

Index